Business Management

BUSINESS MANAGEMENT

Md. Reyazuddin

SERIALS PUBLICATIONS
NEW DELHI (INDIA)

First Published – 2010

ISBN: 978-81-8387-305-5

Published by

SERIALS PUBLICATIONS
4800/24, 1st Floor, Ansari Road
Darya Ganj, New Delhi-110002 (India)
Phone : 23245225. Fax : 91-11-23272135
E-mail: serials@satyam.net.in

CONTENTS

PREFACE

The book is a timely publication of Sixteen multi-disciplined research articles so judiciously selected by the editor for the benefit and information of students and research scholars on various aspects of Business Management. Contributors of the articles are established authorities and uniquely specialize in their concerned field of study. The contributors belong to national and international forum. Many of the articles published were presented at international seminars and contain latest researched information on the subject which can benefit all research scholars. As is wisely said that articles are the forerunner of the books since they contain novel and new information in them.

These articles study many interesting aspects of Business Management eg. Status and impact of IT-Applications on Business Performance: a Study to SMEs of Chandigarh and Mohali region, India, Design of Data Warehousing using the Entity Relationship Model in Business Environment, Regulatory Challenges Strategically Enhance Banking Efficiency and Stability, A note on the law of Capital markets, Social empowerment of Working Women in Bangladesh, Is Inequality Harmful for Botswana's Economy, Growth, Mutual Fund Schemes in India-Can they protect the interest of the retail investors, Indian Strategies for Global Competitiveness, Onslaught of Global Brands, Indian Brands Fight Back, Governance Challenges in India-a perspective, Corporate Governance and its possibility for Business Practices, An alternative Energy-A Comparative Study of E-Bikes and Petrol Bikes, Strategic Management of Manufacturing and some issues, Commercial Mortgage Market of the United States: Financial institutions participation-Does Bank Size Matter? Globalization and State Level Fiscal Reforms in India since 1991

Mutual Fund schemes in India have been a focal point in present day situation. Various Mutual Fund schemes and their regulators alongwith safety and security measures have been discussed. The Mutual Fund Schemes run by ICICI, SBI, Reliance etc. have been streamlined in the article.

A very narrative and comprehensive account of information on Banking Efficiency and stability specially in the East African Countries have been presented by the author. Banking Sector problems in the Sub-Saharan Continent widely detailed. Information statistics in form of Tables as M-2 to GDP Ratio of Various Countries, Ratio of Loans to Private Sectors etc are presented to view the comparative study of facts by the reader. Eritrea, Kenya, Ethiopia Sudan, Uganda form a wide discussion.

Bangladeshi writer has very beautifully brought forward social empowerment of working women in Bangladesh is an interesting fashion but remain factual on all aspects of women Empowerment.

Many of us will be most interested in examining the 'Brand' Scene in India. Foreign Brands have overpowered in Indian Consumer market. Will the Indian Brands survive of the throat-cut competition at national and international level. A reader will be fully satisfied after going through this factual account of Indian 'brands' strategy.

Manufacturing industries pay a vital role in the economy of every developing country including the developed countries. Manufacturing industries have been studied in respect of their Strategic management, business, resources, decision making, global manufacturing- their standards and quality, retail growth factors, technology and performance objectives. Manufacturing in respect of cost, quality, actual delivery, dependability, delivery speed, has been discussed.

If you wish to survive you have to fight strategically and intellectually, the competition at home and in the world. Global competitiveness is order of the day. Indian strategies for global competitiveness is a well research article though brief but compact and logical descriptions of the strategy India is adopting have been provided.

The whole world is worried on the depletion of fossil fuel and new technology is researching ways and means to survive when fossil fuel diminishes and exhausts on the earth with heavy use of resources in the whole of the world. The article brings forth the account of Electrical Bikes which do not use fossil fuel but battery operated, pollution free, less cost, no traffic hazards, easy to operate. The only need o f the hour is a wide awareness about them and their use. The article presents a comparative study of E-Bikes and Petrol Bikes which is very interesting. One must read this account of E-Bikes.

State level fiscal reforms in India since 1991, with an impact of Globalization, is a laboriously worked out article. Globalization has left no field untouched bad or good in every country and its economy. A comprehensive details can be seen in Ratna Vadra's article in the book.

In view of the above, I am of the firm opinion that the book of immense use to all the research scholars in the field of business management. We can lay our hands on fabulous information provided in these articles.

Editor

CHAPTER 1

STATUS AND IMPACT OF IT-APPLICATIONS ON BUSINESS PERFORMANCE: A STUDY OF SMES OF CHANDIGARH-MOHALI REGION, INDIA

Hardeep Chahal
Ruchi Kohli

INTRODUCTION

In the present Internet savvy era, organizations are radically change themselves from traditional operational stage to technological & informative to more collaboration, commercialization and sustain competitive advantage (Bhandari *et al.*, 2004; and Kalakota & Whinston, 2000). Information Technology (IT) plays a prominent and progressive role in the competitive era for enhancing overall efficiency and effectiveness of organizations (Bhandari *et al.*, 2004) and has emerged as a new medium of economic and social exchange. It may be self-owned or outsourced service that works better, costs less and is capable of serving with the partners & customers' needs ease and quick (Argote and Ingram 2000; Rulke *et al.*, 2000 and Teece *et al.*, 1997). The IT and its applications support to e-commerce and e-business activities such as online pricing, reporting, technical support, internal and external communications for customer contact via pillars of systems, network capabilities, or data capabilities and an overall support platform (Kalakota & Whinston, 2000 and Barton & Bear, 1999). E-commerce sparks a variety of new business models for offering products and services that rely on interactivity, direct exchange of information between sellers and vendors, and virtual co-presence (Kalakota & Whinston, 2000). The growth rate of these models is growing at an invigorating speed in the market and this has led experts to argue that the Internet will become so pervasive that in the near future every business will be an internet business (NASSCOM, 2003). At the global level the extent of use of information technology is actually more in service sector than in manufacturing sector (Fulantelli & Allegra, 2003). Some well-known organizations such as Cisco Systems, Dell Computer and General Electric have achieved impressive economic payoffs in terms of return on invested capital (250%), revenue per employee ($650,000) and gross profit margin (64.4%) by leveraging the Internet (Barua *et al.*, 2002).

The Indian IT sector is the fastest growing sector at the rate of 31 per cent (Times Business 2 Business, 2006). According to the latest predictions by Gartner, the total Indian enterprise spending would reach Rs. 739 billion on telecommunication services & equipment, Rs. 172 billion on hardware, Rs. 141 on IT services and Rs. 41 billion on software by year 2006 (Our Delhi Bureau, 2005). Some major Indian industries like Escorts, Ranbaxy, Telco and Dabur etc. have high usage of e-activities and doing well business at global level (CSI *et al.*, 2002). However the pace of information technology is very low in small & medium scale industries in comparison to large industries (CSI *et al.*, 2002).

STUDY METHODOLOGY AND ANALYSIS

The adoption of e-business practices in SMEs has started primarily with computerization, followed by commercialization of Internet (Bhasin, 2003 and Kalakota & Whinston, 2000). These electronic tools and techniques help the SMEs to better manage their internal business processes and to develop interfaces with the environment to have greater effectiveness and efficiencies in the value chain (Wu *et al.*, 2003). As such, SMEs worldwide are striving hard to use these to enhance value addition to stay competitive and face the intense global competition, ushered in by liberalization, privatization and globalization (Daspal, 2003). The overall functional vibrancy of thc SME's in Indian economy is reflected from their overall contribution of 39 per cent in industrial production (Dasgupta, 2005), 34 per cent in total export (Rathore & Dhameja, 1999) and providing employment to over 167 lakh persons in various units (Gadgil & Godgil, 1985; Gupta & Singh, 1978 and Pattanshetti, 1968). The present study is undertaken to study the status and impact of IT–applications on the SMEs performance operating in the Chandigarh-Mohali region. The study will be conducted in two stages. The list of industries operating in the Chandigarh-Mohali region was taken from IAC (2002-03) and approximately 120 SMEs using ICT tools were identified on the basis of their e-mail addresses, which already have given in list. In the first stage 30 industries were surveyed on convenient sample basis and the rest industries would be surveyed in the second stage. The thirty questionnaires distributed to 30 industries: 29 questionnaires were filled up by the specialized managers of different Industries, but one medium-scale manufacturing industry namely Punjab Communications Limited has not given any response. Thus, the data was collected from 29 industries whose demographic profile is given in Table 1.

Table 1
Demographic Profile of SME's

Size	*No.*	*Nature*	*No.*
Small	19	Manufacturing	19
Medium	10	Service	10
Total	29	Total	29

The manufacturing industries were selected from Chandigarh-Mohali Industrial Cluster Areas I and II and service industries from 17 and 35 sectors. The study analyses nature, performance computer hardware, communication hardware and structure cabling, internet, web and e-business solutions, standard & application software and software solutions such as ERP, CRM etc. The various parameters are analyzed underneath:

Establishment of SME's

The establishment of SMEs varies from company to company. More especially, the establishment of SMEs ranges from more than 35 years to less than 15 years. In general, 2 industries before 1970s, 7 industries during 1970-1980 period, 10 industries during 1981-1990 period and 10 industries after 1990s have established their business. Overall, 19 industries out of 29 belonged to small-scale manufacturing and 10 belonged to medium scale service sector (Table 1).

ISO Certification

The process of economic liberalization and market reforms have opened up the Indian SME's to the global competition. In order to enhance the competitive strength of the SME's at the global & national levels, the International Organization Standardization has introduced a certificate of technological upgradation and product quality improvement in 1987 (Chase *et al.*, 2000) for the business and service organizations. Now days, as there is more stress on satisfying the customer by providing them value for money, every company is trying to reduce the cost of products and side by side upgrading the quality (Awasthi & Jain, 1999). ISO-9001, 9002, 9000:2000, 9001:2000 are different standardizations of quality control for products or services, which serve as the benchmark for performance control (Bravener, 1999). In total 19 manufacturing industries, 17% are certified under ISO: 9001, 17% ISO 9002 and ISO 9000:2000, 17% under ISO 9001 & 9002 and 14% under ISO 9001: 2000. In addition to these ISO generally, there are another ISO certification namely 9003 and 9004. In the survey of 19 manufacturing industries, there is not even a single company, which has used ISO 9003, and 9004. The survey also identified that not even a single service organization has been recognized ISO certification.

Specialized Managers

The managers contribute to organizational effectiveness by improving efficiency of the processes, providing and monitoring health care benefits, fulfilling the needs of employees and reviewing cases more rapidly to make quick adjustments to changing economic scenario (Kalakota & Whinston, 2000; Harrison, 1994 and Flippo, 1987).

The survey has evinced that number of managers, working at various levels are ranged between 7 to 12 in medium scale industries. They are involved at various activities such as purchasing of raw material, manufacturing, quality control, material & store management, selling of material, transportation, financing & accounting, human resource management, information technology management and decision-making programs of company. In Small Scale Industries the numbers of managers are ranged between 3 to 4. The small scale sector managers look after generally operational functions such as 'production', 'finance', 'personnel & store keeping' and 'distribution & logistics' in a company. It has been stated by managers that the increased efficiency in the work process is the biggest benefit of implementing ICT in these companies, followed by increased level of services, increased personnel qualification and decreased expenditures.

Computerization, Digitization and Technical Support

The computer technology helps the companies to transform their organization business and functional processes through the application of technologies, philosophies and computing paradigms of the new digital economy (Kumar, 2003; Dalvi, 2002; Murthy, 2002 and Srivastva, 2002). The digital data and documents help in rational decision making in general and messaging & information, procurement & purchasing, marketing, advertising and publishing in particular (Bhasin, 2003).

The implementation of computerization in industries of Chandigarh-Mohali region has started from 1985 onwards. 17% industries in range 1-3 computers during 1985-90 period, 28% industries in range of 4-6 computers during 1991 to 1995 period, 55% industries in range of 4 to 6 between 1996-2000 periods have installed computer systems primarily to increase operating efficiency via information processing. Maximum usage of computer applications in medium-scale industries were found to be used in Finance and Account Department, Human Resource Management Department, Production Department, Marketing & Sales Department and Information Technology Department. The departments namely Human Resources, Warehouse, Material and Technical Foundation, Logistics, etc. possess few computer systems in medium scale industries. However, the usage in small-scale sector is found to be minimal on the whole. Generally, these industries possess 4 to 5 computer systems, on which various functions pertaining to 'production', 'financial & accounting'; 'Human Resource Management & Decision-making', 'Quality control' and 'Payroll' are performed.

Among the computers installed, majority of industries are in possession of branded computers, assembled PCs are very few. The computer brands generally include Wipro, IBM, HP, and HCL. Among these, majority is in possession of Wipro in comparison to other brands. The assembled systems include LG, Samsung for *monitors*, Intel, Celeron, for *processor*, Dot-matrix (HP), Deskjet (Wipro & HP) and Laser (HP) for *printers*. All types of printers found to be equally used by medium as well as small-scale industries. The network operating system in the industries used is generally from Windows NT, Sun and Linux.

Further, the number of communication equipments range generally between 4 to 6 for Intercom and 2 to 3 equipments are connected to local, STD & ISD facilities in small-scale industries. But in medium scale industries communication equipment range from 7 to 25 for Intercom and 7 to 9 communication equipments for local, STD & ISD connected to communicate with their business & trading partners.

Intranets/Extranets

In Service sector, 20% industries namely Bank of Punjab, IndusInd Bank, State Bank of India, Canara Bank, Corporation

Bank, The Punjab State Co-operative Bank Limited are using intranet services to facilitate internal functions such as storing & retrieving of data about varied functions- finance, human resource and material management and to reduce the operating cycle of the functions. 14% banking industries namely Bank of Punjab, IndusInd Bank, State Bank of India, Canara Bank have establish extranet networking to facilitate transactions among different branches and Head –office. These banks are delivering various e-services such as Internet Banking, Tele-Banking, ATM cum Global debit card, Any where Banking, Mobile Banking, Global ebank card and Kiosk machine to access the account for checking, withdraw and deposit the money into bank. In small scale manufacturing Industries, there are no intranets and extranets, but they deal with their trading and business partners through e-mail and website.

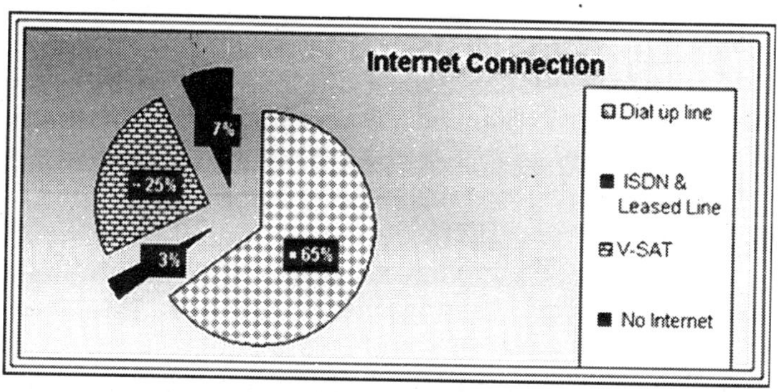

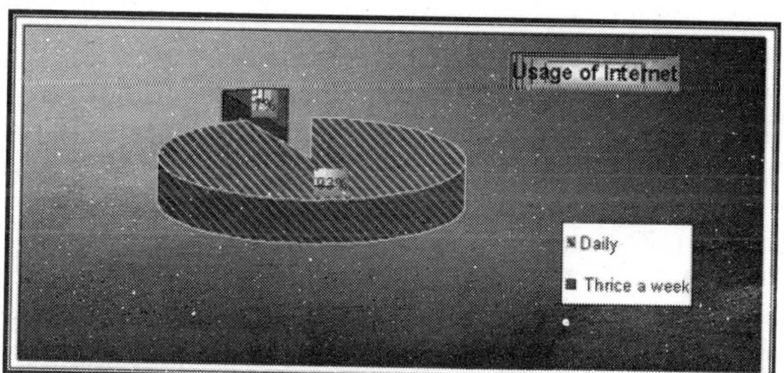

Figure 2

Internet and Website

The pervasive connectivity of the Internet and the attractive graphical user interface of the World Wide Web (www) present enormous opportunities for business of all kinds (Bhasin, 2003 and Kalakota & Whinston, 2000). The Internet and the web support together provide opportunities in selling, customer relationship, product/service design, user support, geographical expansion and logistics & supply chain integration (Bhasin, 2003; Girdhari, 2003; Kalakota & Whinston, 2000 and Murthy, 2002). It performs best in the realm of improving business processes and helps to focus on sharpening a company's competitive edge with quicker time to market and better-tuned customer interaction (Gupta & Sanjay, 2004 and Bhasin, 2003). 68% manufacturing industries are using different channels of connections for internet like Dial up line (65%) and ISDN & leased line (3%) and service industries are connected mostly through V-SAT (24%) i.e banks. 7% industries namely Punjab State Co-operative Bank and Poly Process Private Limited are not connected internet facility (Fig. 1). 86% industries of total, described that they use internet daily and 7% industries thrice a week (Fig. 2). Internet is mostly used for communication (e-mail) by departments viz; Marketing and Sales, Information Technologies, Human Resource Management and Accounts. Among these, just 50% SMEs have developed their own websites and 30% are linked to their head office websites. There are 10% industries namely–Raj Steel Industries, Baba Frozen Foods Private Limited, Primer Tiles Manufacturing Company which are not having their website but are planning to have their website ready by 10 months. As for as website updating is concerned 62% industries are updating their sites regularly, 7% companies are updating website monthly and 7% fortnightly at the head office level, 7% industrialists are not known about website updating and remaining (17%) have not developed their company website refer to Fig. 3. But 7% companies have shown least interest in updating their websites. These companies have developed websites generally to be part of the latest technology adoption.

The website media is primarily used in companies to communicate electronically with their existing and potential customers & suppliers, as mentioned by 50% industries. There are generally few industries, which completely leveraged on IT to beat competition through efficient supply chain, inventory control & finances and business intelligence applications for decision–making (Gupta & Sanjay, 2004 and Kalakota & Whinston, 2000). This scenario is not found in these industries. Further, information related to commercial transactions i.e. invoices, bill of lading, purchase orders, quotations & payment options etc. with business partners & customers and other activities such as downloading statements relating to receipts & payments are used by 30% industries. 17% industries have responded that they are primarily communicating electronically to have information about purchase & supply of materials (excluding payment options) only.

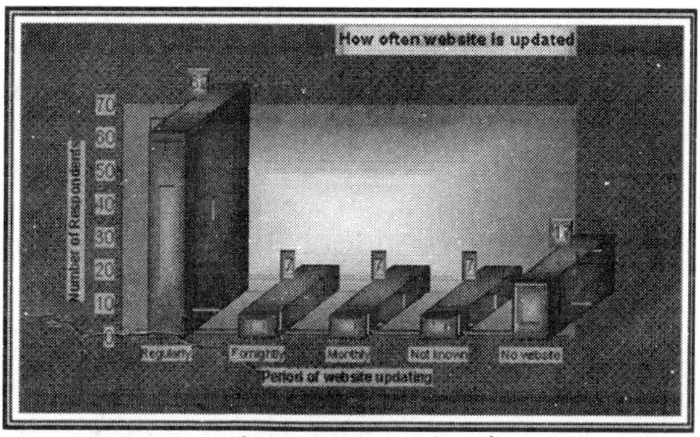

Figure 3

Application of Computer Softwares

This study shows that 10% industries namely Gillard Electronics Private Limited, Suvirs Private Limited and EMCO Switchgears Private Limited are using standard software packages such as MS-Office Product Visio, MS-Project for office automation. But 7% industries such as Poly Process Engineers Company and Leela Confectionary Private Limited plan to use standardized office automation software's with in two-three years. The office packs is for MS Office XP is also in use. There are not only different versions but also even different operating systems are in use. The predominated desktop operating system is found to be MS Windows but MS DOS has been also cited by 7 reputed industries such as Gillard Electronics Private Limited, Suvirs Private Limited, EMCO Switchgears Private Limited, Mahajan Udyog, Vishnu Associates Limited, Shivalik Steels Limited and Nova Industries Private Limited. MS Windows XP penetration has been also seen by some of these industries. 4 industries namely Mahajan Udyog, Vishnu Associates Limited, Shivalik Steels Limited, Nova Industries Private Limited are using only MS DOS. The MS Windows 2000, Linux, MS Windows NT, MS Windows ME, UNIX, Sun Solaris and Novell are also found to be used. The citing of network operating system instead desktop operating system shows that this part of respondents makes a difference between these two types of operating systems. The majority of industries are using self-developed software's in the functional areas such as Accounting Management, Human Resource Management, and Material Management etc. Regarding accounting software, 19 small businesses use Excel, Tally, Foxpro and Busywin or self-developed softwares and about 3 industries plan to change accounting softwares with in six months in their industries. Banks such as namely Andhra Bank, Bank of India, Corporation Bank, Bank of Punjab, Punjab State Co-operative Bank, IndusInd Bank, have installed software's namely Laser, Bank Master, Cibex, IBASE, Filacle, Foxpro and Finware respectively. 3 banks namely State Bank of Patiala, State Bank of India and Canara are using Bank Master in their operating system, use the accounting modules of this software regarding financial and assets management. 29 companies use Enterprise Resource Planning Software, but in the most cases this is being used for accounting programs and not for other specialized areas. MS Excel is also utilized for such purposes. Further, majority of industries have quoted using DBMS software for data base management. The cited names for DBMS include MS Access, MS SQL, and Oracle. Only 5 companies are not using any data base management software but have planned to install such type of software but again the time period have not mentioned for the implementation. Furthermore, Data Application on Tape (DAT) an archiving device is mostly used by SMEs to maintain records for long time. The majority of industries are using self-developed quality control software's. All companies are using Anti-virus software. The software brands used by companies include McAfee, Virus Scan and Norton Anti-virus.

Purpose of Technology Absorption

The main purpose of technology absorption is to enhance quality, reduce cost and converge the business processes in new ways to achieve business goals and respond to challenges such as global competition, rising customer expectations & emerging markets, more effectively than competitors (Roy & Sikdar, 2003). The technology implementation is shifting company's environment from Brick and Mortar to Click & Mortar (Bhasin, 2003 and Kalakota & Whinston, 2000) in the developed regions. About, 40% industries have reported that they have made IT investments in hardware, software, internet and development of the website to access the benefits such as reduce data processing cost, improve service quality for their existing as well as potential trading partners & customers, open new distribution and develop new market channels to streamline the business processes for competitive advantage. It is found that 7% industries have given prominence separately to reduce cost and streamline business processes and 14% industries have installed computerization to reduce total cost & improve service quality of products for their customers. Further, 7% industries are using IT-applications to acquire all benefits excluding focus on the new market development areas. 24% industries are interested to perceive usefulness of IT-applications such as reduce cost, service quality and streamline the business processes but cannot afford to invest for new distribution and develop new markets. 14% organizations such as Khandellia Oil & General Mils Limited, Nova Industries Private Limited, EMCO Switchgears Private Limited and Manu International depicted that they are applying IT-applications to decrease the total cost of products, improve service quality for their existing & potential customers and open new distribution in the competitive market (Roy & Sikdar, 2003). In Chandigarh scenario, surprisingly banking sector has done excellent business through electronical media's such as Internet Banking, Tele-Banking, Anywhere, ATM cum global debit card, Kiosk machine, e-cheque, e-cash, e-draft, transacting through EDI with their upstreamline and downstreamline business suppliers & partners.

Status of SMEs

On the basis of aforesaid analysis, the industries are categorized into three stages namely infancy stage where company implements 10 to 33 per cent of business activities through e-media, partly low usage stage–where companies implement 34 to 66 per cent e-activities, partly high usage stage where 67 to 100 per cent business activities are performed electronically and fully Click & Mortar stage as given in Table 2. Among 29 industries, 7 banks namely Canara Bank, State Bank of India, IndusInd Bank, Bank of Punjab, Corporation Bank, Bank of India and Jammu & Kashmir Bank in IIIrd category i.e. 67 to 100 per cent e-activities for integrating their existing enterprise applications with e-commerce transaction capabilities to manage the flow of business transactions internally& externally across their customer and partners and thus make them more customer-centric. These banks are focused on the scalability of IT-operations, adopting a centralized philosophy and prioritizing efficient back–office operations (Bhasin, 2003). The banks provide services such as generally access accounts round-the clock & even on weekends, check balances online & find out whether cheques or deposits have cleared, transfer fund between accounts, download information directly into personal finance software and receive & pay bills on-line (without check writing, envelopes, or stamps) with the help of data processing, retrieving, data transferring and web promotion activities etc. Banks and financial institutions stand to benefit enormously from e-commerce in the form of reduced transaction costs, improved

Table 2
IT-Adoption Stages

(I) Infancy Stage	*(II) Partly low*	*(III) Partly High/ Fully e-Based*
Computers in various depart-mentsto reduce the manual tedious of clerical, routine and tedious work.	Developed website to communic-ate electronically with their business, trading partners & customers i.e. receiving and placing orders but no electronica-lly transfer of fund.	Electronic Data Interchange withinand outside the company i.e. intran-ets and extranets.
Implementing function specific application package such as Bank Master, Infoysis, Tally, busywin, Excel to reduce operating timei.e. work faster and increase operating efficiency to makefewer mistakes.	Use of IT-Tools i.e. CAD, CAM, to improve the variations as well as quality of products.	Implementing enterprise Solutions i.e. Enterprise Resource Planning, Supply Chain Management.
Adopting e-mail and Internet to communicate with their existing& potential business, trading partners and customers.	Generate and deliver extensive management reports and decision support systems (DSS) to branches/ plants and channel partners.	Implementing e-Commerce activities such as online receiving, placing orders, and online fundtransfer etc. along with other e-activities
Developing website for exposure purpose/ promotional activities.		
% of Industries=		
52%	**24%**	**24%**
Raj Steel Industries, Kansal industries, Gillard Electronics Pvt. Ltd, Mahajan Udyog, Shivalik Steels Ltd., Nova Industries Pvt. Ltd., Poly Process Engineers Co., Leela Confectionary Pvt. Ltd., Khandellia Oil & GeneralMils Ltd., Manu International, Baba Frozen Foods Pvt. Ltd., Primer Tiles Manu-facturing Co., State Bank of Patiala, Andhra Bank, Punjab State Co-operative Bank.	Suvirs (Sales) Pvt. Ltd., Vishnu AssociatesLtd., Bharat Graphics, BNAL Prefabs Pvt. Ltd., Deltron Ltd., EMCO Switchgears Pvt. Ltd., Check Mate International Pvt. Ltd.	Canara Bank, State Bank of India, IndusInd Bank, Bank of Punjab, Corporation Bank, Bank of India, Jammu & Kashmir Bank.

customer service and loyalty and better customer information. They also get benefited from helping businesses handling payments and financial transactions by e- commerce (Bhasin, 2003). The survey identifies that only 24% out of 76% industries namely Suvirs (Sales) Private Limited, Vishnu Associates Limited, Bharat Graphics, BNAL Prefabs Private Limited, Deltron Limited, EMCO Switchgears Private Limited and Check Mate International are operating in partly low usage of e-activities ranged from 34 to 66 per cent. The activities primarily include storing of data, retrieval of data, transfer of documents, and e-mail (receives & sent to their business partners and customers). These industries have also reported that they are also using IT-Tools such as Computer Aided Design, Computer Aided Manufacturing, quality control software's and Total Quality Management in their business processes from long period, which provide maximum benefits to their business customers as well as business partners. Other remaining industries are operating at infancy stage. Further, 14% SMEs, namely Andhra Bank, Punjab State Co-operative Bank, Raj Steel Industries and Kansal Industries described that as to face the competition with their competitors in the market they want to change their operating system software 'Nelito' to 'Infosys' and other remaining industries want to change self-developed software's in standardized or readymade software's such as Infosys, Alex, Busy win & Bank Master etc. The few of industries are finding ways to expand their e-activities and across the country.

CONCLUSION

India, once primarily an agrarian economy, today is better known for its professionals, technocrats and entrepreneurs (Sharma, 1999). The technology innovation, design & process flexibility, quality, productivity & its cost, speed to market and service mix are some of the significant factors on which competitive advantage of any business depends (Shetty, 2004; Roy & Sikdar, 2003 and Nandi, 1995). The changes in the business environment have been more radical in the five years than in the last five decades (Jain *et al.*, 1999). This has been true also for Chandigarh-Mohali region. Overall, it has been seen small-scale manufacturing industries have extended the investment in IT-Tools which help in their production & marketing phases but cannot afford to invest in intranets, extranets and online activities. But service sector play a significant role in implementing the IT-applications, which enabled them overall improvements in co-ordination, improve efficiency of operations and provide organizations with a competitive edge (Gupta & Sanjay, 2004 and Ramachandran & Voleti, 2004). The study tries to find the impact of IT-applications on the business activities. The impact of IT applications is also considered by Fulantelli & Allegra, 2003; Roy & Sikdar, 2003 and Wu et al., 2003 is given in Table 3. As per surveyed about twenty nine industries (96.7%) have stated that after implementation of IT-applications in their business processes the business transactions and customer satisfaction among suppliers, trading partners and distributors have increased. The survey also revealed that adoption of IT-Tools have resulted in decrease in total cost of production in 83.3% of the industries, lead and cycle times in 96.7% of the industries and number of employees in 76.7% of the industries (Fig. 4).

Table 3
Impact of IT–Applications

Financial & Economic	*Technical & Production*	*Social & Organizational*	*Infrastructure Management*
Increase profitability	Improve production process	Skill and capability	Resources/ Assets
Meet competition	Improve product quality	Seeking market	Activity Configuration
Leadership	Increase flexibility	Serving social needs	Partner Network
Save on cost	Target customer	Information	
	Value proposition	Feel and Serve	
	Capability	Trust and Loyalty	

Adapted from Roy, Anjan and Arijit Sikdar (2003), "Technology Absorption in Large and Small Enterprises: A Proposal for Comparative Research" *The Journal of entrepreneurship*, 12(2), 183-199.

On the flip side, it is seen that small-scale industries are not matured in adopting IT-applications such as online purchasing-selling, Intranets-Extranets, Enterprise Resource Planning, Customer Relationship Management, and Electronic Fund Transfer etc. The main reason of low usage of Technology Orientation of small enterprises is because of factors such as resource constraints primarily financial constraints in investment, lack of expert & skilled persons, lack of training to upgrade their knowledge & skill (CSI, 2002; Dalu & Deshmukh, 2001 and Joshi, 2001) and thus, tend to choose technologies which contained apparatus requiring lower involvement of externalities (Roy and Sikdar, 2003). On the basis of this analysis, it can be concluded that the mindset of Chandigarh-Mohali IT-savvy manufacturing and service industrialists is positive for technological integration. As per the statement pointed out by Roy & Sikdar (2003) that small firms can perform better & even compete against large MNC's if they have innovative culture for better adoption to new technology in their operations. To achieve this, some strategies should be considered such as entrepreneurs should take IT as a business strategy and improve links between information system strategy and business strategy. Further, key performance indicators (KPIs) should also be clearly identified

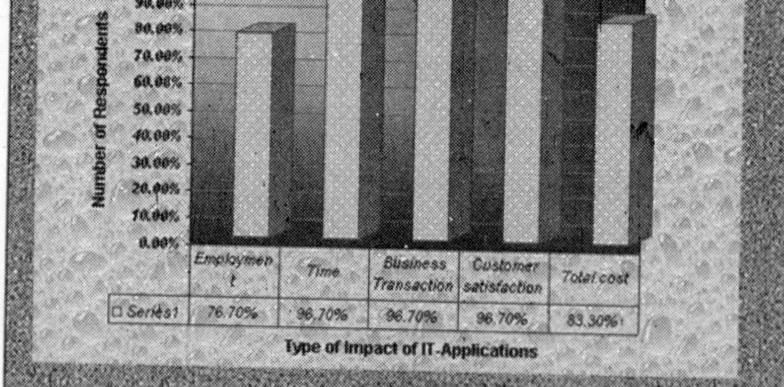

Figure 4

and incorporated into the Information System to monitor the health of the organization. The government organizations such as PhD Chamber of Commerce, CII etc. should provide a platform for the SME's managers and workers to participate & interact in seminars, conferences and training from time to time to aware them about the latest developments. While preparing national level IT-Task Force government should keep in mind different industrial area problems relating to infrastructure, lack of awareness etc. and accordingly provide some subsidies & incentives to motivate the industrialists in implementing the technologies in their industries.

REFERENCES

Argote Linda & Paul Ingram (2000), "Knowledge Transfer: A Basis for Competitive Advantage in Firms," *Organizational Behavior and Human Decision Processes*, Vol. 82, No. 1, pp. 150-169.

Awasthi Anil & Ankur Jain (1999), *"Role of Entrepreneurship in Changing Structure of Organizations,"* in B. S. Rathore and S. K. Dhameja (Ed.) Entrepreneurship in the 21st Century; Rawat Publications, Jaipur, pp. 249-255.

Bhandari Gokul, Michael Bliemel, Allan Harold, & Khaled Hassanein (2004), "Flexibility in e-Business Strategies: A Requirement for Success," *Global Journal of Flexible Systems Management*, Vol. 5, No. 2-3, pp. 11-22.

Bhasin, T. M. (2003), *"E-Commerce in Indian Banking,"* Authorspress, Delhi.

Chase B. Richard, Nicholas J. Aquilano, & F. Robert Jacobs (2000), *"Production and Operations Management – Manufacturing and Services,"* Tata McGraw-Hill Publishing Company Limited, New Delhi, pp. 219-225.

Computer Society of India (CSI) *et al.*, (2002), "E-Commerce Scene in India," *E-Business Digest*, May, pp. 35-46.

Computer Society of India *et al.* (2002), "E-Business Environment in India," *E-Business Digest*, June, pp. 35-48.

Dasgupta Anupam (10-16 Sep, 2005), "Micro and Small Enterprises – Growth Engine of Economy," *Employment News*, pp. 1-2.

Daspal Debasis (April-June, 2003), "e-Commerce to c-Commerce in Textile Supply Chain" *Productivity*, Vol. 44, No. 1, pp. 77-84.

Dalu R. S. & S. G. Deshmukh (2001), "SWOT Analysis of Small & Medium Scale Industry: A Case Study" *Productivity*, Vol. 42, No. 2, pp. 201-209.

Dalvi C. S. (2002), "Wave of Internet Marketing" *Indian Journal of Marketing*, Vol. 32, No. 9, pp. 19-22.

Flippo Edwin B. (1987), "*Personnel Management*," McGraw-Hill Book Company, New York, pp. 3-23.

Gadgil P. G. & P. L. Godgil (1985), "*Industrial Economy of India*," Eurosia Publishing House Private Limited, New Delhi, pp. 365-382.

Girdhari D. G. (2003), "*Global Economy and E-Business*," In N. P. Agarwal & Sajan, C. Jain (Ed.) *Information Technology and e-Commerce*; Raj Publishing House, Jaipur, pp. 155-160.

Gupta M. P and Sanjay (2004), "Information Technology Usage: The Indian Experience" *Vikalpa*, Vol. 29, No. 1, pp. 83-91.

Gupta N. S. & Amarjit Singh (1978), "*Industrial Economy of India*," Light & Life Publishers, New Delhi, pp. 165-195.

Harrison Bennett (1994), "The Small Firms Myth," *California Management Review*, pp. 142-158.

Jain Ankur, Stuli Jain, & Rahul Bahuguna (1999), "*Manufacturing Resource Planning: Concept, Features and Implementation in SSIs*," In B. S. Rathore and S. K. Dhameja (Ed.) Entrepreneur-ship in the 21st Century; Rawat Publications, Jaipur, pp. 242-248.

Joshi Gopal (2001), "Entrepreneurship Development for SMEs in the 21st Century" *Productivity*, Vol. 42, No. 8, pp. 186-190.

Kalakota Ravi, & Andrew B. Whinston (2000), "*Electronic Commerce-A Managers Guide*," Addison-Wesley Longman (Singapore) Pte. Ltd., Indian Branch, New Delhi.

Kumar Mukesh (2003), "E-Commerce Models," *Log in Tribune*, Vol. 2.

Murthy C. S. V. (2002), "*e-Commerce*," Himalaya Publishing House, New Delhi, pp. 393-434.

Nandi S. N. (1995), "Technology Infrastructure and Industry: The Indian Situation," *Productivity*, Vol. 36, No. 2, pp. 246-257.

Our Delhi Bureau (2005), "IT, Telecom Biz to Log Rs 1 Lakh Cr by 2006," *The Economic Times*, Vol. 6.

Pattanshetti C. C. (1968), "*The Dimensions of India's Industrial Economy*," Somaiya Publications Private Limited, Bombay, pp. 156-182.

Ramachandran K., & Sudir Voleti (2004), "Business Process Outsourcing (BPO): Emerging Scenario and Strategic Options for IT-enabled Services," *Vikalpa*, Vol. 29, No. 12, pp. 49-62.

Rathore B. S., & D. D. Sharma (1998), *"Implementing Total Quality in Small Businesses,"* In J. S. Saini and S. K. Dhameja (Ed.), Entrepreneurship and Small Business; Rawat Publications; Jaipur, pp. 127-151.

Rathore B. S., & S. K. Dhameja (1999), *"Entrepreneurship in the 21st Century,"* In B. S. Rathore and S. K. Dhameja (Ed.), Entrepreneurship in the 21st Century; Rawat Publications, Jaipur; pp. 17-34.

Roy Anjan, & Arijit Sikdar (2003), "Technology Absorption in Large and Small Enterprises: A Proposal for Comparative Research," *The Journal of Entrepreneurship*, Vol. 12, No. 2, pp. 183-199.

Rulke Diane Liang, Srilata Zaheer, & Marc H. Anderson (2000), "Sources of Managers' Knowledge of Organizational Capabilities," *Organizational Behavior and Human Decision Processes*, Vol. 82, No. 1, pp. 134-149.

Sharma Umesh (1999), *"Promotion of Small Entrepreneurship: Role of Government,"* In B. S. Rathore and S. K. Dhameja (Ed.), Entrepreneurship in the 21st Century; Rawat Publications, Jaipur, pp. 281-284.

Shetty Pramod (2004), "Attitude Towards Entrepreneurship in Organizations," The *Journal of Entrepreneurship*, Vol. 13, No. 1, pp. 53-68.

Srivastava Chetan (2002), "Marketing in the Internet Age-information Technology as a Strategic Tool," *Indian Journal of Marketing*, Vol. 32, No. 9, pp. 26-28.

Teece D. J., Pisano G., & Shuen A. (1997), "Dynamic Capabilities and Strategic Management," *Strategic Management Journal*, Vol. 8, No. 7, pp. 509-533.

Times Business 2 Business (2006), "IT Boom Continues: Information Technology is Growing at a Steady Pace in the Last Several Years and is Providing Employment to Large Workforce," *The Economic Times*, Vol. 13.

Wu Fang; Vijay Mahajan, & Sridhar Balasubramaniam (2003), "An analysis of E-Business Adoption and its Impact on Business Performance," *Journal of the Academy of Marketing Science*, Vol. 31, No. 4, pp. 425-447.

WEBSITES

Barton Clifton, & Marshall Bear, (1999), "Information & Communication Technologies: Are They Key to Viable Business Development Services for Micro & Small Enterprises? Microenterprise Best Practices Project, U. S. A, available at *www.mip.org/pdfs/mbp/ict.pdf*, Viewed on March 9, 2003.

Barua Anitesh, Prabhudev Konana, Andrew B. Whinston, & Fang Yin, (2002), "Assessing Internet Enabled Business Value: An Exploratory Investigation?" Drafted, Available at *http://crec.mccombs.utexas.edu/works/articles/barua_ konana_whinston_ yin_01311.pdf*, Viewed on April 20, 2004.

Bravener Lee C., (1999), "ISO 9000 in the Next Millennium: What Do We Want It to Be?" Available at *www.ce-mag.com/archive/1999/ mayjune/Bravener.html*, Viewed on March 9, 2003.

Fulantelli Glovanni, Mario & Allegra, (2003), "Small Company Attitude Towards ICT Based Solutions: Some Key-Elements to Improve it," Educational Technology & Society, 6, Available at *www.ifets.messey.ac.nz/periodical/vol-1-2003/fulantelli:html*, Viewed on December 10, 2003.

Industries Association of Chandigarh (IAC), (2002-03), "A Note on Chandigarh Industries," Available at *www.chandigar hindustries. com/html/noteonchdind.htm*, Viewed on March 17, 2003.

NASSCOM, (2001-2002), "Internet & e-Commerce", at *www.ascosys. com/int-ecom*, Viewed on October 15, 2003.

NASSCOM, (2003), "Internet & e-Commerce," at *www.ascosys.com/ int-ecom*, Viewed on October 15, 2003.

Prasad C. S., (2004), "Small & Medium Enterprises in Global Perspective," Employment Generation and WTO Vision 2012; New Delhi, Available at *https://www.vedamsbooks.com/ no37097.htm*, Viewed on December 20, 2005.

UNCTAD Secretariat, (2002), "e-Commerce and Development Report 2002," United Nations Conference on Trade and Development, New York and Geneva, Available at *r0.unctad.org/ecommerce/ docs/ edr02_en/ecdr02_tes.pdf*, Viewed on May 27, 2003.

CHAPTER 2

DESIGN OF DATA WAREHOUSE USING THE ENTITY RELATIONSHIP MODEL IN BUSINESS ENVIRONMENT

Mior Nasir Mior Nazri
Shahrul Azman Mohd Noah
Zarinah Hamid

INTRODUCTION

In today's global business environment, almost all giant corporations are using computer system to run businesses. As the production database become more matured, comprehensive, fast and easily access through out the globe, the focus of organizations requirement has also changed. Organizations have stored large volume of business data in their operational databases. Many of the data have been kept for many years. Corporate executives are looking at ways on how to tap valuable information from these massive data in order for them to make correct planning and right business decision making. Although they have the data themselves, but accessing the production data for analytical processing in not easy. Database from the traditional OnLine Transaction Processing (OLTP) system are not design for analytical processing. The need for OnLine Analytical Processing (OLAP) triggered the design of Data Warehouse.

A data warehouse is a subject-oriented, integrated, time-variant and non-volatile collection of consistent data to support strategic decision making process (Inmon, 1993). As data warehousing become one of the most important tools for business, in 1998 alone, organizations were spending about US$8 billion for hardware and software in the data warehousing market (Sen and Jacob, 1998). The benefit generated from data warehouse can only be acquired if the data warehouse structure has been designed correctly to meet the user queries. The purpose of this paper is to look at techniques of designing data warehouse from the Entity/Relationship (E/R) model. The first focus of this paper is to look at different methodologies being implemented to build data warehouse design from the existing E/R model. Second focus is on the automatic or semi-automatic techniques that have been developed to produce data warehouse design from E/R model.

BACKGROUND AND LITERATURE ON DATA WAREHOUSING

Design process of database can be divided into four major phases starting from user requirement analysis–how to support user business needs, conceptual design–conceptual model on how user perceived data, logical design–concepts related to particular data model, and physical design–describe data definition that correspond to specific DBMS (Batani, *et al.*, 1992). All of the phases are important in designing data warehouse; the focus of this paper is only on the conceptual design phase.

There are several ways of getting requirement for the data warehouse design. The "first principles" approach is by gathering the requirement directly from users through series of meetings and interviews. Another method is by obtaining the requirement from the existing operational system and this method is called source-driven requirement gathering. In this method system designer extracted information from E/R model, reports, user queries, operational manuals and all document that have design value (Ballard, *et al.*, 1998). E/R model was introduced by Chen (1972) has become the standard for conceptual database design. This paper will focus on methodologies that derived data warehouse design from E/R model.

Dimensional model is the most popular model used for designing data warehouse conceptual design. The basic elements for dimensional model are fact, dimension and measure and the most widely used model is the STAR model (Ballard, *et al.*, 1998). Fact represents the vital data for the organization business transaction that can be used for analysis such as Sales. Measure is the numeric attribute for fact which can be aggregated. Examples for measures are Product sold and Price. Dimensions provide business perspective on how to analyze fact such as Sales based on Geography (Cabibbo and Torlone). Dimension can be defined into hierarchies. Example of hierarchy is when temporal dimension is broken into multi level hierarchies such as day, week, month and year.

REVIEW ON PREVIOUS RESEARCHES

This section highlights several researches that have been conducted on designing data warehouse conceptual design from the E/R schema.

Dimensional Fact Model

Golfarelli *et al.*, (1998) proposed graphical conceptual data model for designing data warehouse with a semi-automated methodology starting from operational E/R scheme. The graphical model that he proposed is called Dimensional Fact Model (Fig. 1). The model structured resembles a tree with facts as the root of the tree. The fact is portrayed by a box shape diagram with fact's name and attributes that contain value that can be 'measured'. Vertices branching out directly from the root are dimensional nodes. Dimensional node marks the beginning of hierarchies that extended by new branches to form multiple nodes. All the nodes are represented by circle and carried discrete set of values that can be used for aggregation. The closer the hierarchical nodes of the dimension path to the fact root, the finer the granularity. Some terminal vertices that only carry informative value are called non-dimensional attributes and they are represented by lines instead of circles. Non-dimensional attributes cannot be used for aggregation. Golferelli lay down six steps to build the Dimensional Fact Model and they are as follows:

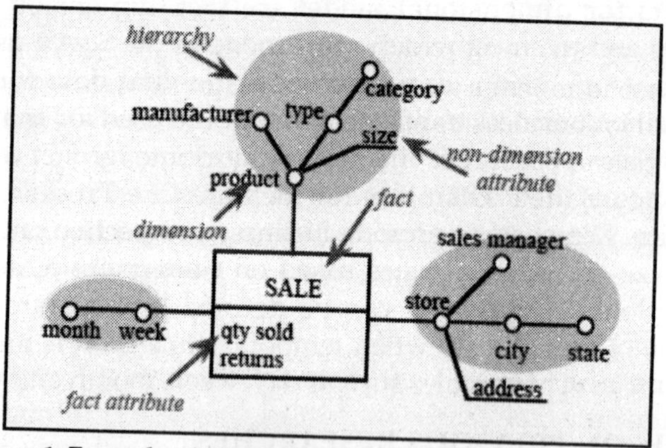

Figure 1: Example of Dimensional Fact Model (Golfarelli *et al.*, 1998)

1. *Defining Fact:* From the requirement study, business analyst selected entity or relationship from the operational ER scheme that represents the highest business interest for decision making process as the model fact. Usually good candidates for selection are those that contained the most frequently update attributes related to the business. Each selected fact becomes the root for each of the fact scheme.
2. *Building Attribute Tree:* Primary key from the selected fact becomes the root and all other attributes form the vertex to the root. Identifiers of other entities that have relationship to the selected fact start another vertex and all its functionally dependent attributes form the sub-branches. The process of building the attribute tree continues until all entities and relationships attached to the fact are utilized.
3. *Pruning and Grafting Attribute Tree:* At this point, the tree structured model contains the maximum number of nodes represented from the E/R scheme. Corporate users do not need very detail amount of information

for their decision making. Next step is to eliminate any unnecessary attributes not required by the Data Warehouse. Pruning is the process to cut off unwanted branches that contains nodes which are not required by users. On the other hand, grafting is the process of cutting a particular node but with the intention of saving the descendents. This is done by replacing the eliminated node with the next descendent node with all its branches. The action resulted in making the granularity of the fact coarser.

4. *Defining Dimensions:* Dimensions are the category of aggregation chosen for the fact in order to execute business making decision. Dimensions will be chosen from the nodes that form the children of the root. Time is a very important candidate to be selected as one of the dimension. If the time node is not an immediate child to the root, grafting the tree should be done in order to move time as one of the dimension.
5. *Defining Fact Attributes:* Fact attributes are used as 'measures' the value of fact using the aggregation functions such as count, sum, average, maximum and minimum. The values of fact attributes are having the most interesting influence on decision making process for the users. Hence, numerical attributes are good candidate for fact attributes. Attributes already selected for dimension will be excluded from this selection.
6. *Defining Hierarchies:* The last step is to define the hierarchies for each dimension. Each sub-tree starting from the dimensional node represents the level of granularity for aggregation. Only one-to-many relationship along the hierarchy's path will be kept while pruning and grafting is performed to eliminate the one-to-one relationship. A new level of hierarchy can also be added by introducing a more summarized node in the branch. For example a new node quarter is a combination of three months can be added in the

time dimension sub-tree. At this point informative attribute labeled as non-dimension attributes and the node is presented as straight line instead of circle in the Dimensional Fact Model. This node cannot be used for aggregation.

Multidimensional Data Model

Cabibbo and Torlone (Cabibbo and Torlone, 1998) proposed designing Data Warehouse conceptual model using Multi Dimensional data model (MD-Fig. 2). Major input for the model is the operational E/R scheme. MD model has two major constructs consist of dimensions and *F*-table. Each dimension contains several level that make-up the hierarchies. Dimensions help business users analyzing transaction data in multiple view points with various aggregations. A single level dimension is called atomic. *F*-table has measures that represent real data which can be translated into meaningful value. In this design methodology, the process starts from analyzing an operational ER scheme and continues in four distinctive steps.

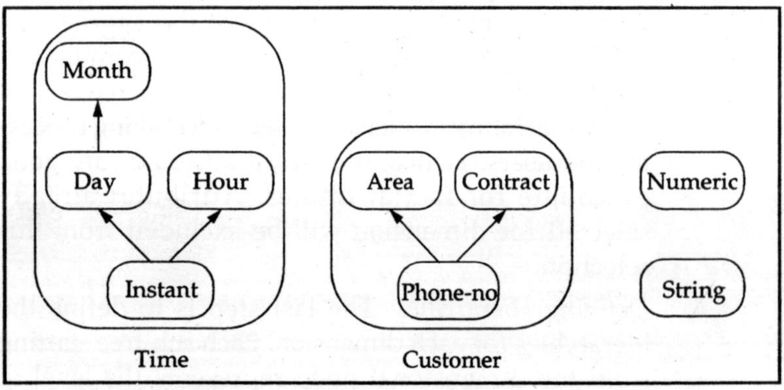

Figure 2: Example of MD Model (Cabibbo and Torlone, 1998)

1. *Identification of Facts and Dimensions:* The first step is for business analyst to evaluate a given E/R scheme for entities, relationships or attributes that are having valuable interest for business decision making process to be selected as facts. Next process is to identify

measures which quantify the property of facts that need to be analyzed. Another important component in the model is dimensions which are used for consolidating facts by certain grouping or category. All the items can be located by navigating the scheme beginning from the selected facts to items surrounding it.

2. *Restructuring of the E/R Scheme:* The objective of this process is to rearrange the ER scheme into a design that can easily be transformed to MD model. The first of the three major steps for the restructuring of the E/R scheme is representing facts as entities. Usually entities will be selected as facts, but attributes and relationships are also good candidate for facts. In those situations, they have to be converted into entities. Next step is to add any missing valuable dimensions such as temporal data into the E/R scheme. The final process is to refine each dimensional hierarchy by selecting levels that contribute in evaluating the facts. The refinement process also identifies levels that are informative in nature which are invalid for aggregations function.
3. *Derivation of a Dimensional Graph:* This process is to convert the restructured E/R scheme into a special graph which is called dimensional graph. Each of the nodes originated from entity or attribute. Entity nodes are presented by the domain of the entity key and attribute nodes are represented by the attribute domain. The dimensional graph consists of four types of nodes; fact nodes converted from fact entities; level nodes that form the dimensional hierarchy; descriptive nodes that are non-aggregated dimensional level; and measure nodes that linked to fact node.
4. *Translation into the MD Model:* In the final process, dimensional graph can be mapped directly into the MD model. Each dimensional graph translated into MD dimension having MD level for each of the

dimension node. The MD level correspond to the hierarchy in the dimensional graph equip with roll-up function. Measure nodes and single level descriptive nodes are converted into atomic dimensions. Descriptive nodes with multiple levels define as MD level description.

StarER Model

Tryfona *et al.*, (1999) proposed designing data warehouse conceptual model by extending the traditional operational database ER model into a model called StarER model (Fig. 3). This model combined the establish Entity Relationship model with the popular star model from the data warehouse environment. The proposed model represents conceptual design understandable by users and easily transform to the next level of design process without any ambiguities and independent of implementation constraint. The methodology for designing the StarER is divided into five phases, namely:

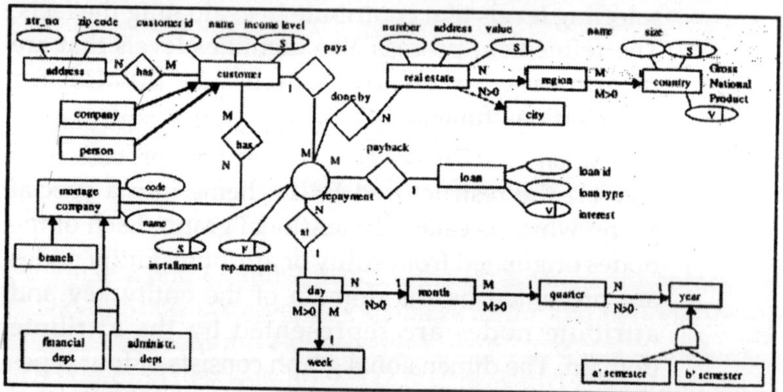

Figure 3: Example of StarER Model (Tryfona *et al.*, 1999)

1. *Identify Facts and Properties:* Facts are the business data required by management for decision making process. They represent the growing data transaction for the organization over time. Facts have properties that measure its values; hence usually numerical data with additive quality and summarizability are selected. Summarizability can be categorized by three different

types; i.e. stock, flow and value-per-unit. Type stock property refers to the value of data that exist at a particular time. Summarization of stock property can only be done in relation to time dimension. On the other hand, type flow property refers to data that change as time pass and this type is natural with summarization. Type value-per-unit is similar to type stock, except that this type cannot be summarized.

2. *Define Temporal Dimension:* Analyzing business trend using data warehouse must always be done in relation to time in order for the result to make sense. For that reason, temporal dimension must be defined in relation to facts.
3. *Represent Object, Properties and Relationship:* Next step is to include objects, their properties and relationship among them that are relevant to the facts. Analysis of the facts is more meaningful when executed in reference with those objects. Object properties can be numeric with additive quality such as summation. Object is related with one another by one of the three types of association; specialization/generalization indicating object as subclasses of another higher object, aggregation signifying object as part of bigger object, and membership showing object as strict or complete member of another object.
4. *Associate Objects to Facts:* Once the related objects have been identified, the objects are semantically connected to the facts. The association between them makes analysis on the data warehouse more complete and comprehensive.
5. *Define Hierarchies:* Facts are analyzed in relation to dimensions. Objects that are linked to the facts are called dimensions. Hierarchy is defined by the type of membership arrangement between objects that resulted in levels of granularities. The further the hierarchy level from the fact, the coarser the granularity.

Multidimensional Normal Form Model

Hüsemann *et al.,* (2000) proposed data warehouse design that follows the traditional data base design process phases starting from requirement analysis and specification, conceptual design, logical design and finally the physical design. The requirement analysis and specification phase started by analyzing the operational E/R schema as the input for the data warehouse design process. The outputs of this phase are important measures, related dimensions and standard multidimensional queries. The next phase is the conceptual design which can be divided into three sequential phases. The objective of this phase is to produce a graphical multidimensional schema conforming to multidimensional normal form (MNF – Fig. 4). The phases of conceptual design are as follows:

1. *Context Definition Measures:* Once measures have been identified, the next step is to determine the functional dependencies (FD) from dimension's levels that are related to the measures. This can be done by identifying the minimum key of the dimension that is functionally determining the corresponding measure. This type of dimensional level will be used as the root for the dimension hierarchies and it is called the terminal dimensional level. At this point the graphical conceptual design will consist of fact schema,

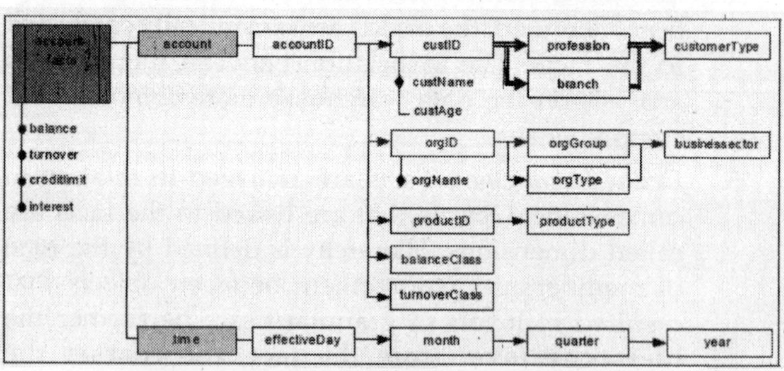

Figure 4: Example of Multidimensional Normal Form Model (Hüsemann *et al.,* 2000)

measures, dimension and terminal dimension level.

2. *Dimensional Hierarchy Design:* In this phase, the remaining of the dimensional hierarchies will be developed based on all the functional dependencies of the dimensional level up to the terminal dimensional. The attributes from the input E/R has to be identified as property attributes or dimensional levels. Next, each dimensional hierarchy will be connected by the dimensional level nodes. Splits between hierarchies have to be identified as the alternative aggregation path for mandatory dimensional level or optional aggregation path for optional dimensional level.
3. *Definition of Summarizability Constraints:* Aggregation functions can be grouped into four levels of restriction. Level 1 indicates that all aggregation functions can be applied. Level 2 is similar to level 1 except for SUM-operator. Level 3 applies only to the count aggregation function and level 4 indicates no aggregation function is allowed. Each of the measures with the corresponding aggregation paths will be assigned to the corresponding aggregation levels of restriction.

Enterprise Models to Dimensional Models

Moody and Kortink (2000) proposed designing data warehouse model directly from an Enterprise E/R model. By using this methodology, data warehouse design is more structured. The fundamental of the design is based on a sound semantic structure of an operational database. The approach also gives more room for changes in the future. Designing process to convert E/R scheme into a data warehouse dimensional model is divided into four major steps as follows:

1. *Classify Entities:* The first step is to classify the E/R entities into three categories. The first category is transaction entities. The entities captured data on the business transaction. The bulk of the operation processes involve this type of entities. They record

activities that happen at particular time with computation measurement. This type of entities is a good candidate for the fact table of star schema. Second category of entities is the component entity. These entities are responsible for capturing information related to the transaction such as customer's profile. They are the best candidate for building dimensional tables. Last category is the classification entities used to subgroup the component entities. These entities carry the natural hierarchy's concept for the dimensional tables. For entities that belong to multiple categories, priority will be given to classify them as transaction entity, followed by classification entity, and the last choice is component entity.

2. *Identify Hierarchies:* Hierarchies play a fundamental concept in designing dimensional modeling. Hierarchies are the link that joined the entities from many-to-one relation going to one direction. Entity from the 'one' cardinality side is the parent for the entity from the 'many' cardinality side. When hierarchy has exhausted the entire link extended upward or downward, the hierarchy is called maximal. The bottom entity of maximal hierarchy with all many-to-one relationships is called the minimal entity and the top entity with all one-to-many relationships is called maximal entity.
3. *Produce Dimensional Models:* There are two operators for converting the E/R models into dimensional models. The maximal hierarchies identified in step 2 can be combined using the 'collapsed' operator. In this process, maximal entity combined with the next entity. But the process produces redundancy and renormalization. This process can be repeated until all the entities have been combined into a single table. The second operator is an aggregation operator. Using

this operator, data can be summarized or group together based on business needs. Aggregation process can only be applied to numeric attributes. For the final dimensional models, user can choose a variety of dimensional models from the simplest but compromised on redundancy to the complex with multiple hierarchies model such as Flat schema, Terraced schema, Star schema (Fig. 5), Snowflake schema and Star cluster schema.

4. *Evaluation and refinement:* Up to this point, the generated dimensional model is produced by following a mechanical and structured methodology. The end result might not suit the user requirement or the model is too complex. Some modification or refinement of the model can be done by combining similar fact tables in order to reduce the number of star schemas. Closely related dimension tables will be merged into single dimensional table. Many-to-many relationship will be deleted or converted to many-to-one relationship in order to avoid "break" in the hierarchical chain.

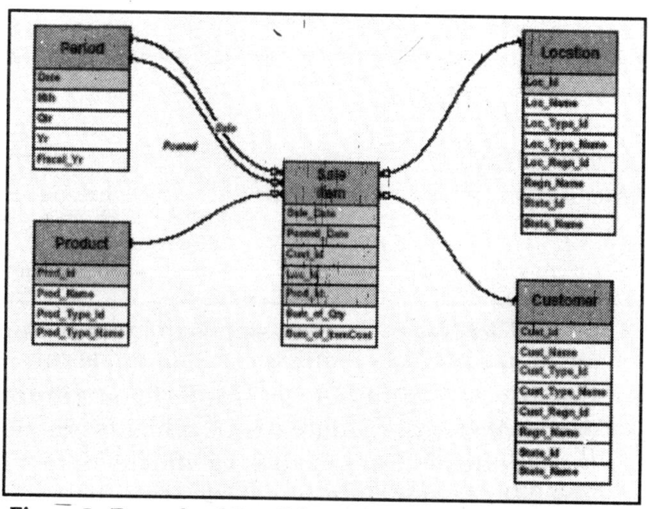

Figure 5: Example of Star Schema (Moody and Kortink, 2000)

Automatic of ME/R Model

Phipps and Davis (2002) proposed automatic algorithms for designing conceptual data warehouse from production E/R schema. The output of their algorithms is the Multidimensional Entity/Relationship (ME/R – Fig. 6) model. Evaluation of the ME/R model is done by running through user queries against the data warehouse model. User queries are treated as function needed by users from the data warehouse. The production E/R model is treated as the framework for the data warehouse design. The automatic algorithms will generate several conceptual candidate schemas from the input E/R schema. The evaluation process helps deciding which schemas to be adopted for the data warehouse design. The algorithm processes require five major steps such as:

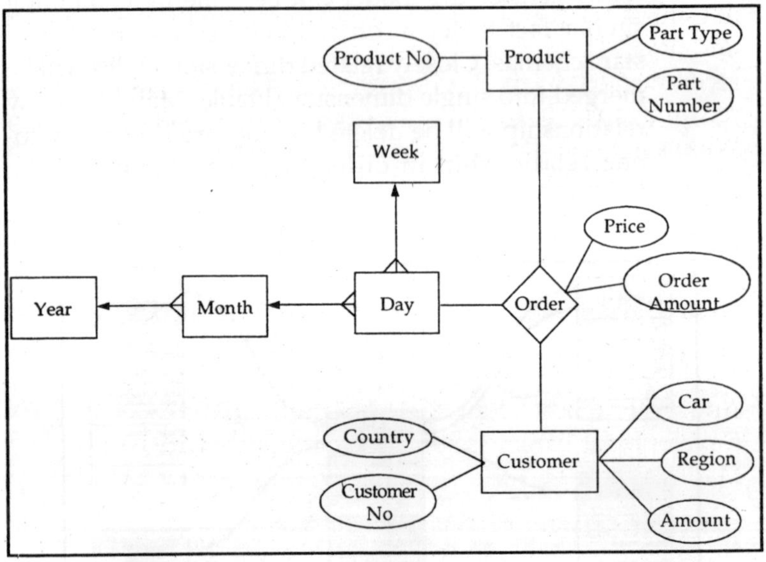

1. *Create Fact Node:* The first step is to identify numeric attributes for each entity by sorting the entities with the highest number of numeric attributes in descending order. Entity with the highest number of numeric attributes is the first candidate for fact node. The ME/R model design starts with the fact node represented by the diamond shape diagram.

2. *Add Fact Attribute:* Next, all the numeric attributes are added as measure for the fact. The measure attributes are depicted as ellipses link to the diamond fact.
3. *Add temporal Dimension:* The next step is the initial attempt to introduce temporal dimension to the model. Attributes with date/time fields are linked to the fact using a hexagon shape diagram. Later in the process, the date/time attributes will be refined with a hierarchical date and time level. If the fact entity does not have any date attributes, temporal dimensions represented by cloud shape are added to the fact node.
4. *Add Other Dimension:* This process is executed if there are still unprocessed attributes left which are non-numeric, non-key or non-date attributes. If the need arise, a dimensional node with the entity's name is created in the shape of a rectangle and all the remaining attributes become its attributes using the ellipse shape.
5. *Add Hierarchical Dimension:* Once all the items from the selected fact entity have been processed, the next step is to 'walk-relations' the rest of the entities in the ER scheme that have relationship to the fact entity. The connected entities to the fact become a level node together with all its attributes. If the connected entity is part of the many-to-one side of the relationship, then the relationship and the linked entity are also applied the 'walk-relations' process which resulted in the creation of another level node with all its attributes. This is a recursive process that has to be repeated until all conditions are met.

DISCUSSION

Six different methodologies for designing conceptual data warehouse from E/R schema have been highlighted in this paper. All the researches have proven that an E/R schema can be a viable option for creating data warehouse. Since the E/R schema represent the semantic operational data for the business, naturally the schema can be converted into data warehouse schema to represent strategic data for user manipulation.

A summary of each methodology are presented in Table 1 from manual transformation, semi-automatic transformation to fully automatic transformation of E/R schema to Data Warehouse schema. Golfarelli et. al. have presented a semi-automatic approach in designing the data warehouse. On the other hand, Phipps and Davis demonstrate the automatic method in designing the data warehouse. The rest of the methodologies are being done manually.

Golfarelli *et al.*, have shown a very systematic method in converting the E/R schema into a conceptual data warehouse design in six steps. The transformation process requires direct involvement of business analyst and data warehouse designer. The Dimensional Fact Model also consists of all the important component of the data warehouse dimensional model. The final model is moderate in complexity.

Cabibbo and Torlone methodology has several intermediate structures starting from E/R schema, modified E/R schema, dimensional graph and finally the MD Model. The final MD Model does not represent a complete conceptual data warehouse model, but consist of building blocks for the construction of the complete conceptual model. In another words, users from different departments have the freedom to construct conceptual model based on their requirement using only the relevant building blocks.

StarER model suggested by Tryfona is a very complex model. Many new symbols are being introduced on top of the existing E/R symbols. Understanding the final data warehouse conceptual model is not easy with the merging of E/R symbols together with the data warehouse symbols. In addition, the steps for transformation process are not clearly identified.

Hüsemann *et al.*, proposed a methodology that utilized the functional dependencies for the creation of dimensional and hierarchies. The final model will contain all the fundamental elements of dimensional model. The model will be based on users' requirement study and input from the business expert.

Table 1
Summary of Researches on E/R Schema Transformation

Researcher	*Model*	*Methodology*
Golfarelli *et al.*, 1998	Dimensional Fact Model – Semi-automatic	– Defining Fact – Building attribute tree – Pruning and grafting attribute tree – Defining dimensions – Defining fact attributes – Defining hierarchies
Cabibbo & Torlone 1998	Multidimensional Data Model	– Identification of facts and dimensions – Restructuring of the E/R scheme – Derivation of a dimensional graph – Translation into the MD model
Tryfona *et al.*, 1999	StarER Model	– Identify facts and properties – Define temporal dimension – Represent objects, properties & relationships – Associate objects to facts – Define hierarchies
Hüsemann *et al.*, 2000	Multidimensional Normal Form Model	– Context definition measures – Dimensional hierarchy design – Definition of summarizability constraints
Moody and Kortink 2000	Dimensional Models	– Classify entities – Identify hierarchies – Produce dimensional Models – Evaluation and refinement
Phipps and Davis 2002	ME/R model – Aautomatic	– Create fact node – Add fact attribute – Add temporal dimension – Add dimension – Add hierarchical dimension

Moody and Kortink proposed a methodology that able to identify the basic components of dimensional model. With the basic components users have the freedom to adjust the final conceptual model that best fit the user requirement. The final model can be as simple as flat schema to the complex star cluster schema.

Phipps and Davis managed to produce a fully automatic methodology for designing multiple candidates for conceptual data warehouse. The candidates have the entire dimensional model component such as fact, attribute, dimensional and hierarchy. The methodology produces all possible candidates for the model which can be massive for a complex E/R model. Some of the candidates selected as facts do belong to suitable hierarchy type. Those candidates should be ignored in the first round. Next, users will perform evaluation process to select suitable candidates to represent the conceptual data warehouse.

For future research, several of the above mention methodologies can be combined in order to produce the most efficient method of producing the conceptual data warehouse model. For example, in order to convert E/R schema automatically to a data warehouse conceptual data model, the automatic methodology of Phipps and Davis will be implemented. Instead of selecting all entities as the fact candidates, only entities identified as transaction entities should be selected as the fact candidate. The classification of transaction entities is based on the Moody and Kortink method. However, not all entities and attributes are needed for the final data model. As suggested by Golfarelli *et al.*, pruning and grafting attribute tree can be implemented at this stage. Several of these techniques can be mixed and matched for the improvement of the data warehouse design methodology.

REFERENCES

Ballard, C. & Herreman, D., *et al.* (1998), Data Modeling Techniques for Data Warehousing, IBM Red Book, San Jose, California.

Batini, C. Ceri, S. & Navathe, S. B., (1992), Conceptual Database Design–An Entity-Relationship Approach. Redwood City, Benjamin/Cummings.

Cabibbo, L. & Torlone, R. (1998), "A Logical Approach to Multidimensional Databases," *Proceedings of EDBT'98: 6th International Conference on Extending Database Technology*, Valencia, Spain.

Chen, P. S. (1976), "The Entity-Relationship Model: Toward unified view of Data," *ACM Trans. Database Systems*, Vol. 1, pp. 9-36.

Golfarelli, M. Maio, D. & Rizzi, S. (1998), "Conceptual Design of Data Warehouses from E/R Schema," *Proceedings of Thirty-First Annual Hawaii International Conference on System Sciences*, Vol. 7, pp. 334.

Hüsemann, B. Lechtenbörger, J. & Vossen G., (2000), "Conceptual Data Warehouses Design," *Proceedings of the International Workshop on Design and Management of Data Warehouses,*

Inmon, W. H. (1993), Building the Data Warehouse, New York: John Wiley.

Moody, D. L. & Kortink, M. A. R. (2000), "From Enterprise Models to Dim. Models: A Methodology for DW and Data Mart Design," *Proceedings of DMDW 2000: International Workshop on Design and Management of Data.*

Phipps, C. & Davis, K. C. (2002), "Automating Data Warehouse Conceptual Schema Design and Evaluation," *Proceedings of DMDW 2002: International Workshop on Design and Management of Data Warehouses.*

Sen, A. & Jacob, V. S. (1998), "Industrial Strength Data Warehousing," *Communication of the ACM*, September.

Tryfona, N. Busborg, F. & Christiansen, J. G. B. (1999), "StarER: A Conceptual Model for Data Warehouse Design," Proceedings of DOLAP '99: 2nd ACM International Workshop on Data Warehousing and OLAP.

CHAPTER 3

REGULATORY CHALLENGES STRATEGICALLY ENHANCE BANKING EFFICIENCY AND STABILITY (THE STUDY OF EAST AFRICAN COUNTRIES)

Ghirmai T. Kefela

INTRODUCTION

If Africa's growth recovery is to be sustained and widespread, effective financial systems are a clear prerequisite. They can ensure that viable business opportunities receive the credit they need, no matter who the entrepreneur may be. The financial sector is made up of the banking sub-sector and the stock or capital market. Again, financial sector development requires growth in the volume of activities as well the rest of the economy. Generally, as the economy develops, the expectation is that the volume of transactions in the financial sector will increase and there will be less reliance on the banking sector, at least, for long-term credit. With an open, competitive and strong financial sector, opportunities are widened and governance improvements underpinned. A rapidly growing number of poor Africans are beginning to feel the benefits of direct access to formal and semi-formal finance – savings facilities as well as credit and other services – at the micro level

Effective finance has a role to play and can speed and improve the provision of physical infrastructure, and the overall governance and business environment.

The primary role of the financial sector, especially in developing countries, is that of mobilizing financial resources from the savers and directing these resources into channels of desired development activities. Against that general background, a useful point of departure is briefly reviewing the nature of the three core functions of national banking systems. The first core function is the mobilization of domestic savings in a safe and efficient manner. This, of course, is the deposit gathering function, which must be rooted in the conviction on the part of the public that deposit balances – especially current account balances – will be paid at par and on demand. The second core function is the channeling of those savings, through the credit decision-making process, to their most efficient uses. To this end, the credit decision-making process must be thorough, objective and balanced; only then will national savings be channeled into the most productive investments. This will, in turn, promote growth and permit borrowers to service their debts in a timely fashion, thereby ensuring the safety of depositors' funds. The final core function is the provision of an efficient, low cost, safe and widely available means of making and receiving payments. Public trust in the banking system will only flourish in a setting in which bank clients – small and large - have virtually complete confidence that they can make and receive payments on a safe and timely basis.

Available data suggests that the financial sector in (SSA) Sub Saharan Africa is lagging behind that of the rest of the world. For instance, the M2/GDP ratio, which was 32 per cent in 1990, increased marginally to 37 per cent by 2003. In the case of East Asia, the corresponding figures are 63.1 and 158.8 per cent respectively. Turning to the SSA stock market, market capitalization, which is one of the measures of size, was about $143 billion in 1990. By 2004, it had doubled to reach $294 billion. Impressive as this seems, it is inferior to the growth of the East Asian stock market size, which increased from about

$87 billion in 1990 to over $1 trillion by 2004. Another measure of size is the number of listed domestic companies. For SSA, there was a decline in the number of listed companies from over 1000 in 1990 to about 900 by 2004, while in the case of East Asia, the number increased from 774 in 1990 to 3,582 by 2004. As economic agents, (household, businesses and government) carry on their consumption and production activities, they need the facilities of credit (short and long-term credit) and equity (financial services) provided by the financial sector (World Bank, 2004).

These financial resources can be injected through the supply (production) channel or through the demand (final consumption) channel. In reality, financial resources are injected into the system through a combination of both channels. However, at any point in time, one of these two channels may be dominant and the imperatives of the predominant channel and the level of development of the economy should influence the role of the state in the financial sector development. An increase in income and or financial resources will lead to an increase in private and government final consumption expenditures. Accordingly, when the banking sector makes more financial resources available to consumers, the immediate effect is for the increased effective demand to put upward pressure on prices. Through higher prices, the increased financial resources will be funneled to the producers. Meanwhile, rising prices will lead to increased output as existing producers step up action and/or new producers, attracted by high profits, come into the economy to set up. Ultimately, the level of economic activities (consumption and production) will be higher.

Resuming normal economic activity will be severely impeded without a revival of commercial banks and insurance companies. The provision of bank finance for working capital, fixed investment, and residential reconstruction must also restart. Banks may take considerable time to restore their capital base, restructure their bad debts, and re-equip and re-staff themselves. In Rwanda, US7 millions was transferred from the network of rural bank co-operatives and into the hands of those responsible for the genocide: the number of bank clients fell to 42,000 compared with 400,000 before the atrocities. Two years after the end of Liberia's civil war, 78 per cent of commercial bank loans were classified as nonperforming. Financial liberalization only works when financial regulation and supervision improves as well (as financial crises over the last two decades demonstrate). Legal reform must also create clear property rights (for collateral-based lending) and punish fraud. For example, Rodrik (1998) argues that there is no evidence in the data that countries without capital controls have grown faster, invested more, or experienced lower inflation. The weaknesses prevalent in the financial systems of developing countries are seen in acute form in conflict-affected countries. These include banking legislations that either omits important prudential regulations or is imprecise; shortages of supervisory skills in financial authorities; and supervisors unwilling to enforce prudential regulations. Considerable technical assistance is required. This requires significant public funds. The key challenge is therefore to rebuild economies so that the benefits of recovery are spread as widely as possible across society, and especially down to the poor.

Banks form the core of financial systems. Thus, whether a country's financial system is "safe and sound" or not depends in large part on the soundness of its banking system. Since the late 1970s, virtually every country on the African continent has experienced banking sector problems. These problems can be quite costly to the country concerned – in both financial and economic terms. Transparency is a cardinal virtue in this domain. Transparency implies openness, communication and accountability. Transparency is introduced as a means of holding public officials accountable and fighting corruption. When government meetings are open to the press and the public, when budgets and financial statements may be reviewed by anyone, when laws, rules and decisions are open to discussion, they are seen as transparent. There is less opportunity for the authorities to abuse the system in their own interest.This is even more reason why we must do our best to understand the causes of banking sector problems and find effective ways to address them, preferably before crises occur.

Usually banks are an instrument of policy in any economy. If the economic system is a capitalist in nature, usually they are owned privately and publicly. If the system is one such as used to be in the Soviet Union (central planning), then banks and other financial institutions are owned by the State, and the State cannot venture to leave huge financial resources outside the purview of the planning agency since it might jeopardize the smooth execution of the plans. From this follows the fact that financial institutions are created as instruments of the major philosophy that guides the economy. They live and die in accordance with the existence of the main philosophy and policy.

REVIEW OF LITERATURE

Causes of Banking Sector Problems

The first order of business is to consider the factors that lead to unsound banking systems. In most cases, banking sector problems begin with lax management within individual banks. Nevertheless, lapses in sound banking practices appear to be pervasive in developing countries – in large part because bank owners and managers often lack strong enough incentives to act prudently. Often there is also a lack of legal and judicial infrastructure, which banks cannot perform properly without and that leads to a breakdown in the credit discipline. One of the principal reasons why incentives are weak is lack of transparency about banks' operations and financial condition, which makes it difficult for market participants–or even bank supervisors–to distinguish the weak institutions from the strong. In many developing countries–as in many industrialized countries–loan valuation and provisioning standards are not rigorous enough to prevent banks from concealing the full extent of non-performing loans. The lack of reliable data and uniform disclosure rules make it difficult for the market–including deposit holders–to compare relative performance. In these circumstances, the market is not in the position to perform the essential role it plays in countries where bank operations are more transparent–that is, rewarding good performers and sanctioning the poor ones.

The problem is compounded when domestic banking supervision is also weak–either because laws and regulations are not comprehensive enough, or because bank supervisors are not free from political interference, or indeed, because the supervisory authority does not have the necessary human and financial resources to carry out its responsibilities effectively. An aggravating factor is the fact that banks in developing countries typically operate in a more volatile economic and financial climate than institutions in industrial countries. Unfortunately, for the most part, banks in developing countries have not responded with appropriate caution, and supervisory authorities have not required sufficiently high capital cushions against the higher risks. Weakness of banking sector can be traced to a variety of sources. It makes sense, therefore, that a successful attack on the problem of unsound banking systems should be launched on several fronts. In fact, a number of constructive steps are already under way.

At the national level, many countries, including Ethiopia, Uganda, Sudan, and Eritrea, have taken or are taking steps to strengthen their banking systems. Banking laws have been updated throughout the region and many countries have made efforts to upgrade their supervision of banks. In particular, Uganda considerably strengthened its banking supervision following its banking crisis in the early 1999s–a terrible one, indeed–and is often used as a model for reforms in the region, and beyond. The region also has begun to see a wave of bank consolidations, as is typical in the rest of the world–or example there have been extensive bank restructurings, mergers, and privatizations in Ethiopia (Geda, 2006) and, to some extent, in Sudan. The Central Bank of Sudan also abandoned treasury bills and government bonds, instruments on which interest was paid. In their place, the Central Bank has issued financial certificates that conform to the Islamic system. One of the main objectives of financial institutions is mobilizing resources (in particular domestic savings) and channeling these to would-be investors. This intermediation role of financial institutions takes different forms in different economic systems. Ethiopia's history of the last three decades clearly shows the validity of this statement.

Uganda has developed regional standards on loan classification and provisioning and on the role of external auditors, and the major milestone that enabled Uganda to move towards full compliance with the Basel Core Principles. The enactment of the new Financial Institutions Act (FIA, 2004) (David Opiokello, 2006) While the Bank of Uganda welcomes the increased use of technology and the growth in financial innovations, there is a challenge in terms of preparing the sector for the implications of increasing globalization. The Bank of Uganda shall endeavor to develop the requisite supervisory and regulatory skills. We expect to have well-capitalized and well-managed financial institutions to face up to the challenges presented by increasing globalization.

The important point is to strengthen the financial system so that it is less prone to crisis, and so that whenever a crisis does occur, the resultant damage to the financial system and to the real sector of the economy is minimized. When banks are not prudently run, not only they allocate resources inefficiently, they also expose themselves to losses at the slightest hint of market turbulence. The Bank of Uganda is therefore determined to insulate the economy from external shocks by adopting prudent monetary policies, a credible exchange rate regime and a well-capitalized, efficient and transparent financial system. To this end, the Bank of Uganda has continued with the structural reforms in the banking sector. The access to finance is an important factor in consumption smoothing and hence poverty reduction. The evidence for a poverty trap is due to liquidity constraint that limits the ability of the rural households on the amount to borrow.

Nevertheless, it is clear from the extent of banking sector problems in some of African countries and elsewhere in the world that major gaps remain in national and international efforts to strengthen banking systems (Camdessus, 1996). At the national level, many of the fundamental causes of unsound banking systems persist, including poor internal governance and a lack of transparency about banks' operations and financial condition, inadequate supervision, and excessive official complacency about problem banks. Moreover, all too often efforts to strengthen domestic banking systems, though welcome, are undertaken only after crisis has struck. It is very important to recognize that this may be the only time when there is sufficient momentum for real reform, as this is very high price to pay. We must be able to do better and avoid such exorbitant costs before the crises exceed 10 percent of GDP.

Financing Growth

Banks are the biggest source of formal finance in developing countries. The banking sector indicators have been developed to extend and complement the financial development that relies heavily on indicators associated to the size, efficiency and stability of the banking sector (World Bank, 2005). The traditional indicators used to assess the size of a country's banking sector are the ratio of M2 (a measure of money supply) to Gross Domestic Product (GDP), and the ratio of private credit to GDP. Both have limitations.

The ratio of private credit to GDP includes non-performing loans and hence disregards the quality of credit allocation. The two traditional indicators of return on assets and the ratio of operating costs to assets are complemented by indicators of competitiveness and by indicators of the efficiency of the banking system structure. Lower profitability and higher bank asset (or deposit) concentration typically related to lower efficiency in the banking sector. The stability indicators are measured by capital adequacy, liquidity, sensitivity to market risk, and asset quality of both lenders and borrowers. One of the foundations of the theoretical literature on banking regulation is that branch banking leads to more stable banking systems by enabling banks to better diversify their assets and widen their depositor base (Gart 1994, Hubbard 1994).

Table 1
Finance Growth Indicators

Banking size indicators	
1.	Central bank assets to GDP
2.	Deposit money banks assets to GDP
3.	Financial system deposits to GDP
4.	M2 to GDP
5.	Private credit to GDP
6.	Private credit to total domestic credit
7.	Private credit to total funding
Banking Sector efficiency indicators	
1.	Returns on assets (adjusted)
2.	Operating costs to total assets
3.	Lending-deposit rates spread
4.	Net interest margin
5.	Three-bank concentration ratio (assets)
6.	Three-bank concentration ratio (deposits)
Banking stability indicators	
1.	Capital adequacy ratio
2.	Non-performing loans ratio
3.	Real credit growth adjusted
4.	Market-to-book-value of equity (borrowers)
5.	Debit-to-book-value of equity (Borrowers)
6.	Interest coverage ratio (Borrowers)
7.	Liquid assets to total assets
8.	Liquid assets to deposits and short-term borrowing
9.	Total return index volatility
10.	Market to book value of equity (banks)

(World Bank, 2005)

Note: The *supply of money* is measured and placed into categories based upon its accessibility. Accessibility refers to how easily you can access and use the money. The first category called *M1*-contains the total dollar amount of currency and coins in circulation, also includes transaction (checking) account balances, traveler's checks that are not issued by banks. The next category of money is called *M2* - contains all balances under M1, and M2 contains savings accounts and time deposits (certificates of deposit) of less than $100,000. M2 also includes money market mutual funds. M2 does NOT contain stock or bond market mutual funds. *M3* contains everything under M2 and M1, and time deposits over $100,000 and includes bank repurchase agreements. Bank repurchase agreements are short-term loans to banks. It contains the overnight Eurodollars are deposits of U.S. currency held at foreign banks, or U.S. currency deposits held by U.S. banks overseas. Overnight refers to the short time period the funds are held on deposit.

Strengthening Africa's Financial Sector

Access to financial services–savings and loans–is lower in SSA than in other developing regions. On the savings side, household deposits in commercial banks have increased slowly relative to GDP since the 1990s. Whereas 90 per cent of households in industrial countries have savings accounts, and one-fourth of households in other low- and middle-income countries have them, only a tenth of households in a large set of SSA countries do. Banks serve mainly governments, the formal sector, and affluent households. Widespread poverty limits both the demand for and the supply of savings facilities. The share of the population having a formal savings account is strongly correlated with poverty rates and per capita income (Gulde and others, 2006). Poor people have only small sums to save, which limits banks' economic opportunities, given the high costs of maintaining small accounts. Banks often respond by charging for opening and maintaining a deposit account, making access to bank services more difficult for small-scale savers. Some countries are reinventing state and development banks to promote more financing. Gabon, for example, is using development banks to channel credit to priority sectors (Pattillo, Gulde, Christenson, 2007). Other countries, such as members of the West African Economic and Monetary Union (WAEMU), are forming state-owned specialized banks to give certain sectors access to desired types of finance.

Many African countries have set up stock markets to help companies raise long-term finance. Whereas there were just five stock markets in SSA in 1989, there are now 15, including the most recently established in Malawi, Swaziland, and Uganda. Corporate financing patterns in certain SSA countries, such as Ghana, South Africa, and Zimbabwe, suggest that stock markets can be a source of finance, but only for a limited number of listed firms. In addition, in all SSA countries except South Africa, stock markets suffer from little turnover and market capitalization partly because of inadequate informational and disclosure rules and supervisory frameworks. Finally, stock markets tend to be more efficient and deliver greater economic benefits when basic financial sector infrastructure and a well-functioning banking system are in place. Most African capital markets are still tiny and fledgling especially in comparison with their counterparts in other regions. In sub-Saharan Africa, the Johannesburg Stock Exchange accounts for nearly 90 per cent of the total value of the region's market capitalization (listed shares). Even the Nigerian exchange, ranked second among sub-Saharan exchanges in 1999, had a market capitalization of just $2.94 bn (equivalent to 6.9 per cent of gross domestic product). In the case of West Africa's other exchanges–the eight-country regional exchange in Côte d'Ivoire and the Ghana Stock Exchange–the amounts were just $1.5 bn (5.5 per cent) and $916 mn (12.1 per cent), respectively. Except for the Johannesburg exchange, most African exchanges share other impediments to their growth and development: too few indigenous companies, small average company size, and low liquidity levels (the value of shares traded in relation to total market capitalization). The number of companies listing shares generally is low, and trading in one or just a few stocks often dominates total trading activity (Irving, 2000).

Remittances to SSA countries, another type of capital inflow, have increased rapidly in recent years. In 2005, they totaled $188 billion–twice the amount of official assistance developing countries received. Moreover, there is evidence that such flows are underreported. Indeed, remittances through informal channels could add at least 50 per cent to global recorded flows. Most of the reported flows go to regions other than sub-Saharan Africa (SSA), but SSA has still been part of the overall rising global trend. Between 2000 and 2005, remittances to the region increased by more than 55 per cent, to nearly $7 billion, whereas they increased for developing countries as a group by 81 per cent (Gupta, Pattillo, and Wagh, 2007). As strong demand for money transfer services continues, spurring needed improvements in the financial sector infrastructure for remittances, more people–including the rural poor–could gain access to financial services. Africa receives just 4 per cent of total remittances–by far the smallest share–to developing countries and just 33 per cent of those to India, the top recipient. In contrast, countries in Latin America and the Caribbean receive about 25 per cent of all remittances, as do countries in the East Asia and Pacific region. However, countries need to reform payment systems to increase the efficiency of remittance services. Predictable legal and regulatory frameworks must be in place that does not discriminate against smaller money transfer operators, and there is a need for competitive market conditions and skills upgrading in the industry. Bringing recipient households into the formal financial sector is only the first step in using remittances more effectively. Country surveys indicate that, although households typically spend a large proportion of their remittances, their propensity to save can be as high as 40 per cent. For policymakers, the challenge is to channel these savings into productive uses.

Beyond developing international guidelines, we also need to find ways to deal with other difficult and even more pressing issues. Such as: how to help countries to take corrective action against problem banks, preferably early while distortions are small; how to close down insolvent banks; how to design payments systems so as to limit contagion; and how to ensure that lender of last resort facilities do not prolong the lives of unsound banks or lead to moral hazard. To do this, the region must improve productivity, increase investment, and dramatically raise levels of domestic savings.

The level of domestic savings in sub-Saharan Africa remains below that of all other developing regions, representing only about 12% of aggregate GDP. Savings rates in Asia, meanwhile, are as high as 30%, and even in South Asia the savings rate is 17%. In addition, it can be done much to increase revenues, without raising marginal tax rates, by eliminating exemptions and broadening the tax base. To encourage private savings, governments must reform property ownership laws and more broadly promote private sector development, improve the investment climate, build infrastructure, and increase access to credit. Strengthening financial sectors is critical to supporting such reforms. In addition, reforming weak banking sectors can have a direct impact on savings, as weak banks tend to have higher loan-to-deposit spreads and thereby discourage savings and investment. A stronger financial sector is also critical to improving income levels. Low-income families, small-to-medium size enterprises, and rural entrepreneurs in developing countries have difficulty obtaining financial services. Banking sector penetration in a typical sub-Saharan African country is around 1% of GDP, far below a more advanced economy like Brazil, where penetration is approaching 25%, or industrialized countries where it is near 85%. Women's World Banking estimates that fewer than 2 per cent of low-income entrepreneurs worldwide have access to financial services. Fragile banking systems not only misallocate resources, but also leave themselves vulnerable to terrorists, money-launderers, capital flight, and others who would abuse the financial system. Financial institutions that simply forward financial resources to the public sector will not be able to play an intermediating role (King, and Levine, 1993, Levine 1997). The financial services to low income households and entrepreneurs in the remote urban and rural areas may be the most effective way to increase monetization, savings, reduce poverty and achieve broad-based economic growth. Yet in Africa, fewer than 2 per cent of low-income producers have access to financial services from the moneylenders. Therefore, financial intermediaries need to adopt new paradigms and take on new and aggressive roles in building financial infrastructure that serves the majority of people and enable the poor to share economic growth.

Table 2

M2 to GDP Ratios of Various Countries, 1993-1998

Country	*1993*	*1994*	*1995*	*1996*	*1997*	*1998*
USA	0.60	0.57	0.57	0.58	0.58	0.60
Italy	0.54	0.51	0.47	0.45	0.47	0.47
Chile	0.40	0.37	0.39	0.39	0.40	0.42
Brazil	0.73	0.38	0.28	0.24	0.28	0.28
Ethiopia	0.28	0.32	0.28	0.25	0.25	0.21
Kenya	0.17	0.16	0.15	0.15	0.14	0.13
Sudan	0.12	0.24	0.14	0.11	0.10	N/A
Eritrea	0.02	0.01	0.01	0.01	0.01	0.01

Source: IMF (2000)

Table 3
Ratio of Loans to the Private Sector to Total Domestic Loans of Various Countries, 1993-1998

Country	*1993*	*1994*	*1995*	*1996*	*1997*	*1998*
USA	0.81	0.82	0.8	0.83	0.83	0.85
Argentina	0.70	0.76	0.71	0.71	0.72	0.73
Nigeria	0.31	0.32	0.42	0.68	0.64	0.71
Kenya	0.63	0.54	0.59	0.62	0.67	0.58
Ethiopia	0.12	0.16	0.26	0.38	0.44	0.44
Sudan	0.21	0.28	0.28	0.32	0.34	0.31
Eritrea	0.39	0.41	0.14	0.14	0.29	0.27

Source: IMF (2000)

Challenges for Reform

While several Sub-Saharan African countries have already made substantial progress in reforming and modernizing their financial sectors, there is still much work to do:

(a) Banking systems often still operate with a substantial degree of government ownership or control. Many African countries faced external shocks; the primary cause of financial distress of banks is political, in the form of pressure not to recover debts, or to lend to weak borrowers including parastatals, politically connected private sector borrowers, and the government itself.

(b) Bank supervision remains weak, enforcement tools inadequate, and management standards low. Most African financial sectors need reform in the areas of prudential regulations, banking supervision, bankruptcy laws and contract enforcement law. Compliance with international codes and standards is also an area in need of reform.

(c) The depth and size of Sub-Saharan Africa's financial markets are inadequate. The banking industry is highly concentrated (in a study of 5 Sub-Saharan African countries, 60% of banking sector assets were concentrated in, at most, 4 banks); loan portfolios are not diversified, reflecting national economies; capital markets are shallow; and insurance and pension systems are not well developed:

(d) Mobilizing the Diaspora was the latest step that aims to promote greater investment on the African continent. The African Diaspora is already playing an important role in African development. Each year it remits an estimated $45 billion. Mobilizing the Diaspora sought to explore how these funds could be better structured to promote sustainable development on the continent. It is also considered that the African Diaspora is stimulating the transfer of intellectual resources and creative business practices (Hampshire, 2004). However, just 6% of remittances are actually channeled into investments. There is an appetite within the Diaspora to invest in Africa: 91% of those questioned said they would be interested in doing so if certain obstacles were tackled, such as a lack of reliable information of the business environment in Africa is discouraging investment (Banjoko, 2004–Africa Recruit). Amongst the investment vehicles available to the Diaspora, bank accounts and property are the most readily available. A private equity fund is the investment vehicle with the greatest potential to create employment and create a multiplier effect in the economy, particularly if it is private equity investment into small and medium-sized enterprises (SMEs). Governments must promote private equity investments in Africa by creating tax incentives for the Diaspora. Without reforms in these areas, financial systems will continue to experience high levels of non-performing loans, interest rates that do not adequately reflect the level of risk, and the crowding out of the private sector. In Africa, as in most other developing regions, the predominant source of banking stress is nonperforming loans. A loan is seldom classified as nonperforming until payments due under the contract have fallen six or more months in arrears.

The financial sector has an economy-wide effect. All other sectors rely on financial intermediation for growth. Second, perhaps more than in any other economic sector, a stronger, deeper financial sector can protect an economy from external as well domestic shocks. Therefore, financial sector openness can promote stability. As financial institutions aggregate capital, they must move it into the business and industry sectors where they can earn the best risk-adjusted returns for their savers. That means investing in the businesses that can make the best use of their capital–in other words, those that offer the highest productivity. Moreover, rising productivity–output per worker–is at the root of raising living standards. Ghana took a very systematic approach to reforming its financial sector in the early 90s. In the first phase of those reforms, the government placed ceilings on net bank credit to the government to avoid crowding out the private sector. While administrative controls on interest rates remained in place, they were gradually relaxed. The second phase of reform focused on liberalizing controls on interest rates and bank credit. The third phase was a gradual shift from a direct system of monetary controls to an indirect system that utilized market-based policy instruments.

Individual banks experience stress when the cash flows generated by their earning assets prove insufficient to service their deposits and other debt. As long as a bank is perceived either to be intrinsically solvent or to be supported at least implicitly by credible government guarantees, its managers can manage the stress by selling liquid assets and by borrowing funds from new depositors and from other institutions. This paper seeks to show that, during the last two decades, the banking systems of most African countries have been under more or less permanent stress and to explain why. The explanation combines two factors: First, depositors' vulnerability to loss: the constant difficulties individual depositors encounter both in obtaining timely and reliable information and, regulatory strategies that did not efficiently counteract the weaknesses because of the limited fiscal capacity and the regulatory policymakers operate. Financial instability occurs when the reliability of information about savings and investment opportunities deteriorates sharply enough to disrupt the flow of savings and investment.

THE BANKING SYSTEM IN EAST AFRICAN NATIONS

Eritrea

According to the International Monetary Fund, commercial banks in Eritrea–all government owned and operated–appear to comply with prudent regulations. Although the commercial banking sector is largely profitable, mostly owing to income from foreign exchange transactions, a high proportion of non-performing loans burdens the sector. The Commercial Bank of Eritrea (CBE) deploys only 29% of the funds collected from its depositors. At the same time, a lack of finance for small firms in Eritrea is an important obstacle for the development of the country. Core lending activities do not generate sufficient income to cover operating costs at most commercial banks (Journal of Eritrean Studies, Vol. 1, No.1, p. 59-74). Helping Eritrea move out of the current crisis requires close attention and thoughtful adaptation of Bank instruments; it will not be enough to take standard instruments from the shelf and expect them to yield success. At the same time small firms, which are considered major actors in the economy, are constrained in their growth by a restricted access to credit. According to the National Survey (1995), the small firms in the country have financial, marketing, transportation, personal and other constraints. Finance is reported as the major barrier for start-ups and as the second after marketing during normal operations of small firms: 43 per cent have financial constraints at the start-up and 20 per cent face such constraints during normal operation. The bank's corporate policies are reflected in the Country Program's emphasis on promoting growth, human development, private sector development, environmental sustainability and financial management. Despite some early difficulties, bank assistance has ultimately been in line with the processes of the Comprehensive Development Framework (World Bank, 2004).

Kenya

Kenya acquired its first separate currency on 14 September 1966, when the IMF announced the initial par value for the

Kenya shilling. The powers of the CBK were reduced in the early 1990s with the liberalization of the financial sector. The commercial banks are free to set their own interest and exchange rates. The banks rapidly rising loan-able resources from the banking system to the private sector, increased access to social services, growing confidence of the business sector, and better prospects for the economy. The central bank of Kenya adopted a monetary policy in 2003 that sought to support economic recovery while ensuring macroeconomic stability with particular focus on inflation, stable interest rates and the exchange rate. As a result, the measures they took created conditions for increased competition among commercial banks for a limited supply of Government securities. In the financial year 2004/2005, the bank of Kenya focused on an exit strategy from high inflation environment and by June 2005, overall inflation had eased significantly. Further easing continued through October 2005 when overall inflation fell to 3.7%. Throughout the period since 2003, economic activity continued to expand with real GDP growth rising from 2.8% in 2003 to 4.6% in June 2005 and at 5% or more by June 2006.

The bank of Kenya is responsible for two other important assignments besides monetary policy. The first is to ensure that those who are placing their resources in banks and financial institutions are protected. The Central Bank is required to ensure that banks and financial institutions are competently managed and completely transparent. The second responsibility of the Central Bank is to ensure that banks act as efficient financial intermediaries utilizing the nation's savings effectively to create jobs and improve national welfare. The central bank has also revised prudential regulations based on global experience. During the past two years, the Bank's supervision process identified infringements to the banking laws and regulations. These include the problems of an inadequate legal framework for enforcing remedial action and gaps in supervisory capacity to perform critical transaction testing and to form an independent opinion on the value of securities that collateralize non-performing loans. They set out to tackle these challenges by complementing professional skills available within the Central Bank with highly specialized skills that were sourced externally. The central bank's new in-depth approach to the supervision of banks and financial institutions activities has become the norm for the routine supervision missions. An important challenge faced by the banks has been the disposal of collateral used to secure non-performing loans. These changes to the methods for disposal of collateral have the benefit of improving credit allocation in favor of credit worthy borrowers, maintaining financial discipline among borrowers and early recognition of bad debts (Mullei, 2005). Going forward, the Central Bank of Kenya sees three main pillars, which constitute their vision for their banking sector. First is the achievement of a sound legal framework for the banking sector. Second is the achievement of an efficient and stable financial sector. Third is increased access to financial services. The Government has given a firm commitment to limiting its domestic borrowing to manageable levels and it will be creating a favorable environment for expansion of credit to the private sector and increasing economic growth with enhanced access to financial services.

Ethiopia

The establishment of the Abyssinian Bank in 1905 marked the start of modern banking in Ethiopia. With the fall of the Derg in 1991, the new government faced the difficult tasks of organizing the demobilization as well as starting the transition to a market economy (Hansson 1995). War and the Derg's policies had left a crippled economy and an impoverished people. Economic reform began soon after the new government took power. Despite five years of rapid economic growth based on sound economic policies and high levels of aid, Ethiopia remains one of the world's poorest countries. The economy is estimated to have grown at a rate of 6.8 per cent in real terms in 2004/05 and is approaching the 7 per cent growth rate needed to reach the Millennium Development Goals (MDG).

Due to the nature of the Ethiopian financial sector, in which there are no foreign banks, a non-competitive market structure the state-owned banks have the dominant role and strong capital controls. The Ethiopian economy would benefit from financial sector liberalization, especially from the entry of foreign banks and the associated privatization of state-owned banks (Kiyota, Peitsch, & Stern, 2007). Ethiopia appears unique compared to its East African neighbors (namely Kenya, Tanzania, and Uganda) and many other developing countries in that it has not yet opened its banking sector to foreign participation. The Ethiopian banking sector remains isolated from the impact of globalization. Although Ethiopian policy makers understand the potential importance of financial liberalization, it is widely believed that liberalization may result in loss of control over the economy and may not be economically beneficial. Ethiopia's financial sectors remain closed and are they are less developed than its neighbors are. Ethiopia has no capital market and very limited informal investing in shares of private companies. A series of financial sector reforms has been introduced since 1994, when private banks were allowed to be re-established. Nevertheless, the three large state-owned banks continue to dominate the market in terms of capital, deposits and assets.

Sudan

Before Sudanese independence, there had been no restrictions on the movement of funds between Egypt and Sudan, and the value of the currency used in Sudan was tied to that of Egypt. In 1959, the Bank of Sudan was established, and in February 1960, the Bank of Sudan began acting as the central bank of Sudan, issuing currency, assisting the development of banks, providing loans, maintaining financial equilibrium, and advising the government. Work started in implementing the Banks Restructuring Program announced in 2000, with the objective of establishing large and sound banking units to meet the international competition in the banking industry. One of the main functions of Bank of Sudan is to perform the role of "Lender of last resort", by assisting banks in overcoming problems of temporary liquidity shortages and reducing the finance gap for the important economic sectors (Bank of Sudan,

2004). Meanwhile, Dubai Islamic Bank (DIB) has acquired 60% of Sudan's Al Khartoum Bank. The Government of Sudan had owned 99% of the bank's total shares and Sudanese investors, the remaining 1%. DIB will own the majority of shares in Al Khartoum Bank, Sudan's first bank, established in 1913. Mr. Khalil General Manager - points out that until recently, Sudanese banks were used to paying a rate of return on deposits and investment certificates much higher than those paid by banks and financial institutions outside of Sudan. "The purpose was to attract the liquidity both in local and foreign currencies circulating outside the banking system, to encourage savings and turning it into real investments. The banks have been freed from government control over their sectoral lending, but in the second stage of reform, all Sudan's banks have until 2003 to meet the Basel criteria. If they fail, they will be forced to sell out or close (Bank of Sudan Governor, Sabir Al Hassan). "Al Khartoum Bank has recorded high growth rates during the past few years. The bank was able to increase profits to US$7 billion in 2004 as compared to US$3.5 billion in 2003. These results reflect its ability to grow and we are confident that performance will further improve" (Kooheji, 2005). Economic reforms have been successfully applied, and the activation of all economic sectors and other activities has caused an increase in the average growth of the industrial section to 4.6%, according to the last report issued by the International Monetary Fund. The Central Bank of Sudan continued to play its role as the bank for the central and regional governments, and for government and semi-government institutions, contributing to their capital formation and keeping their accounts in both local and foreign currencies.

Uganda

The Bank of Uganda was established on 16 May 1966 as the bank of issue, undertaking the function previously served by the East African Currency Board in Nairobi. The government-owned Uganda Commercial Bank (UCB) provided a full commercial banking service, complementary to and in competition with other commercial banks in the country. The financial sector in Uganda is strong and resilient. Public confidence in the banking sector has increased as indicated in the rising level of total deposits. The government supported the establishment of a stock exchange in Kampala, and it inaugurated the Capital Markets Authority in 1995/96. The initial stage of capital market development concentrated on the inner-bank market and the sale of Treasury bills, which the Bank of Uganda started selling in 1992 at weekly auctions. The exchange was officially opened in 1997, but in 1999, had not been active since inception. The IMF finds a strong link between Uganda's improved record of accomplishment in that regard and a series of steps the country took in 2002 to strengthen the sector. The IMF study finds a marked improvement in the health of Uganda's banking system after distressed banks were closed, a risk-based approach to supervision was introduced, and the country's dominant state-owned Uganda Commercial Bank was sold to an international bank (IFC, 2006). There is also a need to widen the outreach banking services into the rural areas. Therefore, Bank of Uganda shall continue to encourage the growth of Microfinance institutions (MFIs) to improve access to financial markets.

CONCLUSION

An effective domestic banking system is one of the most basic prerequisites for robust economic performance over time all financial sector development is critical to stronger economic growth, improved productivity, increased investment rates and better savings rates. A competitive and open financial sector can play a critical role in this process. Over the past twenty years, all the above-mentioned East African countries have experienced major problems within individual banking institutions or entire banking systems. While there are so many reasons for the banking failure, and those reasons may vary from country to country, the following common denominators have been present in virtually all such episodes. Among those are (a) a rapid changes in the macroeconomic and macro-financial environment, (b) inadequate internal controls and procedures, together with lapses in official supervision, and (c) concentrated patterns of credit or market risk exposure.

Even though countries have used a variety of devices to spread costs over a long period, it has been common a direct fiscal costs ranging from 5% to 10% of GDP. Literally tens, if not hundreds, of billions of dollars of precious domestic savings have been poured into a bad credits in a setting in which such savings are in very short supply. The paralyzing effects of banking crises on both lenders and borrowers have also severely restrained the GDP growth. The erosion of public confidence in the banking system should be considered and reforms are needed to remedy the prevailing problems that are so vital to the long run success of those countries in question. The road ahead will be beset with problems and challenges that will not be easily overcome. Given the dynamic nature of the banking industry, it can only be expected that routine, technical, and operational issues will emerge from time to time and move forward. Since the level of saving in Africa is low for any meaningful and transformational investment, the alternative weapon they may have among others is through increased monetization or credit creation. To achieve these results, an efficient banking system, prudential controls and a friendly, non-distorted macroeconomic framework are required.

REFERENCES

Adelman, Irma (1999), "The Role of Government in Economic Development," Working Paper 890, Giannini Foundation of Agricultural Economics, Department of Agricultural and Resource Economics and Policy, University of California at Berkeley.

Ajakaiye, Olu (2004), "Centrality of Planning to Alternative Development Paradigm in Africa," In: Bade Onimode (Ed.), *African Development and Governance Strategies in the 21st Century: Essays in Honour of Adebayo Adedeji at Seventy*, Zed Books, London and New York, Chapter 5.

Ajakaiye, Olu (2002), "Banking Sector Reforms and Economic Performance in Nigeria," In: Howard Stein, Olu Ajakaiye and

Peter Lewis (Eds.), *Deregulation and the Banking Crises in Nigeria: A Comparative Study*, Palgrave, UK.

Ajakaiye, D. O. (1995), "Short Run Macroeconomic Effects of Bank, Lending Rates in Nigeria, 1987-91: A General Equilibrium Analysis," AERC Research Paper No. 24, African Economic Research Consortium, Nairobim – (1992), "Challenges of the Nigerian Banking Sector.

A Macro-Claessens, Stijn (2005), "*Access to Financial Services: A Review of the Issues and Public Policy Objectives*," Policy Research Working Paper No. 3589 (Washington: World Bank), Gulde, Anne-Marie, and Catherine Pattillo, 2006, "Adding Depth," Finance & Development, June (Washington: International Monetary Fund).

——, & Jakob Christensen, with Kevin Carey & Smita Wagh, (2006), "*Sub-Saharan Africa: Financial Sectors – Issues, Challenges and Reform Strategies*," (Washington: International Monetary Fund).

Sy, Amadou (2006), "*Financial Integration in the West African Economic and Monetary Union*," IMF Working Paper No. 06/214 (Washington: International Monetary Fund).

http://www.unepfi.org/fileadmin/publications/atf/sustainable_banking_africa_2004.pdf

http://siteresources.worldbank.org/INTAFRSUMAFTPS/Resources/MFWfAFinalNov2.pdf

http://www2.bc.edu/~kaneeb/BankRuns.pdf

http://www.bou.or.ug/bouwebsite/export/sites/default/bou/bou-downloads/annual_supervision/2001/BSAnnualReports_2001.pdf

http://www.bis.org/review/r060901f.pdf

http://rru.worldbank.org/fpdforum/presentations/5aJustineBagyenda.pdf

http://www.imf.org/external/pubs/ft/issues/issues23/index.htm

http://www.bceao.int/internet/bcweb.nsf/files/colloque12005e.pdf/$FILE/colloque12005e.pdf

http://www.geocities.com/~dagmawi/News/Aug21_ Erit Econ_USEmb.html

http://www.wider.unu.edu/publications/dps/dp2001-55.pdf

Geda

http://www.sudantribune.com/spip.php?article22650

http://www.bankerme.com/bme/2006/may/sudan.asp

http://www.bi.go.id/NR/rdonlyres/DBA4F7E1-6C81-4D19-957C-A1FA70A4B844/1925/Bankers_Dinner05_eng.pdf

http://www.centralbank.go.ke/downloads/gov_speeches/kib111105.pdf

http://lnweb18.worldbank.org/oed/oeddoclib.nsf/DocUNIDViewForJavaSearch/6380291B1D8CBE1B85256E 9F0056CCE6/$file/cae_eritrea.pdf

http://lcweb2.loc.gov/frd/cs/profiles/Eritrea.pdf

http://www.imf.org/external/NP/fsap/fsap.asp

http://www.imf.org/external/np/vc/2001/022301.htm

http://www.financial-indicators.org/banking_financing.php

http://hei.unige.ch/mpfsrp/papersmpfsrp/collier-pap.pdf

http://www.uneca.org/eca_resources/Major_ECA_Websites/6finmin/cmffin1.htm

http://homepage.eircom.net/~phonohan/diagnosing.pdf

http://www.fondad.org/publications/africaworld/Fondad-AfricaWorld-Chapter7.pdf

http://www.ustreas.gov/press/releases/kd3805.htm

http://www.worldbank.org/afr/findings/english/find276.htm

http://dissertations.ub.rug.nl/FILES/faculties/eco/2005/h.t.mehrteab/c3.pdf

http://www.bankofsudan.org/english/Periodicals/annual/annual04e/chapter_2.pdf

(Sudan)

http://www.worldbank.org/mdf/mdf2/papers/benefit/finance/abouali.pdf

CHAPTER 4

A NOTE ON THE LAW OF CAPITAL MARKETS

Athanasios Koulakiotis
Apostolos Dasilas
Nicholas Papsuriopoulos

INTRODUCTION

The aim of this study is to rank the level of harmonisation on disclosure accounting rules, bankruptcy protection rules and shareholder protection rules on European capital markets for cross-listed companies that decide to list in these stock exchanges. For this purpose, we have studied the paper of La Porta *et al.*, (1998) in order to rank the European capital markets according to their exposure to high, low or similar regulatory environments between the foreign market and home market. The difference between our study and that of La Porta *et al.*, (1998) is that we summarize some of the results of La Porta et al. study on financial law in order to provide a list of 'Law Ranks' on European capital markets.

THE LAW OF CAPITAL MARKETS

The tables below refer to the accounting disclosure standards, bankruptcy protection rules and shareholder protection rules differences between foreign and home European markets for cross-listed companies. Table 1 measures the accounting differences between home and foreign European markets and show that companies that listed from London Stock Exchange (LSE) to the rest of European stock exchanges are listed in an environment with low accounting standards. However, exception is the case of the Stockholm Stock Exchange (SSE) where the accounting standards are higher than the home market. With the same way, we can interpret the rest of the results of the Table 1.

Accounting Disclosure Standards' Differences

Table 1 presents La Porta *et al.*, (1998) regulatory classification index. Data on regulatory classification were obtained from La Porta *et al.*, findings for European home equities that traded on European foreign markets in December 1998. For each stock eligible for dual listing, we identify the difference in accounting disclosure rules between the home and foreign European markets. La Porta *et al.*, (1998)[1] constructed this index by examining and rating a minimum of three companies in each country using 1990 annual reports, studying the inclusion or omission of 90 items. These items fall into seven categories: general information, income statements, balance sheets, funds flow statement, accounting standards, stock data, and special items. The companies represent a cross section of various industry groups; industrial companies represent 70 per cent, and financial companies represent the remaining 30 per cent. 'M' means that the foreign cross-listing is located in a market with more onerous accounting disclosure rules compared to the home listings. 'L' refers to less onerous accounting disclosure rules compared to the home listings and 'TS' refers to exchanges that have similar accounting disclosure rules.

At first glance, we see that the accounting disclosure rules between London Stock Exchange and the rest of European stock markets and between Stockholm Stock Exchange and the rest of European stock markets are low. On the other hand, the accounting disclosure rules between Brussels Stock Exchange and the rest of European stock markets are high. For the rest of European stock markets the results are mixed.

Table 1
Accounting Disclosure Standards' Differences

Markets	*LO*	*IRL*	*BRU*	*FR*	*IT*	*NET*	*SP*	*AU*	*GER*	*SWI*	*DEN*	*FIN*	*NOR*	*SWE*
LO		N/A	L	L	L	L	L	L	L	L	L	L	L	M
IRL	N/A		N/A	N/A	N/A	N/A	N/A	N/A	N/A	N/A	N/A	N/A	N/A	N/A
BRU	M	N/A		M	M	M	M	L	M	M	M	M	M	M
FR	M	N/A	L		L	L	L	L	L	L	L	M	M	M
IT	M	N/A	L	M		M	M	L	TS	M	TS	M	M	M
NET	M	N/A	L	M	L		TS	L	L	M	L	M	M	M
SP	M	N/A	L	M	L	TS		L	L	M	L	M	M	M
AU	M	N/A	M	M	M	M	M		M	M	M	M	M	M
GER	M	N/A	L	M	TS	M	M	L		M	TS	M	M	M
SWI	M	N/A	L	M	L	L	L	L	L		L	M	M	M
DEN	M	N/A	L	M	TS	M	M	L	TS	M		M	M	M
FIN	M	N/A	L	L	L	L	L	L	L	L	L		L	M
NOR	M	N/A	L	L	L	L	L	L	L	L	L	M		M
SWE	L	N/A	L	L	L	L	L	L	L	L	L	L	L	

Note: LO stands for London Stock Exchange, IRL stands for Dublin Stock Exchange, BRU stands for Brussels Stock Exchange, FR stands for Paris Stock Exchange, IT stands for Milan Stock Exchange, NET stands for Amsterdam Stock Exchange, SP stands for Madrid Stock Exchange, AU stands for Vienna Stock Exchange, GER stands for Frankfurt Stock Exchange, SWI stands for Zurich Stock Exchange, DEN stands for Copenhagen Stock Exchange, FIN stands for Helsinki Stock Exchange, NOR stands for Oslo Stock Exchange, SWE stands for Stockholm Stock Exchange, N/A means not available.

Creditor Bankruptcy Protection Rules' Differences

Table 2 makes reference to the bankruptcy protection rules differences according to the creditor rights index that has been identified in the study of La Porta *et al.*, (1998). Data on creditor rights index were obtained from La Porta *et al.*, (1998) findings for European home equities that traded on foreign European markets in December 1998. For each stock eligible for dual listing, we identify the difference in creditor rights between the home and foreign European markets. The index is formed when (a) the country imposes restrictions, such as creditors' consent or minimum dividends to file for reorganization; (b) secured creditors are able to gain possession of their security once the reorganization petition has been approved (no automatic stay); (c) secured creditors are ranked first in the distribution of the proceeds that result from the disposition of the assets of a bankrupt firm; and (d) the debtor does not retain the administration of its property pending the resolution of the reorganization. The index ranges from zero to four[2]. 'M' means that the foreign cross-listing is located in a market with more onerous bankruptcy protection rules compared to the home listings. 'L' means less onerous bankruptcy protection rules compared to the home listings and 'TS' refers to exchanges that have similar bankruptcy protection rules.

The results from Table 2 show that the bankruptcy protection between London Stock Exchange and the rest of European capital markets is high. Exception is the home market of Dublin in comparison with the foreign European markets. In particular, low bankruptcy protection rules apply for the foreign capital markets of London, Brussels, Milan, Amsterdam, Madrid, Vienna, Frankfurt, Copenhagen, Oslo, and Stockholm, while high regulatory environment appears to have the Paris stock exchange and a similar regulatory environment has the Zurich stock exchange and the Helsinki stock exchange. For the rest of European stock markets the results are not so clear.

Shareholder Protection Rules' Differences

Table 3 presents La Porta *et al.*, (1998) ownership concentration index. Data on ownership concentration index were obtained

Table 2
Creditor Bankruptcy Protection Rules' Differences

Markets	*LO*	*IRL*	*BRU*	*FR*	*IT*	*NET*	*SP*	*AU*	*GER*	*SWI*	*DEN*	*FIN*	*NOR*	*SWE*
LO		M	M	M	M	M	M	M	M	M	M	M	M	M
IRL	L		L	M	L	L	L	L	L	TS	L	TS	L	L
BRU	L	M		M	TS	TS	TS	L	L	M	L	M	TS	TS
FR	L	L	L		L	L	L	L	L	L	L	L	L	L
IT	L	M	TS	M		TS	TS	L	L	M	L	M	TS	TS
NET	L	M	TS	M	TS		TS	L	L	M	L	M	TS	TS
SP	L	M	TS	M	TS	TS		L	L	M	L	M	TS	TS
AU	L	M	M	M	M	M	M		TS	M	TS	M	M	M
GER	L	M	M	M	M	M	M	TS		M	TS	M	M	M
SWI	L	TS	L	M	L	L	L	L	L		L	TS	L	L
DEN	L	M	M	M	M	M	M	TS	TS	M		M	M	M
FIN	L	TS	L	M	L	L	L	L	L	TS	L		L	L
NOR	L	M	TS	M	TS	TS	TS	L	L	M	L	M		TS
SWE	L	M	TS	M	TS	TS	TS	L	L	M	L	M	TS	

Note: LO stands for London Stock Exchange, IRL stands for Dublin Stock Exchange, BRU stands for Brussels Stock Exchange, FR stands for Paris Stock Exchange, IT stands for Milan Stock Exchange, NET stands for Amsterdam Stock Exchange, SP stands for Madrid Stock Exchange, AU stands for Vienna Stock Exchange, GER stands for Frankfurt Stock Exchange, SWI stands for Zurich Stock Exchange, DEN stands for Copenhagen Stock Exchange, FIN stands for Helsinki Stock Exchange, NOR stands for Oslo Stock Exchange, SWE stands for Stockholm Stock Exchange, N/A means not available.

from La Porta *et al.*, (1998) findings for European home equities that traded on European foreign markets in December 1998. For each stock eligible for dual listing, we identify the difference in ownership concentration between the home and foreign European markets. La Porta *et al.*, (1998) use ownership concentration in 10 largest private firms as an index of investor protection. The index is constructed using the average percentage of common shares owned by the three largest shareholders in the 10 largest non-financial, privately owned domestic firms in a given country. A firm is considered privately owned if the state is not a known shareholder. 'M' means that the foreign cross-listing is located in a market with more onerous shareholder protection rules, compared to the home listings. 'L' means less onerous shareholder protection rules compared to the home listings and 'TS' refers to exchanges that have similar shareholder protection rules.

The results from Table 3 document some ownership concentration in companies, since large shareholders might monitor managers and, consequently, increase the value of a firm. It is also evidenced that concentration of ownership is an adaptation to poor legal protection and countries that, for some reasons, have heavily concentrated ownership. As a result small stock markets might have little use of good accounting standards, and therefore, they fail to develop them. In addition, good accounting standards and shareholder protection measures are associated with a lower concentration of ownership, indicating that concentration is indeed a response to poor investor protection (La Porta *et al.*, 1998). In particular, poor investor protection rules appeared to be in the foreign stock markets[3] of London, Paris, Amsterdam, Copenhagen, Helsinki, Oslo and Stockholm in comparison to the home markets of Brussels, Milan and Vienna. However, the accounting standards are found to be high between the above foreign capital markets and the Brussels Stock Exchange (see fifth row of Table 1), while the law of bankruptcy protection rule applied shows that there is a variety in the standards between the home market of Brussels and the other European foreign markets (see fifth row of Table 2).

Table 3
Shareholder Protection Rules' Differences

Markets	*LO*	*IRL*	*BRU*	*FR*	*IT*	*NET*	*SP*	*AU*	*GER*	*SWI*	*DEN*	*FIN*	*NOR*	*SWE*
LO		M	M	M	M	M	M	M	M	M	M	M	M	M
IRL	L		M	L	M	TS	M	M	M	M	M	L	L	L
BRU	L	L		L	M	L	L	M	L	L	L	L	L	L
FR	L	M	M		M	M	M	M	M	M	M	M	M	L
IT	L	L	L	L		L	L	TS	L	L	L	L	L	L
NET	L	TS	M	L	M		M	M	M	M	M	L	L	L
SP	L	L	M	L	M	L		M	L	L	L	L	L	L
AU	L	L	L	L	TS	L	L		L	L	L	L	L	L
GER	L	L	M	L	M	L	M	M		L	L	L	L	L
SWI	L	L	M	L	M	L	M	M	M		M	L	L	L
DEN	L	L	M	L	M	L	M	M	M	L		L	L	L
FIN	L	M	M	L	M	M	M	M	M	M	M		L	L
NOR	L	M	M	L	M	M	M	M	M	M	M	M		L
SWE	L	M	M	M	M	M	M	M	M	M	M	M	M	

Note: LO stands for London Stock Exchange, IRL stands for Dublin Stock Exchange, BRU stands for Brussels Stock Exchange, FR stands for Paris Stock Exchange, IT stands for Milan Stock Exchange, NET stands for Amsterdam Stock Exchange, SP stands for Madrid Stock Exchange, AU stands for Vienna Stock Exchange, GER stands for Frankfurt Stock Exchange, SWI stands for Zurich Stock Exchange, DEN stands for Copenhagen Stock Exchange, FIN stands for Helsinki Stock Exchange, NOR stands for Oslo Stock Exchange, SWE stands for Stockholm Stock Exchange, N/A means not available.

CONCLUSIONS

This note uses the results of La Porta *et al.*, (1998) in order to show that for some cases good accounting standards are related with poor investor protection and various bankruptcy protection rules (e.g. Brussels home market and other foreign European markets). This is in accordance to La Porta *et al.*, findings and proved to be the case here for the rank that we have made for all the home and foreign European markets in order to provide a list for the European cross-listed companies that seek markets to list in Europe and elsewhere. We expect that this ranking level of harmonisation will be useful for those investors that seek a listing abroad and decide to list on capital markets with low or high or similar law rules in comparison to their home markets.

REFERENCE

La Porta R., F. L. De Silanes, A. Shleifer, & R. W. Vishny, (1998), "Law and Finance," *Journal of Political Economy*, Vol. 106, pp. 1113-1155.

NOTES

1. See La Porta *et al.*, (1998) in page 1125.
2. See La Porta *et al.*, (1998).
3. Poor investor protection rules appeared to be, to less extent, in the foreign stock markets and to less in Dublin, in Madrid, in Frankfurt and in Zurich.

CHAPTER 5

SOCIAL EMPOWERMENT OF WORKINGWOMEN IN BANGLADESH: AN EMPIRICAL STUDY

Kazi Nazmul Huda
Md. Rezaul Karim
Ferdous Ahmed
Amir Mohammad Nasrullah

INTRODUCTION

Almost every society does have within some minority groups that feel incapable of controlling their own destiny (Newstrom and Davis, 2005). There are some marginal groups feel incompetents of molding their own socio-economic future particularly in the developing countries. Likewise, many communities do have class of people who believe themselves to be dependent on others' charity and that they have a conviction that their efforts will have a little impact on their family and the society. This subjection contributes to the vexing practice of low self-efficacy. Again, the perceptions existing in people retard them to successfully perform many socio-economic activities, which virtually frustrate them of making any substantial contributions to the family and society. This pitiable scenario is visible in the developing countries, particularly in Bangladeshi women-folk. Due to the socio cultural phenomenon, most of the Bangladeshi women seem to be socio-powerless and lack of raising voices on issues that indeed related to their interests. Directly and indirectly it also shatters our socio-economic growth; as statistics shows nearly half of the total population i.e., women, are unproductive, logically speaking. It is well-accepted in modern development economics domain that empowerment is a tool of practice to overcome the aforesaid issues by involving women in the economic activities, which would consequently lead them to a greater autonomy both in the society and family. The development economists are experimenting many development theories mainly in the rural areas of Bangladesh, and in some cases, like micro credit, it is bringing about fractional success by providing financial support to the rural women. But the women, who are financially solvent and generating regular income, are they empowered in the real sense of the term? Is financial solvency the only tool of women empowerment? Why are they subject to various discriminatory treatments in the current social structure? Hence, many more things are required to ensure empowerment to women in addition to their financial strength, which is the main focus of this study.

BACKGROUND OF THE STUDY

The phrase empowerment of women implies the amplification and bringing in full recognition of potentials of women (Begum, 1995). But the setback is all the empowerment activities of development organizations in Bangladesh are centered around the rural women-folk neglecting or evading another big and emerging working women class in the urban areas most of whom are engaged in the public and private service sectors and they are already financially solvent. Despite their financial strength why still there exists a social disparity in terms of women empowerment? Therefore, the question that automatically creeps in whether the financial solvency alone matters much, to social empowerment of women or there are other social factors needed for their sustainable empowerment in the family and society as a whole. This paper makes an in-depth study on the social empowerment of these workingwomen through financial solvency and if it is not, what else remains to be probed into in the light of 'inclusion and participation', which is deemed as an element of empowerment.

OBJECTIVES OF THE STUDY

1. To identify the level of financial solvency of working women.
2. To know the degree of social empowerment through financial solvency.
3. To know the auxiliary issues of social empowerment other than financial solvency.
4. To suggest some recommendations on the basis of the findings.

SCOPE OF THE STUDY

The study was limited to 65 workingwomen who are serving in government and private sectors as mid-level executives within the age limit of above 30 years. This study gave much importance from macro and micro economic point of view because empowerment is not a social issue but it has a lot of contributions in solving socio-economic problems. Women are no more a social class but a great human capital of production and economic activities. To bring out the productive capabilities of women, the society must try to empower them socially and mainly in the family. They must be considered as a subject of economic activities socially where social participation and inclusion are important beside financial solvency.

The findings of the study may help the policy makers, NGO entrepreneurs and foreign donors in designing projects for urban workingwomen to expedite the empowerment process socially.

RESEARCH METHODOLOGY

Social empowerment of workingwomen is principally an advanced socioeconomic issue. Since it was an empirical study both primary and secondary sources were used for collecting data. Here the researchers used specifically, both the survey and observation methods for the purpose.

Collection of Primary Data

For collecting primary data a set of pre-designed questionnaire were used to dig out the degree of empowerment of workingwomen's. With this end in view, 65 working women serving in government and private sector organizations as mid-level executives within the age limit of above 35 years were interviewed randomly.

Collection of Secondary Data

For collecting secondary data various literature, published and unpublished books, articles, websites were used.

Data Analysis

For analyzing the collected primary data simple statistical tools were used.

KEY CONCEPTS DEFINED

Empowerment refers to increasing spiritual, political, social or economic strength of individuals and communities. It often involves the empowered to develop their confidence in own capacities (Wikipedia). It is the process of enhancing the competence of individuals or groups to make choices and to transform those choices into preferred actions and outcomes. Vital to this practice are actions, which both build individual and collective assets, and improve the competence and fairness of the organizational and socio-institutional context which govern the use of these assets (World Bank).

Empowerment that is enhancing an individual's or group's capacity to make choices and transform those choices into desired actions and outcomes, is an increasingly familiar term within the World Bank and many other development agencies. Targeting practitioners engaged in the analysis of projects and policies that have empowerment components, to provide guidance on how to unpack the concept in order to measure empowerment (World Bank).

Types of Empowerment

The term empowerment has various aspects. These are as follows:

Social Empowerment

Sociological empowerment often addresses members of groups that social discrimination processes have excluded from decision-making processes through, for example, discrimination based on race, ethnicity, religion, and gender (Wikipedia).

Managerial Empowerment

In the sphere of management and organizational theory, "empowerment" often refers loosely to processes for giving subordinates (or workers generally) greater discretion and resources: distributing control in order to better serve both customers and the interests of employing organizations. The use of the word appears somewhat at odds with other usage, which most often assumes the empowerment of groups and of individuals to better serve their own interests (Wikipedia). Empowerment is any process that provides greater autonomy to employees through the sharing of relevant information and the provision of control over factors affecting job performance (Newstrom and Davis, 2005)

Economic Empowerment

In economic development, the empowerment approach focuses on mobilizing the self-help efforts of the poor, rather than providing them with social welfare.

Personal Empowerment

In the arena of personal development, empowerment forms an apogee of many a system of self-realization or of identity (re-) formation. Realizing the solipsistic impracticality of everyone anarchistic ally attempting to exercise power over everyone else, empowerment advocates have adopted the word "empowerment" to offer the attractions of such power, but they generally constrain its individual exercise to potentiality and to feel-good uses within the individual psyche (Wikipedia).

A Framework for Empowerment

There are thousands of examples of empowerment strategies that have been initiated by poor people themselves and by governments, civil society, and the private sector. Although there is no single institutional model for empowerment, experience shows that certain elements are almost always present when empowerment efforts are successful. There are four key elements of empowerment that must underlie institutional reform are:

- Access to information
- Inclusion and participation
- Accountability
- Local organizational capacity.

COMPILATION AND ANALYSIS OF DATA AND MAJOR RESEARCH FINDINGS[1]

In this study total sample size was 65 Working women of whom 19 living with single family, i.e., with spouse & children, and 46 living with joint family, i.e., with parents in laws, spouse & children.

Simple statistical analysis was considered as feasible for this study, so no complex analytical correlation was tried upon. The core independent variables were education and financial phenomena. Due to the length and number of variables the number of analytical tables have been segregated and analyzed differently, but in the decision-making conclusions, all the independent tables, which are deemed to be feasible-and applicable, considered.

Empowerment of Women on the Basis of Income and Education; their Contribution to the Family and Power in the Decision Making Process in the Society and Family

A number of 65 married working women were taken randomly from the population as sample to conduct the study which were segregated as per family nature, viz., living with joint family (Parents in law, spouse and offspring) and single family (Spouse and offspring). In the sample population 31were found Post-graduates, 26 Graduates, and the rest 8 were Non-graduates. The trend of higher education for women was visualized in this study. While analyzing the salary structures 43 (66%) were earning between 5-10 thousand per month from the jobs they are doing. The highest range of salaries drawn by women found as 20-30 thousand per month 7% only. Which indicates the believes that women are not yet in a position to grab the top most jobs in the market, which is an indicator for less empowerment of women too. Further most of the women yet to be engaged in the production or manufacturing sectors, for that reason the income range of women still found as low as minimum in comparison with their educational competences. The reasons could be the limitations on women's part not to be challenging and full time devotion outside home environment, in other words women are yet to be debarred to work freely with cross sections of people. One of the reasons could be the men colleague's attitudes and social taboo against women folks. It was presumed that by educating and working outside is an opportunity for women to be empowered drastically, but it was not a generic phenomenon. For cultural taboo or family upbringing in our society women are still as lenient as ever, that is why even after contributing fully in the home-financing they couldn't become independent of taking vital decisions on various parts like Savings, Children's education, matrimonial decisions, family planning decisions; or, they are not yet free from the control of spouse and senior members of the family with whom they share homes. Table 1 and Table 2 can be shown for more details.

Degree of Women's Participation in Family Level Decision-Making Process in Comparison with Men (Husband): Single-Family Scenario versus Joint Family Scenario

In the case of joint family working women (19) who contribute 60-100% of their incomes 2 out of 3 have their voices in the case of children's education, Family planning and assets

APPENDICES

Table 1

Empowerment on the Basis of Income, Education and Women's Contribution to the Family

Sample Popul.	*Education*	*Organization Type*	*Form of Organization*	*Designation*	*Members in the Family*	*Salary 000*	*Children's' Education*	*Family Contribution*
Total Joint families 19	MA = 10 BA = 7 Others = 2	S = 16 M = 3	Prvt = 11 Public = 8	Teacher = 10 Official = 9	2 pers = 2 4 pers = 7 5 pers = 3 6-10 p = 7	5-10 = 11 10-15 = 5 15-20 = 1 20-30 = 2	S = 3 H = 4 B = 11	10-20% = 7 40-50% = 9 60-100% = 3
Total Single families 46	MA= 21 BA= 19 Others = 6	S = 44 M = 2	Prvt = 35 Public = 11	Teacher = 30 Official = 16	2pers = 6 3pers =14 4pers =17 5pers = 6 6pers = 3	5-10 = 32 10-15 = 9 15-20 = 2 20-30 = 3	S = 3 H = 8 B = 35	10-20% = 13 40-50% = 21 60-100% = 12

Source: Field Survey

Table 2

Women's Power in the Decision-making Process in the Society and Family

Sample Popul.	*Matrimonial Decision*	*Who decides for Savings/ Insurance*	*Family Planning Decision*	*Assets Accumulations*	*Assets Title*	*Assets Owning*	*Job Change Decision*	*Empower Perceptions in the Family*	*Empower in the Society*
Total Joint families 19	S = 4 H = 5 B = 11	S = 2 H = 5 B = 12	S = 3 H = 2 B = 14	S = 3 H = 5 B = 11	S = 2 H = 9 B = 8	N/A = 4 5-10% = 3 20-50% = 8 > 50% = 4	S = 10 H = 2 B = 7	E = 11 F = 4 SS = 4	E = 7 F = 6 SS = 6
Total Single families 46	S = 2 H = 5 B = 39	S = 9 H = 10 B = 27	S = 2 H = 3 B = 41	S = 3 H = 11 B = 32	S = 4 H = 18 B = 24	N/A = 1 15-10% = 6 20-50% = 20 > 50% = 9	S = 20 H = 3 B = 23	E = 22 F = 7 SS = 17	E = 17 F = 11 SS = 18

Source: Field Survey

Table 3
Degree of Women's Participation in Family Level Decision-making Process in Comparison with Men (Husband): Single Family Scenario

Joint/Family Contribution	*Children's' Education*	*Matrimonial Decision*	*Who decides for Savings/ Insurance*	*Family Planning Decision*	*Assets Accumu-lations*
60-100%	Self	H	H	Self	Self
60-100%	S	S	S	S	S
60-100%	B	B	B	B	H
40-50%	H	H	H	B	B
40-50%	B	B	B	B	B
40-50%	B	B	B	B	H
40-50%	B	B	B	B	B
40-50%	B	B	B	B	B
40-50%	B	B	B	B	B
40-50%	H	S	H	H	H
40-50%	H	H	S	S	H
40-50%	B	B	B	B	B
10-20%	B	H	B	B	H
10-20%	B	B	B	B	B
10-20%	H	H	H	H	H
10-20%	S	S	B	B	B
10-20%	B	B	B	B	B
10-20%	B	B	B	B	B
10-20%	B	S	H	B	S
Total = 19					

Source: Field Survey

Table 4
Degree of Women's Participation in Family Level Decision Making Process in Comparison with Men (Husband): A Joint Family Scenario

Single/Family Contribution	*Children 's' Education*	*Matrimonial Decision*	*Who decides for Savings/ Insurance*	*Family Planning Decision*	*Assets Accumu-lations*
60-100%	B	B	B	B	B
60-100%	B	Others	B	B	B
60-100%	B	B	B	B	H
60-100%	B	B	B	B	B
60-100%	B	B	H	B	H
60-100%	B	B	S	B	B
60-100%	B	B	S	B	B
60-100%	B	B	B	B	B
60-100%	B	B	B	B	B
60-100%	B	B	B	B	B
60-100%	B	B	B	S	B
60-100%	B	B	B	B	B

Contd.

Single/Family Contribution	Children 's' Education	Matrimonial Decision	Who decides for Savings/ Insurance	Family Planning Decision	Assets Accumu-lations
40-50%	B	B	Self	B	B
40-50%	H	H	Self	B	H
40-50%	H	H	B	B	H
40-50%	H	H	H	B	H
40-50%	B	B	S	B	H
40-50%	B	B	H	H	B
40-50%	B	B	B	B	B
40-50%	H	S	S	B	S
40-50%	B	B	B	B	B
40-50%	B	B	B	B	H
40-50%	S	B	B	B	B
40-50%	B	B	B	B	B
40-50%	B	B	B	B	B
40-50%	B	B	B	B	B
40-50%	B	B	B	B	B
40-50%	B	B	H	B	B
40-50%	B	B	H	B	H
40-50%	B	B	B	B	B
40-50%	B	B	B	B	B
40-50%	B	B	B	B	B
40-50%	H	B	H	B	B
10-20%	H	B	S	B	B
10-20%	B	B	H	B	H
10-20%	B	B	H	B	B
10-20%	B	B	B	B	S
10-20%	H	H	H	H	H
10-20%	H	H	B	B	B
10-20%	B	B	B	B	B
10-20%	S	S	S	S	B
10-20%	B	B	B	B	B
10-20%	B	B	B	B	B
10-20%	B	B	B	B	B
10-20%	B	B	S	B	S
10-20%	S	B	H	H	H
Total = 46					

Source: Field Survey

accumulation decisions; for matrimonial & savings' cases 1 out of 3, which seems that there are still some barriers and problems in women's decision-making process. This might be due to other senior guardians who are living in the family. It is also found only 16% contributed 60-100% of their earnings in the joint family. 26%working women who are living in a single family found to be spending 60-100% of their income. 40-50% incomes spend for the families were found about 47%

in the both types of families. See Table 3 and Table 4 for more details.

Women's Power Regarding Assets Holding, Job Changing, Along with the Empowerment Perceptions in View of Family and Societal Perspectives: Joint Family versus Single Family

The study shows that even spending 60-100% of their earnings in the joint family women did have the title of assets 1 in 3 proportions i.e., 33% which is 8% in the single family. This indicates the women's natural sacrificing and unselfishness attitudes of Bengali women in our society, if positively focused. If the feminists point of philosophy is taken it deemed, as women still have not been empowered though they are contributing significantly to the family. The cultural practice and social taboo is still playing a greater role in our society even above the educational qualification and earnings, as our sample-working women are well educated. In the job change factor women, who are contributing 60-100% of their earnings, are free to take their decisions in 67% cases living in the joint family which is 50% for the single living family, i.e., 59% averagely best contributing women folks could take their own decision regarding job choices. Table 5 and table 6 show more details.

Table 5
Women's Power in the Joint Family Regarding Assets Holding, Job Changing, Along with the Empowerment Perceptions in view of Family and Societal Perspectives

Joint/Family Contribution	*Assets Title*	*Assets Owning*	*Job Change Decision*	*Empower Perceptions in the Family*	*Empower in the Society*
60-100%	H	10%	Self	Finance	Education
60-100%	S	100%	S	SS	SS
60-100%	H	20%	B	E	E
40-50%	Self	N/A	B	F	F
40-50%	B	60%	B	E	F
40-50%	B	20%	S	E	F
40-50%	H	50%	B	E	E
40-50%	B	N/A	S	SS	SS
40-50%	B	50%	S	F	F
40-50%	H	50%	S	F	E

Contd.

Joint/Family Contribution	*Assets Title*	*Assets Owning*	*Job Change Decision*	*Empower Perceptions in the Family*	*Empower in the Society*
40-50%	H	50%	H	SS	E
40-50%	H	N/A	B	E	E
10-20%	H	5%	Others	E	F
10-20%	H	9%	H	SS	F
10-20%	B	50%	S	E	E
10-20%	B	N/A	B	E	SS
10-20%	B	50%	S	E	SS
10-20%	B	50%	S	E	SS
10-20%	H	60%	S	E	SS
Total = 19					

Source: Field Survey

Table 6
Women's Power in the Single Family Regarding Assets Holding, Job Changing, Along with the Empowerment Perceptions in View of Family and Societal Perspectives

Joint/Family Contribution	*Assets Title*	*Assets Owning*	*Job Change Decision*	*Empower Perceptions in the Family*	*Empower in the Society*
60-100%	B	100%	B	E	E
60-100%	H	N/A	B	SS	F
60-100%	H	N/A	B	SS	F
60-100%	B	20%	S	E	SS
60-100%	H	50%	S	SS	E
60-100%	S	50%	S	F	SS
60-100%	B	50%	S	F	F
60-100%	H	50%	B	E	E
60-100%	B	70%	S	SS	SS
60-100%	H	50%	B	E	E
60-100%	B	50%	S	E	SS
60-100%	B	30%	B	F	SS
40-50%	H	30%	S	E	SS
40-50%	H	N/A	H	F	SS
40-50%	H	10%	B	E	E
40-50%	H	15%	S	F	F
40-50%	B	50%	S	E	SS
40-50%	B	70%	S	E	SS
40-50%	H	50%	S	E	SS
40-50%	B	100%	S	SS	SS
40-50%	B	N/A	B	SS	E
40-50%	B	100%	S	SS	SS
40-50%	B	50%	S	F	E
40-50%	B	50%	B	F	E

Contd.

Joint/Family Contribution	*Assets Title*	*Assets Owning*	*Job Change Decision*	*Empower Perceptions in the Family*	*Empower in the Society*
40-50%	H	100%	B	E	SS
40-50%	S	60%	S	SS	SS
40-50%	B	N/A	B	E	E
40-50%	B	40%	S	E	F
40-50%	H	N/A	S	E	E
40-50%	B	50%	B	E	SS
40-50%	B	N/A	B	SS	E
40-50%	B	N/A	B	E	E
40-50%	B	6%	H	E	F
10-20%	B	55%	S	SS	SS
10-20%	H	5%	H	E	F
10-20%	H	N/A	B	SS	F
10-20%	H	50%	S	E	E
10-20%	H	4%	Others	SS	F
10-20%	H	50%	B	E	E
10-20%	S	N/A	B	E	E
10-20%	H	30%	B	F	F
10-20%	B	40%	B	SS	F
10-20%	B	45%	B	F	F
10-20%	S	50%	B	F	E
10-20%	B	N/A	S	E	E
10-20%	B	6%	B	E	F
Total = 46					

Source: Field Survey

Summary of Table 5 & 6

While interviewed about the perceptions of empowerment of women in the family 58% women who are living in the joint family responded Education as the key factor, while who are living with single family turned out to be 48%. But what makes them empowered in the 'society' is responded differently; for joint and single family women responded Education is still the case 37%. For single living women Social status is more valuable 39% than education, 37%. Averagely For empowerment in the 'society' issue education is voted 24 (7 + 17) (37%), Finance (6 + 11) 26%, Social status (6 + 18) 37%. While the family empowerment Education is (11 + 22) 51%, Finance (4 + 7) 17%, and social status (4+17) 32%. See Table 7 for details.

From the above study it is found that women have an opportunity to make a choice about at least some key elements relating to their interests in the family. Secondly, they at least have some opportunity to use their 'says' on some aspects of family. Thirdly, there are evidences that the choice resulted in the desired result of the women folks and the rate is in a positive trend.

Table 7
Summary of Table-5 & 6

Family Type	*Empower Perceptions in the Family*	*Empowerment in the Society*
Joint	E = 11 (58%) F = 4 SS = 4	E = 7 (37%) F = 6 (32%) SS = 6 (31%) J
Single	E = 22 (48%) F = 7 (15%) SS = 17 (37%)	E = 17 (37%) F = 11 (24%) SS = 18 (39%) S
Total: 65		

Clarification: E = Education, F = Finance, SS = Social Status
Source: Field Survey

Women who are working and contributing to the family economy have achieved the right of participation in different forms. The four key elements viz., access to information, inclusion and participation, accountability and local organizational capacity, have been found in an encouraging mode of action and trends are found to be farther improving. To conclude the empowerment of women in our society is not depending upon any one or two factors which we normally deemed to be, rather this is a complex socio-economic cultural issues that are molded together to create phenomenon which make a women empowered in the family and society in our country. Lastly more in depth psychological research is needed for a longer period of time to find our which changes society, values and perceptions in our society. But generally the study shows indeed education, and financial contribution give working women at least some footholds both in the society and family. This makes the society to understand women as human being irrespective of gender focused views.

SUMMERY OF MAJOR FINDINGS

1. It was observed that in Bangladesh women who live with their mother in-laws or in the joint families, their husbands misinformed or misled with misinformation or incited with one reason or other by the mother in-laws or sister in-laws or so on. Upon which the male partner found to be doing misbehave with wives. So merely empowerment of women financially would not be enough to dismantle the mindset of our women folks.
2. This is our Bengali or sub continental culture that usually husbands do agree to allow their spouses to be involved in economic activities, which in most of the cases opined negatively by the peer-women in the name of social taboo.
3. The objectivity of education in the eyes of society or the perception of educating people needed to be changed. It was found that males and females do get their education with different perspectives, viz., males for jobs, females for a competitive edge in marital market.
4. It was found that when any problem was emerged male and female genders move to share with same gender colleagues. It was also found that in most of the cases opposite sex counseling bring forth positive results.
5. General perception on our society is that women are vulnerable and they are deemed as caliber too, or the other hand after 12 or 14 years of studies they will be married and in most of the cases turned out to a good house wives (i.e., giving birth to children, raring them and do the household chores), so women don't go for studying technical subjects which might force them to denote more study and research. So women in our society mostly go to study arts and culture, and non-business subjects; but there are exceptions also.
6. It was observed that women are considered in our society as weak and feeble. In most of the cases they get a sympathetic consideration both in the queue or in the job. In government service there are quotas preserved for the women. So this created an impression that women could take a place easily without competition and hardship,

which make them more weaker and non-competitive. In the childhood the gender issue needed to be unspoken, rather all should be treated as human being, not as girls and boys, as it was the case we observed.

7. It was found that the women's empowerment is considered piecemeal basis not as a whole. That's why it cannot derive as a comprehensive and just solution rather the vested interest is found while the issue of empowerment covers. Women who are educationists focusing only in education. NGO workers on their own field or micro credit, legal workers or legal bases- all needed to be a combination.
8. It was found that development practitioners do not put their enough efforts or legal and cultural sectors, particularly the motivational aspects or altering the perceptions remain absent in our country.

RECOMMENDATIONS

1. Empowerment of women should be a social movement. Attitude of women in the family is needed to be changed positively. Most of the cruelties, family feuding and physical and mental torture of women occur by women directly or indirectly. It is widely said that women are women's foes.
2. Senior and other non-working women folks in the family veto opinion against Women's working outside, not by men. So the attitude of the women to women should be changed positively.
3. Total educational focus needs to be changed in a way to change the values and beliefs of women and society.
4. Any human resource problems derived in the office could be successfully resolved if opposite genders are negotiated rather than same sexes. So it should be practiced.
5. Empowerment in social, economic, and personal sectors improved significantly over the past few decades. Only the other managerial empowerment is found to be lagging behind slightly. One of the main reasons is that traditionally business education has been considered as the subject for men; women were normally choosing or

induced to choose subjects like non-business which made them non-efficient in the field of business or economics. This trend or practice also needs to be changed.

6. Gender issues to be carefully addressed in the childhood at schools, not in the office. All men and women should be taken as human beings not merely as men and women. It is not also recommended to do positive discriminations or other favors that would make women inefficient and ineffective or eventually put them in a vicious circle of worthless loss for the organization. Let them stand and fight, fight for their rights and that would empower them best.
7. Social empowerment should be an integrated empowerment (see Fig. 1) practice in combination of educational empowerment, economic/financial empowerment, managerial empowerment, legal empowerment, political empowerment and finally the socio-cultural empowerment.
8. To work on empowering the workingwomen, the development practitioners should emphasize on the legal and cultural sectors by developing awareness project, legal advising project, corporate level seminars and symposiums and mostly through motivational campaign.

CONCLUSION

Terminologically, 'empowerment of women' refers to making the women folk socially powerful and independent having the equal and legitimate rights to offer opinion in any decision-

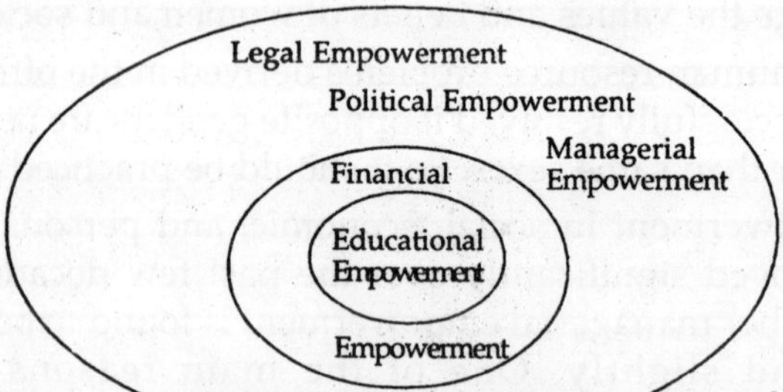

Figure 1: Model of Integrated Social Empowerment Process

making matters like her male counter parts and thus establishing a solid social stance to live with honor and dignity. It is a recent concept, which has gained stupendous significance in the contemporary development literature. However, this very idea is conceived to be as old as civilization itself with social stratification when powerlessness prevails upon many and the powerful ruled upon the powerless and exploit them. Social Empowerment of workingwomen is a multi-dimensional phenomenon. There is no denying fact that, financial solvency although has infused empowerment among the women in general but in case of working women integration of other empowerment issues should get upper hand to create a true practice. With this end in view, Bangladesh Government, NGDOs and related agencies to play a vital role to promote empowerment in socio-economic standpoint and to promote the empowerment scenario of Bangladesh, we must try to change the social value system, which is still a great challenge for many developed countries also, indeed.

REFERENCES

Begum L. N., (1995), "Empowerment of Women with Special Reference to Bangladesh: An Evaluation," Chittagong University Studies, Vol. XVI, No. 1.

(http://web.worldbank.org/WBSITE/EXTERNAL/TOPICS/EXTPOVERTY/EXTEMPOWERMENT/0,,contentMDK: 20245753~pagePK:210058~piPK:210062~theSitePK:486411,00.html)

http://siteresources.worldbank.org/INTEMPOWERMENT/Resources/41307_wpc3510.pdfrelated processes and outcomes. 2

http://en.wikipedia.org/wiki/Empowerment

Newstrom, J. W. & Davis K., (2005), *Organizational Behavior, Human Behavior at work*, Tata McGraw-Hill Publishing Company Ltd, New Delhi, India

www1.worldbank.org/prem/poverty/empowerment/whatis/locorg.htm

NOTE

1. *J* = Joint family, *S* = Single family, *O* = other qualifications below *BA*. *S* = Self, *B* = Both, *H* = Husband, *E* = Education, *F* = Financial, *SS* = Social Status.

Chapter 6

IS INEQUALITY HARMFUL FOR BOTSWANA'S ECONOMY GROWTH?

Albert Makochekanwa

INTRODUCTION

Since its independence in 1966, and nearly for the past four decades, Botswana has enjoyed accelerated[1] economic growth than any other African country. Through fiscal and sound management, the country has transformed itself from one of the poorest countries in the world to middle-income country with a per capita GDP of US$11200 in 2006 (World Bank). In fact, the country shows that mineral wealth can be a benefit in a country that has the appropriate political development in place. The country has experienced by far the highest rate of growth in SSA: 8.4% per year over the entire 1965-1990 period and a still-high 5.1% in the 1990-2005. Thus, since its independence, the country has gone from being among the poorest countries in world to one with a greater per capita income than Turkey, Thailand, or Brazil (Todaro and Smith, 2006). This sustained economy growth is true whether economic growth is measured using the change in total output of goods and services (GDP) or changes in output per person (GDP per capita) (See Fig. 1).

Despite this positive economic growth, Botswana has also high income inequality. According to Samson (2007: 11),

"Botswana is one of Africa's (and the world's) most unequal countries". The country's inequality has been slightly rising over the years. For instance, although income inequality measured by the Gini coefficient[2] was just below 60 in the 1970s, this coefficient has been above 60 since the 1990s to date (see Fig. 2). The combination of comparatively rapid economic growth and high and relatively rising income inequality raises a question: Has income inequality contributed to Botswana's economic growth? Or is the economic growth performance of Botswana essentially unrelated to its large and relatively growing income disparities.

Although the relationship between income distribution and economic growth has been a field of ongoing research for

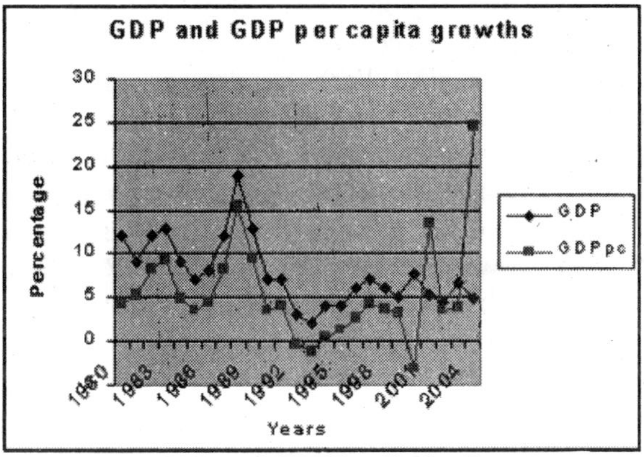

Figure 1: GDP and GDP Per Capita Growth Trends

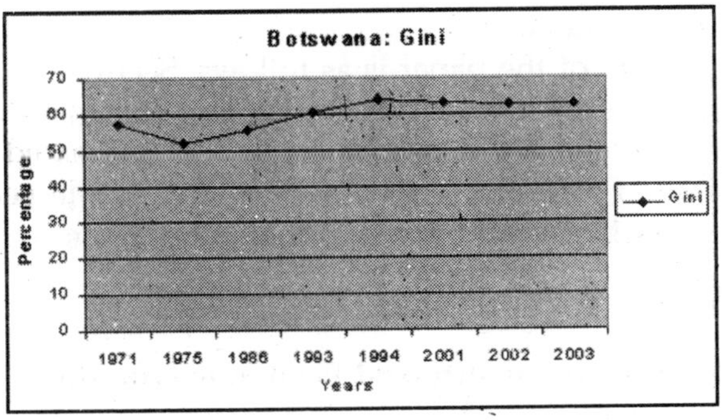

Figure 2: Gini Coefficient for Botswana
Source: WIDER database

over five decades, controversies still exist on the relationship between income inequality and economy growth.

Views of earlier scholars like Lewis (1954) and Kuznets (1955), as represented by the much-debated Kuznets hypothesis, was that rising inequality was an unavoidable concomitant of economic growth in the initial stages of development (Bhatta, 2001). On the other hand, researches of contemporary economics have been concerned with how inequality affects economic growth rather than the other way round. Although the jury is still settled, there seems to be equal evidence for both views. For instance, Morrisse *et al.*, 2002; Aghion *et al.*, 1999, Perotti, 1996; Alesina & Rodrick, 1994; Banerjee & Newman, 1993; Persson and Tabellini, 1994; are among the authors whose work support the view that inequality is harmful for economic growth. On the other hand, Burtless, 2003; Bhatta, 2001; Forbes, 2000; Li and Zou, 1998 and Partridge, 1997; are some of the scholars who reported evidence to the fact that inequality is positively related to economic growth. Barro (1999) presented findings which supported both views when he found a negative relationship between inequality and growth for low-per capita GDP countries and a positive relationship for high per-capita GDP countries.

Objectives of the Study

Following the preceding brief exposition of the inequality-growth nexus, the study's main objective is to empirically explore how income inequality and economic growth are related in Botswana.

The outline of the paper is as follows. Section 2 provides literature review with section 3 detailing the methodology employed to achieve the study's objective. Estimated results are presented and discussed in section 4, while section 5 provides conclusion and policy recommendations.

LITERATURE REVIEW

Links Between Inequality and Economic Growth

Burtless (2003) alluded to the fact that literature on growth and economic performance, on the one hand, and inequality, on the other, was not especially large a decade ago, but rather it grew tremendously in the past half-dozen years.

The seminal work of Kuznets (1955) is probably the most appropriate starting point for reviewing the links between inequality and (urban) economic growth. By paying particular attention on the movements of people from peasant rural agriculture to industry in town, Kuznets hypotesized that income inequality increases in the early stages of an economy's development as a result of the exodus of people from the large, relatively poor and egalitarian agriculture/rural sector to the small, industrial/urban sector that is richer but relatively unequal (Bhatta, 2001). In the latter stages, however, as people move in masses to urban sector, wages of poorer workers will relatively increase in both urban and rural sectors, and various government policies will also be implemented to reduce intra-and-inter-sectoral income inequality. Hence, overall income inequality in the country will decrease in the latter stages of development.

Another leading theory of economic performance and inequality was described by Okun (1975). His theory highlighted the efficiency sacrifices that countries make when they set up regulatory frameworks or income-distribution programs to ensure equality in the final income distribution. According to Okun, the efficiency cost of income redistribution and economic regulations, such as the minimum wage, can sometimes be large. In such a case, it follows that a policy regime with more redistribution–and less inequality–may generate less national income than a regime where redistribution is lower (Burtless, 2003).

Theories Supporting that Inequality Retard Economic Growth

Following Morrissey et al (2002), the following theories are classified as those which support the view that income inequality negatively affects economic growth.

Political economy models of growth and inequality links a country's level of income inequality with the political measures taken to reduce inequality and the social consequences that follow when income disparities grow unchecked. The notion behind these models is that inequality can have important consequences for growth, because the degree of inequality in a society can affect the policy measures it adopts and the willingness or ability of citizens to undertake measures that contribute to growth. For instance, it is argued that if income of the majority median voters lies below the mean income, they may vote in favour of redistributive taxes that reduce investment incentives and consequently reduce economic growth (Alesina and Rodrick, 1994; Perotti, 1993). Alternatively, a very unequal income distribution might induce social unrest, which in turn discourages productive investments. Finally, a very unequal distribution might reduce the percentage of the population that can make worthwhile investments in its own education and training, thus depressing both present and future economic growth (Burtless, 2003).

The *social conflict* approach indicates that an unequal distribution of resources is a source of political tension and social conflict. In such a socio-political environment, property rights are insecure and this discourages investment accumulation. When the gap between the rich and the poor is very high, there will be greater probability or temptation to engage in rent seeking and this in turn reduces investment and constrains the ability of the government to respond to shocks (Benabou, 1996; Rodrik, 1998). At the same time, Alesina and Perotti (1996) argue that greater inequality leads to less political stability and consequently sub-optimal investment levels.

The *credit markets* channel (Tsiddon, 1992) is premised on the basic fact that investments are lumpy and access to credit depends on the existence of collateral. Given unequal initial distribution of assets, there will be credit constraint and the end result is that economic growth will be hindered as the majority will be excluded from tapping investment funds from the financial sector. In this context, inequality of land holdings represents a constraint on growth in the agriculture sector, typically the major productive sector in poor developing countries.

The other approach is based on the argument that high inequality reduces the *X-efficiency* of workers. X-efficiency refers to a measure of workers' productivity holding constant all other inputs into the production process including workers' skills (Leibenstein, 1966, cited in Birdsall *et al.*, 1995). According to Morrissey *et al.*, (2002), workers' productivity is limited by a 'virtual' glass ceiling as they do not visualize themselves progressing beyond a certain point and this discourages effort and perpetuates a vicious cycle of low incomes and therefore high inequality. In such a case, inequality has a disincentive effect that retards growth.

Theories Supporting that Inequality Positively Affect economic Growth

Forbes (2000) reviewed models which predict a positive relationship between inequality and economic growth. For instance, study by Gilles Saint-Paul and Thierry Verdier (1993) argued that the actions of the median voter in more unequal societies may also promote growth. Specifically, they argued that in an unequal society, median voter will vote for a higher taxation rate to finance public education, which will in turn increase aggregate human capital and hence economic growth.

Benabou (1996a) developed a model based on heterogeneous citizens in a given country and showed that if the degree of complementarity between individuals' human capital is stronger in local than global interactions, then segregated and more unequal societies can experience higher rates of economic growth (at least in the short run).

Lastly, Galor and Tsiddon (1997a, b) developed two theories which explain why inequality and economic growth may be positively related. In the one model, a home environment externality helps determine an individual's level of human capital and if this externality is strong enough, a high level of inequality may be necessary for growth to "take off" in a less-developed economy (Forbes, 2000). Galor and Tsiddo's second model argues that inequality increases during periods of major technological inventions, which, by enhancing mobility and concentration of high-ability workers in technologically advanced sectors, will generate higher rates of technological progress and economic growth.

Empirical Review

Morrissey *et al.*, 2002 carried a cross-section study on 44 developing countries whose main objective was to investigate the links between economic growth, inequality and trade liberation in these countries. They found two results. Firstly, the study found out that, within the sample, there was no evidence that those countries which were initially poorer were also more unequal. Secondly, and most importantly, the study concluded that inequality appeared to have a negative effect on economic growth in these 44 countries in the long run, although no evidence was found for the short run.

Bhatta (2001) investigated the link between income inequality and economic growth in a number of metropolitan statistical areas (MSA) of the United States of America. His results showed a positive association between initial MSA income inequality and subsequent MSA per capita personal income (PCPI) growth rates. The study also concluded that, the fact that the positive correlation between these two variables was maintained in the regression for all the income classes testified to the robustness of this positive relationship.

Forbes' (2000) research conclusion is among the results which showed a positive colleration between economic growth and income inequality. After applying panel data estimation technique on a sample of 45 countries, the study challenged the current belief that income inequality has a negative relationship with economic growth. The paper estimated economic growth as a function of the following variables: initial inequality, income, male and female human capital, market distortions, and country period dummy. The results showed that the coefficient on initial inequality was positive.

The study by Persson and Tabellini (1994) affirms the negative effects of income inequality on economic growth. Covering a period of more than 150 years (from 1830 to 1985) for nine developed countries, the research estimated growth equation as determined by variables such as income inequality, education, and GDP gap. The estimated results indicated a negative coefficient on inequality, implying that the latter retard economic growth.

METHODOLOGY

Model Specification

The empirical model used in investigating the impacts of income inequality and economic growth can theoretically be derived from an overlapping-generation model (see for instance Persson and Tabillin (1994. pg. 602-604)). The empirical model used in this analysis is similar to that used in most empirical work in this area (such as by Morrissey *et al.*, 2002; Forbes, 2000, and Perotti, 1996), although with some slight modifications. The dependent variable is economic/GDP growth (GDPGR). Economic growth literature points to the importance of economic activity at any point in time (GDP_t) as also explaining subsequent growth. Another additional variable is the measure of the increases in the stock variables. The increase in the capital stock is captured by gross capital formation. Given that the study is mainly concerned with inequality, the basic specification estimated, is:

$$\text{Log GDPGR} = \beta_0 + \beta_2 \text{ Gini} + \beta_2 \text{ logOPEN} + \beta_3 \text{ logGDP} + \beta_4 \text{logGCF} + \mu \qquad (1)$$

Where GDPGR = GDP growth rate
Gini = Gini income inequality coefficient
OPEN = trade openness [(= exports + imports)/GDP]
GDP = Gross domestic product
GCF = Gross capital formation

From the reviewed theory, the coefficient of Gini is indeterminate *a prior*. The coefficients of trade openness, GDP and investment as represented by gross capital formation are all expected to positively affect economic growth.

Data Analysis

The study employs annual time series data covering the period 1980 to 2004 to investigate the effects of inequality on economic growth in Botswana. All data series, with the exception of the Gini coefficient, are from World Bank's World Development

Indicators (WDI-CDROM). Gini coefficients are from WIDER's World Income Inequality Database, as well as from Botswana's Household Income and Expenditure Surveys (HIES).

Stationarity Tests

The drawback to using non-stationary economic series in the study would be that the presence of deterministic time trends in any paired series could lead one to misinterpret what is essentially a pro-cyclical movement of the series over time for a deeper relationship between them. Thus to avoid inappropriate model specification and to increase the confidence of the results, time series properties of the data are investigated. Although there are a number of methods used to test for stationarity and the presence of unit roots, the methods used here are the Augmented Dickey-Fuller (ADF) and the Philips Peron (PP) tests. By definition a series is stationary if it has a constant mean and a constant finite variance. On the contrary, a non-stationary series contains a clear time trend and has a variance that is not constant overtime. If a series is non-stationary, it will display a high degree of persistence i.e. shocks do not die out. A series X_t is said to be integrated of order d, denoted as $I(d)$, if it must be differenced d times for it to become stationary. For example, a variable is said to be integrated of order one, or $I(1)$, if it is stationary after differencing once, or of order two, $I(2)$ if differenced twice. If the variable is stationary without differencing, then it is integrated of order zero, $I(0)$. The ADF regression test can be written as:

$$\mathrm{Dc}_t = \mathrm{b}_0 + \mathrm{lc}_{t-1} + \mathrm{b}_1 t + \sum_{t=2}^{p} \mathrm{g}_i \mathrm{Dc}_{t-1} + \mathrm{e}_t \qquad (2)$$

Where t is the time trend, p is the number of lags; e_t is a stationary disturbance error term. The null hypothesis that x_t is non-stationary is rejected if l_1 is significantly negative. The number of lags (n) of $\mathrm{D}x_t$ is normally chosen to ensure that regression residual is approximately white noise. To this end, Table A1 of the Appendix provides unit root test results (ADF and PP tests) and the tests indicate that all the variables are stationary at first difference, that is, they are $I(1)$ variables.

RESULTS

Long run Model results

The estimated coefficient of the Gini index as presented in Table 1 shows that, for Botswana, income inequality is negatively related to economic growth as evidenced by a significant coefficient of minus 0.056, which is significant at ten percent level of significance. Thus, a one per cent increase in income inequality will cause a 0.06 per cent decline in economic growth. This result is in line with theoretical perspectives which suggest that inequality retards economic growth. Also the results are similar to the findings of Persson and Tabellini (1994) and Morrissey *et al.*, (2002) among others who concluded that inequality was harmful for economic growth.

Table 1
Long Run Regression Results: Dependent Variable log of Log_GDPGR

Variable	*Coefficient*	*Standard Error*	*t-statistic*	*Probability*
GINI	–0.056	0.0299	–1.869	0.076
LN_OPEN	2.08	1.074	1.937	0.067
LN_GDP	0.474	0.125	3.784	0.078
LN_GCF	–0.199	0.094	–2.136	0.058
C	–10.69	10.89	–0.982	0.338
R^2	0.66	*F*-statistic	15.56	
Adjusted R^2	0.63	Prob (*F*-statistic)	0.0000	

Gross capital formation; unexpectedly, negatively affect economic growth. Whilst conversional wisdom is that, the former should propagate economic growth, hence expected to have a positive correlation with the latter, Botswana's case seems to prove otherwise. A possible explanation maybe the fact that most of the capital formation over the years has been mainly in the mining related activities, with relatively few or meaningful investments in other non-mining sectors. Given diminishing marginal returns to output per each additional gross capital formation in the mining sector; the fact that investments in this sector is more capital intensive, rather than labour intensive; and possible 'crowd-out' of other non-mining investments, overall economic growth may have been negatively affected.

The relationship between economic growth on one hand, and trade openness and GDP on the other hand is according to economic theoretical expectations. The results indicates that a one percent increase in trade openness will result in a 2.1 per cent increase in economic growth, while a unit percentage increase in GDP will cause economic growth to rise by 0.47 per cent.

The long-run estimation indicates that the model fits the data well as evidenced by relatively high values of both R^2 (adjusted R^2) which are above 63 per cent, and F-statistic tests whose significant values is above 15 per cent. The adjusted R^2 which measures the "goodness of fit" of the equation (after taking account of degrees of freedom) is satisfactory high at 63 per cent, indicating that 63 per cent of the variations in GDP growth in Botswana is explained by variations in the changes in the Gini coefficient, trade openness, GDP and gross capital formation. The F-test statistic of 15.56, with a p-value of 0.00, indicates that all the explanatory variables jointly determine economic growth in Botswana.

Short Run Model Results

The results from the parsimonious error correction model (ECM) are presented in Table 2. To avoid any estimations bias from the results, the ECM model was tested for such econometric assumptions as normality, heteroskedasticity, serial correction and mis-specification and these tests are presented in the Appendix Table A2. Generally, the tests confirm that the shot-run model is statistically good.

The statistical fit for the short run dynamic equation for economic growth in Botswana appears to be good as indicated by higher values of both the R^2 and the F-statistic values. At the same time, as expected, the coefficient of the error correction term (ECM) has a negative sign and more importantly that it lies within the bound of negative 1 and zero. This significant negative sign on the ECM ensures that the all the explanatory variables in ECM work together for economic growth to get to equilibrium in the short run.

Table 2
Short Run Regression Results: Dependent Variable log of DLN_GDPGR

Variable	*Coefficient*	*Standard Error*	*t-statistic*	*Probability*
ECM_{1-t}	–0.380795	0.199194	–1.911675	0.0704
DLN_GDP	1.083837	0.559636	1.936682	0.0670
DLN_INF	–0.680742	0.350759	–1.940767	0.0665
C	–0.155565	0.086869	–1.790804	0.0885
R^2	0.63	*F*-statistic	13.04	
Adjusted R^2	0.57	Prob (*F*-statistic)	0.0000	

CONCLUSION

The paper employed a time-series econometrics techniques to investigate the links between economic growth and income inequality. The study's results shows that income inequality has a negative effect on Botswana's long run economic growth. Such results points to one main policy recommendation. That is, to reduce the negative impacts of income inequality on potential economic growth, the country needs to institute redistributive policies and programmes which try to reduce income inequality.

REFERENCES

Aghion P., Caroli E., & C., Garcia-Penalosa (1999), Inequality and Economic Growth: The Perspective of the New Growth Theories, *Journal of Economic Literature*, Vol. 37, pp. 1615-1660.

Alesina A., & D. Rodrick (1994), Distributive Politics and Economic Growth, *Quarterly Journal of Economics*, Vol. 109, pp. 465-490.

Alesina Alberto, & Roberto Perotti (1996), Income Distribution, Political Instability and Investment, *European Economic Review*, Vol. 81, No. 5, pp. 1170-1189.

Banerjee A. V., & A. F. Newman (1993), Occupational Choice and the Process of Development, *Journal of Political Economy*, Vol. 101, No. 2, pp. 274-298.

Barro R. (1999), Inequality, Growth and Investment, *National Bureau of Economic Research*, NBER Working Paper 7038.

Benabou Roland (1996), Unequal Societies, New York University C. V. Starr Center Economic Research Report: 9617.

Benabou Roland (1996a), Heterogeneity, Stratification, and Growth: Macroeconomic Implications of Community Structure and School Finance, *American Economic Review*, Vol. 86, No.3, pp. 584-609.

Benabou Roland (1996b), Inequality and Growth, In Ben S. Bernanke and Julio J. Rotemberg, (Eds.), NBER Macroeconomics Annual, Cambridge, MA: MIT Press, pp. 11–74.

Bhatta S. (2001), Are Inequality and Poverty Harmful for Economic Growth: Evidence from the Metropolitan Areas of the United States? University of Illinois at Chicago, USA.

Birdsall N., Ross D., & Sabot R. (1995), Inequality and Growth Reconsidered: Lessons from East Asia, *World Bank Economic Review*, Vol. 9, No. 3, pp. 477-508.

Burtless G. (2003), Has Widening Inequality Promoted or Retarded US Growth, *Canadian Public Policy*, Vol. 29, S185-S201.

Forbes K. J. (2000), A Reassessment of the Relationship Between Inequality and Growth, *American Economic Review*, Vol. 90, pp. 869-887.

Galor O., & D. Tsiddon (1997a), The Distribution of Human Capital and Economic Growth, *Journal of Economic Growth*, Vol. 2, No. 1, pp. 93-124.

Galor O., & D. Tsiddon (1997b), Technological Progress, Mobility, and Economic Growth. *American Economic Review*, Vol. 87, No. 3, pp. 363-382.

Gilles Saint-Paul, & Thierry Verdier (1993), Education, Democracy, and Growth, *Journal of Development Economics*, Vol. 42, No. 2, pp. 399-407.

Kuznets J. (1955), Economic Growth and Income Inequality, *American Economic Review*, Vol. 45, pp. 1-28.

Lewis W. A. (1954), Economic Development with Unlimited Supplies of Labour, Manchester School, pp. 139-191.

Li H., & H., Zhou (1998), Income Inequality is Not Harmful for Growth: Theory and Evidence, *Review of Development Economics*, Vol. 2, pp. 318-334.

Morrissey O., J. Mbabazi, & C. Muller (2002), Inequality, Trade Liberalization and Growth, Centre for the Study of Globalization and Regionalism, The University of Warwick.

Partridge M. D. (1997), Is Inequality Harmful for Growth? Comment, *American Economic Review*, Vol. 87, No. 5, pp. 1019-1037.

Okun A. M. (1975), Equality and Efficiency: The Big Tradeoff, Washington, DC: The Brookings Institution.

Perotti R. (1996), Growth, Income Distribution and Democracy: What the Data Say? *Journal of Economic Growth*, Vol. 1, pp. 149-187.

Perotti R. (1993), Political Equilibrium, Income Distribution, and Growth, *Review of Economic Studies*, Vol. 60, No. 4, pp. 755-776.

Persson T., & Tabellini G. (1994), Is Inequality Harmful for Growth, *The American Economic Review*, Vol. 84, No. 3, pp. 600-621.

Rodrik D. (2004), Growth Strategies, Harvard University, UK.

Rodrik D. (1998), Globalization, Social Conflict and Economic Growth, *World Economy*, Vol. 21, No. 2, pp. 143-158.

Samson M. (2007), The Impact of Social Transfers on Growth, Development, Poverty and Inequality in Developing Countries. Paper Presented at the 1st Annual Conference, Charlote Manye Maxeke Collaboration, Pilansburg, South Africa.

Todaro M. P., & S. C. Smith (2006), Economic Development, (9th Ed.), Pearson Education Limited, England.

Tsiddon D. (1992), A Moral Hazard Trap to Growth, *International Economic Review*, Vol. 33, pp. 299-321.

www.worldbank.org

NOTES

1. Rodrick (2004: 15) defined growth acceleration as an increase in an economy's per-capita GDP growth of two percentage points or more (relative to the previous 5 years) that is sustained over at least 8 years.
2. Gini coefficient is a measure of inequality, and takes values between 0 and 1, or can be multiplied by 100 to obtain the Gini coefficient index which varies between 0 and 100. Values close to zero indicate perfect equality while values close to 1 (or 100) indicate high levels of inequality.

APPENDIX

Table A1
Univariate Characteristics of all the Variables

Series	Model	ADF Lags	$\tau\ \tau_\mu\ \tau_\tau$	$\phi_3\ \phi_1$	Lags	PP	Conclusion
LN_GDPGR	τ_τ	0	–2.22	2.56	2	–2.35	Non-Stationary
	τ_μ	0	–2.05**	4.2*	2	–2.12	
	τ	0	–0.86	–	2	–0.86	
GINI	τ_τ	0	–1.53	1.26	2	–1.71	Non-Stationary
	τ_μ	0	–1.49	1.22	2	–1.26	
	τ	0	0.54	–	2	0.54	
LN_OPEN	τ_τ	4	–2.93	2.39	2	–2.36	Non-Stationary
	τ_μ	0	–0.71	0.51	2	–0.48	
	τ	1	–1.85*	–	2	–1.76*	
LN_GDP	τ_τ	1	–2.2	3.45	2	–1.66	Non-Stationary
	τ_μ	0	–0.54	2.47	2	–0.33	
	τ	1	1.91	–	2	2.88	
LN_GCF	τ_τ	1	-2.84	4.17	2	–2.09	Non-Stationary
	τ_μ	1	-1.17	2.4	2	–0.92	
	τ	3	1.34	–	2	1.06	
DLN_GDPGR	τ_τ	0	–4.27***	9.11**	2	–4.23**	Stationary

Contd.

		ADF					
Series	*Model*	*Lags*	$\tau\ \tau_\mu\ \tau_\tau$	$\phi_3\ \phi_1$	*Lags*	*PP*	*Conclusion*
	τ_μ	0	–.437***	19.09***	2	–4.35***	
	τ	0	–4.47***	–	2	–4.46***	
D_GINI	τ_τ	0	–4.51***	10.22***	2	–4.52***	Stationary
	τ_μ	0	–4.59***	21.02***	2	–4.58***	
	τ	0	–4.61***	–	2	–4.61***	
DLN_OPEN	τ_τ	0	–6.44**	21.1***	2	–6.31***	Stationary
	τ_μ	0	–6.53***	42.7***	2	–6.41***	
	τ	0	–5.96***	–	2	–5.88***	
DLN_GDP	τ_τ	0	–2.64	3.53	2	–4.61**	Stationary
	τ_μ	0	–2.71***	7.38**	2	–2.67**	
	τ	0	–1.85*	–	2	–1.72*	
DLN_GCF	τ_τ	2	–3.36*	3.25	2	–3.10	Stationary
	τ_μ	2	–3.43**	4.49*	2	–3.16**	
	τ	0	–3.03***	–	2	–3.10***	

*(**)[***] Statistically significant at a 10(5)[1]% level

Key: τ_τ : Means Trend and Intercept

τ_μ : Means intercept

τ : Means None?

(LN_GDPGR = log of economic/GDP growth, LN_OPEN = log of trade openness, LN_GINI = log of Gini coefficient, LN_GDP= log of GDP and LN_GCF = log of gross capital formation). The univariate ADF and PP tests indicates that all the variable are stationary after first difference, that is they are $I(1)$.

Table A2
ECM's Diagnostic Tests

Test	H_0	*Test Statistic*	*p-Value*	*Conclusion*
Jarque-Bera	Normally distributed	JB = 1.36	0.51	Normally distributed
Ljung-Box Q	No Serial Correlation	$LB_Q = 4.68$	0.59	No Serial Correlation
Breusch-Godfrey	No Serial Correlation	$nR^2 = 0.03$	0.98	No Serial Correlation
ARCH LM	No Heteroskedasticity	$nR^2 = 0.92$	0.63	No Heteroskedasticity
White	No Heteroskedasticity	$nR^2 = 7.48$	0.29	No Heteroskedasticity

Stability Test

Test	H_0	*Test Statistic*	*p-Value*	*Conclusion*
Ramsey RESET	No Misspecification	LR = 0.14	0.93	No Misspecification

CHAPTER 7

MUTUAL FUND SCHEMES IN INDIA–CAN THEY PROTECT THE INTEREST OF THE RETAIL INVESTORS?

J. N. Mukhopadhyay
Veena Vishwanathan

INTRODUCTION

According to Association of Mutual Funds of India (AMFI), a Mutual Fund (MF) is a trust that pools the savings of a number of investors who share a common financial goal. It is basically an avenue for pooling of resources of small investors for deployment both in primary & secondary markets. The figure below describes broadly the working of a mutual fund:

The MF started in 1963 in India with the formation of Unit Trust of India by an act of the Indian Parliament. It has witnessed a phenomenal increase with the Assets under Management (AUM). at Rs. 505152 crores (US$ 126.29 B) in March 2008.

As the small investors have low risk bearing capacity & lack the requisite expertise to directly invest in the capital market, the MFs were supposed to be an avenue whereby the surplus of the household sector could be diverted to the capital market. Furthermore, it was expected that MFs could with their professional management outperform the stock market while diversifying away the risk.

Against this backdrop, we have attempted to study the performance of some of the leading MF schemes during the last couple of years commencing from 1st April 2006. Though considerable research has been done in the area of mutual funds, this paper includes new datasets, up to a period of March 2008. The period of our study has been momentous for the Indian stock Market. This period includes a couple of high volatile periods–the period when the Nifty reached a high of 3754 on 10th May 2006 and quickly declined to 2632 on 14th June 2006. Similarly it dropped sharply from 6288 on 8th January 2008 to 4503 on 17th March 2008. Therefore the drop during this period was a staggering 29.9% and 28.4% respectively.

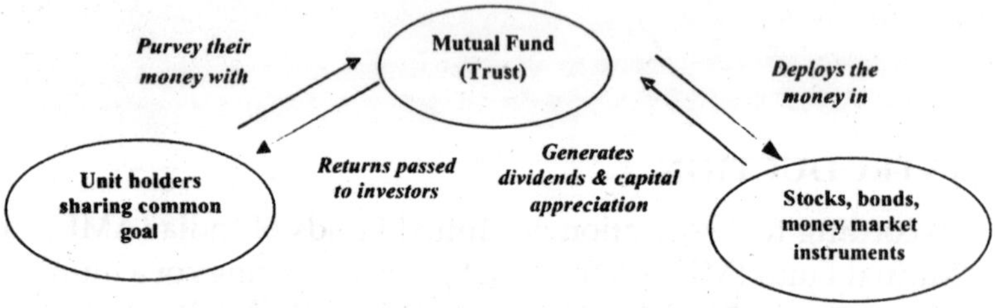

Figure 1: Working of a Mutual Fund*

* *Adapted from, Mukhopadhyay J. N. and Vishwanathan V (2007), "Mutual Funds In India – A Study of their Growth and Behavior", Globsyn Management Journal, 1(1)*

Using a case-study methodology, with some of the leading MFs, this article examines whether mutual funds could actually impart more value than the stock market & protected the interest of the investors even during the downturn.

The plan of this paper is as follows:

In Section II, we present a brief history of the mutual funds in India, with their growth during the different phases. In Section III, we give the classification of the different schemes according to their investment objectives. In Section IV, we compare the Indian mutual funds with the USA mutual funds along some dimensions. In Section V, graphical analysis and parametric test like Pearson test is used to analyze the recent performance of the mutual funds. Section VI presents the conclusions.

BACKDROP

The graph indicates the growth of AUM in the Indian MF industry over the years.

The growth of the mutual funds in the 4 different phases is shown in the Table 1.

With the bifurcation of the erstwhile UTI & with recent mergers taking place among different private sector funds, the MF industry has entered its current phase of consolidation and growth.

It may be noticed here from Table 2 that though the 3rd phase had been a relatively low growth period, the growth in the MF industry picked up in the 4th phase and that the CAGR had accelerated to 60.66% for the 5 years since February 2003.

Table 1
Growth of MFs in India

First Phase – 1964-87	UTI all the way • Unit Trust of India (UTI) started its operations in 1964 by launching its first scheme • It still continues to be one of the largest players in the domestic MF industry with an AUM of Rs. 38,603 crores (US$ 8.39 B) as on 28th February 2007.
Second Phase–1987-1993	Entry of Public Sector Funds • 1987 marked the entry of non–UTI, public sector MF set up by public sector banks and Life Insurance Corporation of India (LIC) and General Insurance Corporation of India (GIC) • SBI MF was the first non – UTI MF established in June 1987. At the end of this phase, the MF industry had AUM of Rs. 47,000 crores (US$ 10.22 B).
Third Phase–1993-2003	Entry of Private Sector Funds • Both domestic and foreign players entered the market • The erstwhile Kothari Pioneer (now merged with

Contd.

	Franklin Templeton) was the first private sector MF registered in July 1993. • International players like Morgan Stanley, Jardine Fleming, and JP Morgan entered the market • By the end of this phase, there were 33 MF with total AUM of Rs. 1,21,805 crores (US$ 26.48 B)
Fourth Phase–since February 2003	UTI's restructuring and beyond In February 2003, following the repeal of the UTI Act 1963, UTI was bifurcated into two separate entities: (i) Specified Undertaking of the UTI, under the Government of India had AUM of Rs. 29, 835 crores (US$6.49 B) as at the end of January 2003, representing broadly, the assets of US 64 scheme, assured return and certain other schemes. (ii) UTI MF Ltd, sponsored by State Bank of India (SBI), Punjab National Bank (PNB), Bank of Baroda (BOB) and Life Insurance Corporation of India (LIC)

www.amfiindia.org

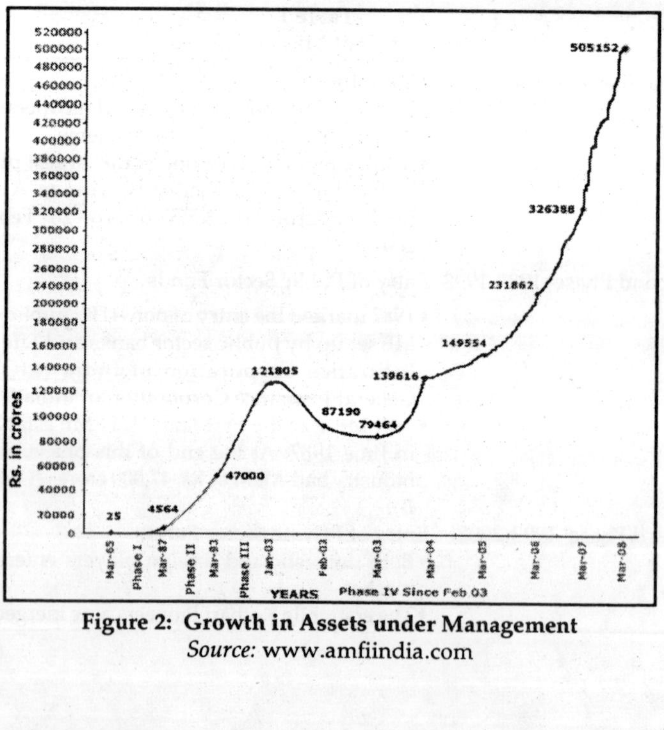

Figure 2: Growth in Assets under Management
Source: www.amfiindia.com

Table 2
Growth of MF

Phases	CAGR of AUM
First Phase – 1964-87	25.40%
Second Phase – 1987-1993	47.50%
Third Phase – 1993-2003	9.99%
Fourth Phase – (till Mar'08)	60.66%

CLASSIFICATION OF SCHEMES

The mutual funds have numerous schemes. The schemes can be classified according to Investment Objective as follows– Growth scheme, income scheme, or balanced scheme considering its investment objective.

Growth/Equity Oriented Scheme

The aim of growth funds is to provide capital appreciation over the medium to long- term. Such schemes normally invest a major part of their corpus in equities and have comparatively high risks.

Income/Debt Oriented Scheme

The aim of income funds is to provide regular and steady income to investors. Such schemes generally invest in fixed income securities such as bonds, corporate debentures, Government securities and money market instruments and are considered less risky compared to equity schemes.

Balanced Fund

The aim of balanced funds is to provide both growth and regular income as such schemes invest both in equities and fixed income securities in the proportion indicated in their offer documents.

Over the years the mutual fund industry has seen the transformation & inception of a number of innovative schemes like the following:

Money Market Mutual Fund (MMMF)

These funds are also income funds and their aim is to provide easy liquidity, preservation of capital and moderate income.

These schemes invest exclusively in safer short-term instruments such as treasury bills, certificates of deposit, commercial paper and inter-bank call money, etc. UTI Money Market Mutual Fund was the 1st MMMF to be launched in April 1997.

Gilt Fund

These funds invest exclusively in government securities and have no default risk. Kotak Mutual Fund was the 1st mutual fund to launch Gilt Plan in December 1998.

Index Funds

Index Funds replicate the portfolio of a particular index such as the BSE Sensitive index, S&P NSE 50 index (Nifty), etc. These schemes invest in the securities in the same weightage comprising of an index. IDBI Index Fund launched the first index fund in 1999.

Fund of Funds (FOF)

A fund of fund scheme invests in other mutual fund schemes. FOF schemes invest in specific funds, which have more weightage of certain stocks & can exit from those schemes when growth prospects of those sectors are not good. Franklin Templeton launched the first fund of fund in 2003.

Exchange Traded Funds (ETF)

It is a security that tracks an index, a commodity or a basket of assets like an index fund, but trades like a stock on an exchange, thus experiencing price changes throughout the day as it is bought and sold. By owning an ETF, one gets the diversification of an index fund as well as the ability to sell short, buy on margin and purchase as little as one share. The Nifty BeES launched by Benchmark MF in January 2002 was the 1st ETF to be traded.

Gold ETFs

The Gold ETF is a new concept, an instrument that enables one to buy and sell gold in demat form. The gold is held by a mutual fund house which offers investors gold in units for as little as Rs. 100. The fund houses invest the money collected from investors in standard gold bullion and issue 'gold receipts'. Currently, there are two mutual funds, which offer Gold ETFs in India. Benchmark Mutual Fund launched India's first gold Exchange-Traded Fund (ETF) on February 15, 2007 and listed as Gold BeES on NSE this year. Benchmark was soon followed by UTI Mutual Fund's gold scheme on March 1, which will list on the NSE in April 2007.

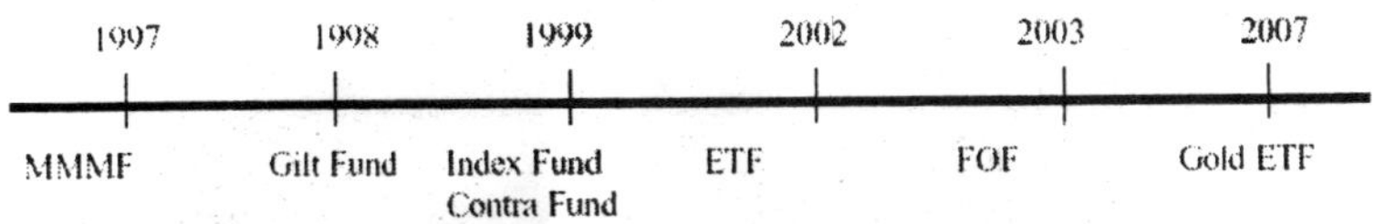

Figure 3: Time Line Depicting Inception of Some Innovative Schemes

Contra Fund

A fund with an investing strategy, that seeks the stock of out of favor companies, with good fundamentals such as low debt or good potential earnings, with the belief that the stock will increase in value in the long run. SBI Mutual Fund launched the Magnum Contra Fund in August 1999. This was the 1st contra fund to be launched.

The following time line captures the inception of the various schemes in India.

Therefore, it can be seen from Figure 3 that schemes, which were considered exotic in the Indian context till phase II, got introduced in India also in phase III & phase IV.

Apart from these there are sector specific funds/schemes, which invest in the securities of only those sectors, or industries as specified in the offer documents. e.g. Pharmaceuticals, Software, Fast Moving Consumer Goods (FMCG), Petroleum stocks, etc. The returns in these funds are dependent on the performance of the respective sectors/industries

In Figure 4, based on the data from The Association of Mutual Funds in India, we see that out of the total AUM, income funds contribute 44%, followed by growth funds, which contribute 31%. The money market mutual funds contribute 17% of the total AUM. The Equity linked saving schemes and the balanced funds each contribute 3% and the Gilt funds & ETFs contribute 1% each.

Since the first MF was born in USA, and also as the largest MF industry exists in USA, we give in the following section, a backdrop of the MFs in USA.

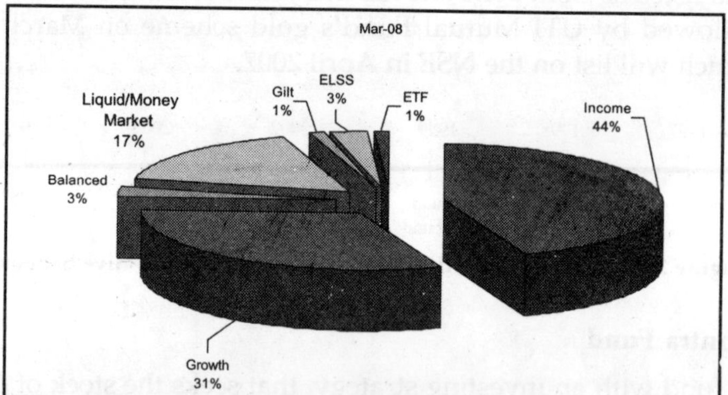

Figure 4: Scheme Wise Break up of MF in March 2008

MUTUAL FUNDS IN THE UNITED STATES

When three Boston securities executives pooled their money together in 1924 to create the first MF, they had no idea how popular MFs would become. On March 21st, 1924 the first official mutual fund was born. It was called the *Massachusetts Investors Trust.*

After one year, the Massachusetts Investors Trust grew from $50,000 in assets in 1924 to $3,92,000 in assets (with around 200 shareholders).

The stock market crash of 1929 slowed the growth of mutual funds. In response to the stock market crash, Congress passed the Securities Act of 1933 and the Securities Exchange Act of 1934. These laws require that a fund be registered with the SEC and provide prospective investors with a prospectus. The SEC helped create the Investment Company Act of 1940, which provides the guidelines that all funds must comply with today.

Strong economic growth in the United States during much of the past quarter century has provided the underpinning for the growth in household demand for discretionary financial assets in general, and mutual funds in particular.

Poterba and Samwick (1995) in their study found that the market value of corporate stock in the United States increased by nearly one trillion dollars between December 1994 and July 1995 and hence the gains from the stock price rise.

Mutual funds have become very popular, known for ease-of-use, liquidity, and unique diversification capabilities. There are various reasons, which have contributed to the popularity of the mutual funds in USA. In the US, the regulatory system is very strong which is designed to achieve only one goal, which is investor protection. The presence of multiple distribution channels make mutual funds easily accessible to investors. Moreover, direct-marketed funds are sold through the mail, by telephone or at office locations.

The U.S. mutual fund market, with $12 trillion in assets under management as of year-end 2007, remains the largest in the world, accounting for 46 percent of the $26.2 trillion in mutual fund assets worldwide according to the Investment Company Institute's official survey of the mutual fund industry.

However, the growth of MFs is not an unmixed blessing. Marcis, West and Chambers (July 1995) in their paper mention that with the rapid growth in mutual funds in the 1990s, economist Henry Kaufman has expressed the concern that mutual funds may now pose a systemic risk to financial markets. They fear that a large and sudden drop in stock or bond prices could cause massive redemptions of mutual fund shares that would force portfolio managers to dump securities, thereby sending securities prices well below their fundamental values.

Dow Jr. and Elmendorf (1998) in their study noted that during the 1990s, households have sharply increased the share of their portfolios held in equities and mutual funds and sharply reduced the share held in bank accounts. They showed that this reallocation has substantially increased the impact of financial-market developments on the demand for money. Specifically, both increases and decreases in the Wilshire 5000 have boosted the demand for money funds during the 1990s, although they had little effect on money funds during the 1980s. The estimated effects in the 1990s are generally statistically significant and economically important.

We now examine the contribution of the US households in the nation's MF industry.

It is seen from Figure 5, that the percentage of households owning mutual funds has been steadily increasing over the years. In 2007, an estimated 50.6 million U.S. households, or 43.6 per cent of households, owned mutual fund, up from only 5.7% in 1980.

Covrig, Lau and Ng (May 2006) mention the phenomenal growth of the mutual fund assets worldwide, which rose to $12.83 trillion at the end of the third quarter of 2003, an increase of about 38% from 1998.

We go further in our paper & examine the mutual fund assets worldwide till the end of the 1st quarter of 2006.

Figure 6 shows the trend in the worldwide mutual fund assets since 2005. The USA mutual fund industry has grown to be the largest in the world with AUM Mutual fund assets worldwide were $22.72 trillion at the end of 2007.

Table 3
Largest Asset Management Firms in USA (2005)

Company	*AUM (US$ M)*
State Street Global Advisors	1,367,269
Fidelity Investments	1,299,400
Capital Group Companies	1,050,435
The Vanguard Group	852,000
JP Morgan Asset Management	782,646
Total	5,351,750

Source: www.wikipedia.org

We briefly study some of the large asset management firms in USA individually, which have achieved phenomenal size by global standards. The AUM of the top 5 asset managers, as shown in the table below sums up to US$ 5,351,750 M whereas

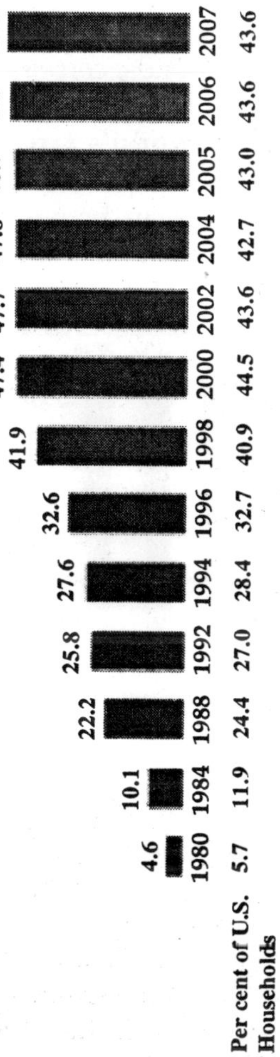

Source: www.ici.org

Figure 5: More than Four in Ten U.S. Households Own Mutual Funds

that of the top five Indian MFs sums up to US$ 29,820 M, which is just 0.56% of the US Figure.

State Street Corporation is a financial services company and provides a full range of products and services for portfolios of investment assets and focuses its services on institutional investors and investment management. Its customers include mutual funds and other collective investment unds, corporate and public pension funds, corporations, unions and not-for-profit organizations Fidelity is one of the world's largest investment management organizations The company's two largest mutual funds are Contrafund and Magellan, both with more than $50 billion in assets. The Magellan Fund was for many years the largest in the United States.

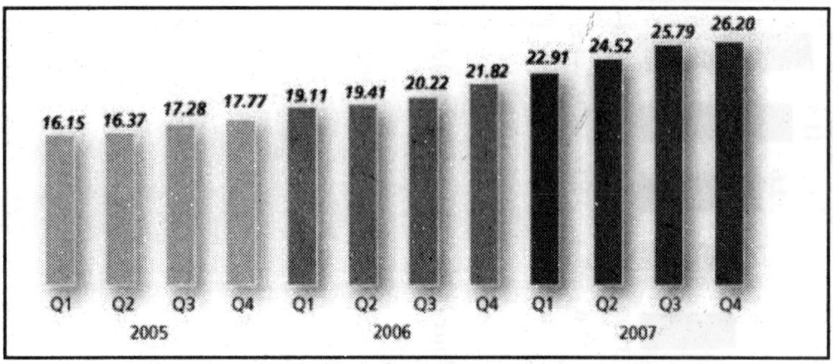

Figure 6: Worldwide Mutual Fund Assets (*Trillions of U.S. dollars, end of quarter*)
Source: www.ici.org

Capital Group Companies is also among the world's largest investment management organizations. The American Funds, managed by the Capital Group Companies, marched past Fidelity Investments in 2005 in total managed assets through September – $738 billion for American Funds, $716 billion for Fidelity. American Funds has quietly and unassumingly become home to six of the 10 largest stock funds in the U.S.– including the biggest of them all, the $117 billion Growth Fund of America.

Vanguard, one of the largest mutual funds began operations on May 1, 1975, with 11 mutual funds and approximately $1.8 billion in assets. In 1976, John C. Bogle opened the first retail index fund called the First Index Investment Trust. It is now called the Vanguard 500 Index fund and in November of 2000 it became the largest mutual fund ever with $100 billion in assets. In contrast one of India's largest MF, Prudential ICICI Mutual Fund has only Rs 31,431 crores AUM (US$ 6.83 B). In other words it is just 6.8% of assets of Vanguard 500 Index Fund.

More than $1 of every $3 plunked into a fund these days goes to American Funds. Vanguard gets about $1 of every $5; Fidelity just $1 of every $50.

JP Morgan asset management is a part of the JPMorgan Chase & Co. a financial holding company, a leading global financial services firm and one of the largest banking institutions with over $1.27 trillion USD in assets.Formed in 2000 with the merger of the Chase Manhattan Corporation and J.P. Morgan & Co., the firm is a leader in investment banking, financial services for consumers and businesses, financial transaction processing, investment management, private banking and private equity. In 2004, the company acquired Bank One of Chicago.

Most American funds like the above emphasize on an investment philosophy of long-term value oriented approach. E.g., Vanguard says, "You cannot regard an approach based on short-term trends or performanc e as an investment philosophy. And the risk of price declines in the bond and stock markets is too significant to hazard money that you will need for short-term goals. Therefore, consider as investment only money that you won't need for a minimum of five years."

The different types of funds available in US are as follows

- Stock funds
- Hybrid fund
- Bond fund
- Money market fund

The pie chart below gives an idea about the assets under management of the different types of funds.

A comparison of the nature of the distribution of funds in India & USA from Figure 4 & Figure 7 shows that whereas

Equity funds comprise a major chunk (54 %) of the total funds invested in MFs in USA the income funds were more popular in India since 2005. The trend reversed in 2006 as can be seen from Figure 8 below.

The trend again reversed in 2007 and income funds again became more popular in India and stood at 44% of AUM in March 2008.

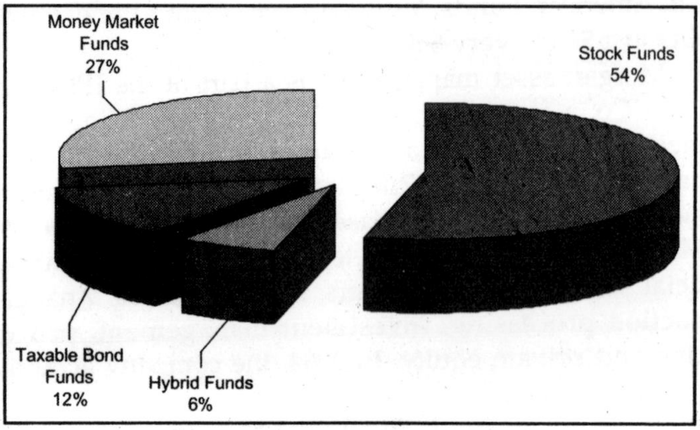

Figure 7: AUM In USA (Mar 2008)
Source: www.ici.org

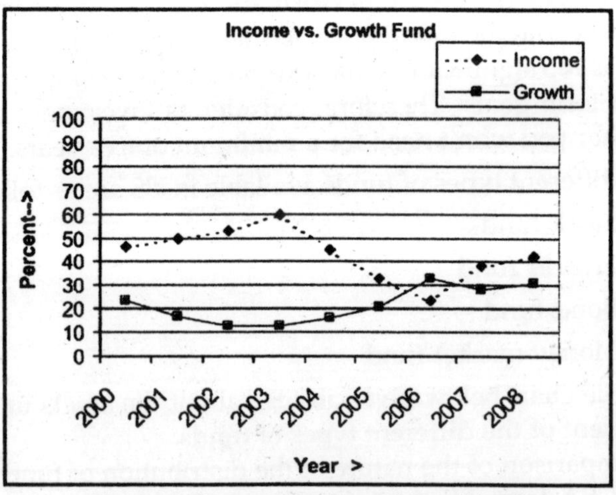

Figure 8: Income Vs. Growth Fund (India)

We shall for the purpose of this paper, focus only on equity diversified funds as their performance can be evaluated by comparing with the performance of Nifty, which is taken as the proxy of the Indian stock market.

ANALYSIS OF RECENT PERFORMANCE OF MUTUAL FUNDS

Fischer and Jordan (1995) mention, "It has often been said that large investors such as mutual funds perform better in the market than the small investor does becaus e they have access to better information." However, researchers have found that mutual funds do not seem to be able to earn greater net returns (after sales expenses) that those that can be earned by investing randomly in a large group of securities & hold ing them. Furthermore, these studies indicate, mutual funds are not even able to earn gross returns (before sales expenses) superior to those of the naive buy-and-hold strategy.

A number of key empirical tests have been conducted to answer questions such as – "Can mutual funds do better for an investor than he can do for himself". The answer is negative; that is, mutual funds contained in the sample taken did not, on the average, outperform the returns that could be earned by following a naive strategy over the sample period.

The Securities Exchange Commission (SEC) as part of its Institutional Investor Study found some evidence that, in its sample, mutual funds outperformed the market by very small amounts. Its study was carried out on a risk-adjusted basis. Another finding of this study was that there was no consistency with respect to which funds provided the investor with superior performance. Specifically, during the five year period 1960-64 the least volatile funds in the sample tended to provide the strongest performance, while during the five-year period 1965-69 the more volatile funds in the sample taken by them provided the best performance. The mutual funds in the study demonstrated a considerable lack of consistency in terms of which type of funds provided regular, superior performance.

We now analyze the performance of the MF industry in India, during the last two years.

We have considered for our case study UTI, Prudential & Reliance MF, as they are the largest as per Assets Under Manage ment as on Mar 2008. Moreover, we study only equity schemes as they primarily invest in the stock market and their performance is evaluated and compared with the stock market. (Nifty is considered as the proxy of the Indian stock market)

As seen from the Table below, these mutual funds have a large number of equity schemes.

Table 4
Top MF Schemes with Date of Inception

Name of the Scheme	*Date of Inception*
UTI Mutual fund	
UTI-Mastershare Unit Scheme	19th September 1986
UTI-Equity Fund (Formerly UTI-Mastergain Unit Scheme)	20th April 1992
UTI-Mastergrowth	18th January 1993
UTI-Master Value Fund	1st June 1998
UTI-Growth & Value Fund	28th October 1999
UTI-Dynamic Equity Fund	10th September 2003
UTI-Opportunities Fund	20th July 2005
UTI-Leadership Equity Fund	9th January 2006
Prudential ICICI Mutual Fund	
Prudential ICICI Growth Plan	4th June 1998
Prudential ICICI Dynamic Plan	7th October 2002
Prudential ICICI Emerging STAR Fund	6th September 2004
Reliance Mutual Fund	
Reliance Growth Fund	30th September 1995
Reliance Equity Fund	16th October 2004
Reliance Equity Opportunities Fund	14th February 2005

Furthermore, for the purpose of focusing our analysis, we have considered the three oldest equity diversified schemes from these three MFs.–UTI Master share Unit Scheme, Prudential ICICI Growth Plan, and Reliance Growth Fund and compare them with the Nifty.

As mentioned earlier, particular focus is given on the period 10th May to 14th June 2006 and 8th January to 17th March 2008 as the market slid sharply by approximately 30% and 28% during these periods respectively. It can be seen clearly from the dataset, that in 2008, we have captured the lowest point

17th March 2008 and also the highest point in its vicinity i.e. 8th Jan 2008.

Similarly in 2006, the lowest point was 14th June 2006 and to analyze the volatility and risk, we took the nearest point when the Nifty index was very high i.e. 3754 on 10th May. The results of the performance of the different schemes and Nifty are presented in the table below.

Table 5
Performance in Different Time Periods

Period	*Nifty*	*UTI-Mastershare Unit Scheme*	*Prudential ICICI Growth Plan*	*Reliance Growth Fund*
10/5/2006 – 14/6/2006	–29.87%	–30.55%	–30.97%	–34.27%
8/1/2008 – 17/3/2008	–28.38%	–30.04%	–24.08%	–33.65%
1/4/2006 – 31/3/2008	26.64%	21.45%	19.86%	30.84%

It is seen from the graph and the table above, that during the sharp downturn in the markets from 10th May 2006 to 14th June 2006 these same sche mes not only gave negative returns but also under-performed the index. Whereas the Nifty went down by –29.87% during this period the funds from UTI, Prudential & Reliance MF went down by –30.55%, –30.97% and –34.27% respectively. Similarly, in the sharp downturn of 8th January to 17th march2008, whereas the market again went down by –28.38% the 3 funds under study also went down steeply by –30.04%, –24.08% and –33.65% respectively i.e., except the Prudential ICICI growth plan scheme, the other two schemes in our study under performed the index.

On the other hand, for the two years period, all the three funds gave positive returns and only Reliance growth fund scheme outperformed the index. This clearly shows that even for a longer duration the MFs are not able to outperform the broad based index and generate superior returns for their investors.

However, the investment philosophy propagated by India's oldest and of the biggest MFs in India viz., UTI Mutual Fund is

"...to deliver consistent and stable returns in the medium to long term with a fairly lower volatility of fund returns compared to the broad market"

Investors, who have low risk taking capacity and lack the professional skills of fund management, are generally advised not to invest directly in the stock market but through the mutual funds route. Mutual funds are also supposed to provide for high liquidity. But from the above graph and table it appears that the MF are exposing the investors to high risk and therefore the investors are loosing even compared to the broad based index Nifty during a downturn.

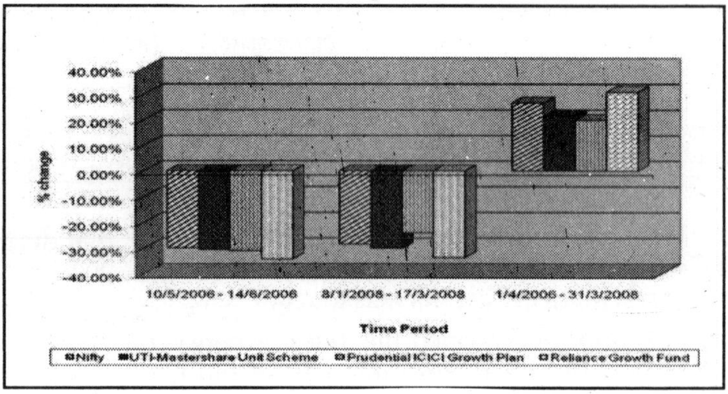

Figure 9: Graphical Representation

Johnson (2004) analyzes the distribution of investment horizons in a large, proprietary panel of all shareholders in one no-load mutual fund family. A proportional hazards model shows that there are observable shareholder characteristics that enable the fund to predict reliably on the day each account is opened whether the account will be short-term or long-term. Simulations show that the liquidity costs imposed on the fund by the expected short-term shareholders are significantly greater than those imposed by the expected long-term shareholders. Combining these results, the analysis argues that mutual funds do not provide equitable liquidity-risk insurance.

Diamond (1999) studied whether the time horizons of investors, on average, have changed or will change. While the question of how time horizon should affect asset demands raises subtle theoretical issues (Samuelson 1991), longer horizons and sufficient risk aversion should lead to greater willingness to hold stocks given the tendency for stock prices to revert toward their longterm trend (Campbell and Viceira 1999). Thc evidence on trends in investor time horizons is mixed. For example, the growth of explicit individual retirement savings vehicles, suggests that the average time horizons of individual investors may have lengthened.

Finally, individual stock ownership has become less concentrated (Poterba and Samwick 1997), which suggests a shorter time horizon as less wealthy investors might be less concerned about passing assets on to younger generations.

Our study also tries to examine, whether a unit holder of MF in India is actually having a medium to long-term investment horizon & hence will not react to short-term market changes.

We now see empirically, whether there was change in the pattern of MF inflows during this downturn. It is interesting to note, that whereas the average mutual fund net inflows per day (for a 10 day period) during 10th May 2006 was (+) Rs. 237 crores it had dramatically changed to (for a 10 day period) during 14th June 2006 to (–) Rs. 134 crores. In other words, there was a negative swing of Rs. 371 crores per day in the average net inflows for the mutual funds during this period (10th May to 14th June 2006). Similarly, for the period of 8th January 2008 to 17th March 2008, the daily negative swing in the average net mutual fund inflows stood at Rs. 427.22 crores. Here, the daily average mutual fund net inflows (for a 10 day period) during 8th January 2008 was (+) Rs. 329.5 crores and changed to (for a 10 day period) during 17th March 2008 to (–) Rs 97.72 crores.

It therefore appears that the Indian mutual fund investor may actually be succumbing to the herd mentality and giving in to selling, when the market goes down.

Since the above trends are for a short period, we examine the correlation of the mutual fund inflows with the market for longer periods also and run Pearson test.

Pearson's Correlation Test

Correlation is the degree of association between two or more variables. Pearson correlation coefficient is a statistic, which estimates the correlation between two random variables. i.e. a measure of how well a linear equation describes the relation between two or more variables.

The mathematical notation of this correlation coefficient is,

$$r = \Sigma (x - \mu_x)(y - \mu_y)/n\, \sigma_x \sigma_y$$

where, $\sigma_x = \sqrt{(X - X)^2 / n}$

and $\sigma_y = \sqrt{(Y - Y)^2 / n}$

The numerator is the Sum of The Product of Deviations of X and Y from their respective means, σ_x and σ_Y. This summation is then divided by the number of observations times the Standard Deviation of X and Y.

The coefficient correlation 'r' ranges from –1 to 1, where a value of +1 show a positive perfect linear relationship & –1 shows a negative perfect trade off between variables.

The Population Correlation Co-Efficient

The statistic 'r' is used to estimate ρ and to carry out tests of hypotheses, since we don't know population correlation coefficient. The most common test is whether $\rho = 0$, that is whether the correlation is significantly different from zero.

The coefficient of correlation provides a method of determining numerically the existence of causal relationship between variables. The proportion of variation explained by regression is equal to the square of correlation coefficient, i.e. $\mathbf{r}^2$ = ESS/TSS, i.e. $\mathbf{r}^2$= Proportion of variation explained by regression. It helps in estimating the value of the dependent variable given the value of independent variable.

As can be seen from the table below, the Pearson correlation for a one-year data from 14 June 2005 to 14 June 2006 between Nifty and MF equity inflow is significant at 1% level and the Pearson correlation coefficient is 0.169.

Table 6
Pearson Correlation for the Data from 14/6/05 – 14/6/06

		Nifty	*MF*
Nifty	Person Correlation		.169**
	Sig. (2-tailed)		.007
	N	250	250
MF	Person Correlation	.169**	1
	Sig. (2-tailed)	.007	
	N	250	250

If the correlation test is done only again for one year period from 10th May 2005 to 10th May 2006, it is found that the correlation is significant at 1% level and the Pearson correlation coefficient is higher at 0.281.

Table 7
Pearson Correlation for the Data from 10/5/05 – 10/5/06

	Nifty		*MF*
Nifty	Person Correlation	1	.281**
	Sig. (2-tailed)	.000	
	N	231	228
MF	Person Correlation	.281**	1
	Sig. (2-tailed)	.000	
	N	228	228

We also examine the Pearson correlation coefficient for shorter periods from 10th May 2006 to 14th June 2006 and 8th January to 17th March 2008 and find that the correlation coefficient is 0.369 and 0.114 respectively.

We can therefore say from the Pearson test results that there is correlation between the mutual fund inflows and the stock market index.

CONCLUSION

Mutual funds started in 1963 with the formation of UTI. UTI was the sole player till 1987 when others were allowed to float their own schemes. Subsequently, with the entry of the private players, MF industry has witnessed a phenomenal increase in their AUM.

As the small investors have low risk bearing capacity & lack the requisite expertise to directly invest in the capital market, the MFs were supposed to be an avenue whereby the surplus of the household sector could be diverted to the capital market. Furthermore, it was expected that MFs could with their professional management outperform the stock market while diversifying away the risk.

Against this backdrop, we have attempted to study the performance of some of the leading MF schemes during the last couple of years commencing from 1st April 2006. Though considerable research has been done in the area of mutual funds, this paper includes new datasets, up to a period of March 2008. The period of our study has been momentous for the Indian stock Market.

This period includes a couple of high volatile periods – the period when the Nifty reached a high of 3754 on 10th May 2006 and quickly declined to 2632 on 14th June 2006. Similarly it dropped sharply from 6288 on 8th January 2008 to 4503 on 17th March 2008. Therefore the drop during this period was a staggering 29.9% and 28.4% respectively.

Using a case-study methodology, with some of the leading MFs, this article examines whether mutual funds could actually impart more value than the stock market & protected the interest of the investors even during the downturn.

It is observed from the analysis that during the sharp downturn in the markets from 10th May 2006 to 14th June 2006 these same schemes not only gave negative returns but also underperformed the index. Whereas the Nifty went down by –29.9% during this period the funds from

UTI, Prudential & Reliance MF went down by –30.6%, –30.97% and –34.3% respectively.

Similarly, in the sharp downturn of 8th January to 17th March 2008, whereas the market again went down by –28.38% the 3 funds under study also went down steeply by –30.0%, –24.1% and –33.7% respectively i.e., except the Prudential ICICI growth plan scheme, the other two schemes in our study under performed the index.

On the other hand, when the schemes are studied for the longer two years period, all the three funds gave positive returns but only Reliance MF outperformed the index. This clearly shows that even for a longer duration the MFs are not always able to outperform the broad based index and generate superior returns for their investors.

We now see empirically, whether there was change in the pattern of MF inflows during this downturn. It is interesting to note, that whereas the average mutual fund net inflows per day (for a 10 day period) during 10th May 2006 was (+) Rs. 237 crores it had dramatically changed to (for a 10 day period) during 14th June 2006 to (–) Rs. 134 crores. In other words, there was a negative swing of Rs. 371 crores per day in the average net inflows for the mutual funds during this period (10th May to 14th June 2006). Similarly, for the period of 8th January 2008 to 17th March 2008, the daily negative swing in the average net mutual fund inflows stood at Rs. 427.22 crores.

Pearson Correlation test was carried out which shows that there is correlation between the mutual fund inflows and the stock market index.

It therefore appears that the Indian mutual fund investor may actually be succumbing to the herd mentality and giving in to selling, when the market goes down sharply, suffering serious losses on their investment.

REFERENCES

Campbell Y. John, and Viceira M. Luis M., (1999), "Consumption and Portfolio Decisions When Expected Returns are Time Varying," *The Quarterly Journal of Economics*, Vol. 114, No. 2.

Diamond A Peter, (September 1999), "*What Stock Market Returns to Expect for the Future*? An Issue in Brief – Center for Retirement Research At Boston College, No. 2.

Dow Jr. P. James, and Elmendorf W. Douglas, (May 1998), "The Effect of Stock Prices on the Demand for Money Market Mutual Funds," Paper Provided by Board of Governors of the Federal Reserve System (U.S.) in its Series Finance and Economics Discussion Series with Number 1998-24

Fischer E. Donald, and Jordon J. Ronald, (1995), *Security Analysis and Portfolio Management* (Sixth Edition): Prentice-Hall of India, pp. 542.

Johnson T. Woodrow, (2004), "Predictable Investment Horizons and Wealth Transfers Among Mutual Fund Shareholders," *The Journal of Finance*, Vol. 50, No. 5.

Marcis Richard, West Sandra, and Leonard-Chambers Victoria, (July 1995), "Mutual Fund Shareholder Response to Market Disruptions," *Investment Company Institute*, Vol. 1, No. 1.

Poterba J. M., & Samwick A. A., (1996), "Stock Ownership Patterns, Stock Market Fluctuations, and Consumption," *Working Papers* 96-2, Massachusetts Institute of Technology (MIT), Department of Economics.

Poterba J. M., and Samwick A. A., (1997), "Household Portfolio Allocation Over the Life Cycle," *NBER Working Papers* 6185, National Bureau of Economic Research, Inc.

Vicentiu Covrig, Sie Ting Lau, and Lilian Ng. (May 2006), "Do domestic and Foreign fund Managers Have Similar Preferences for Stock cCharacteristics? A Cross-Country Analysis", *Journal of International Business Studies*, 37.3: p. 407 (23).

http://www.amfiindia.com/ – Last Accessed on 31st March 2008

http://www.ici.org/ – Last Accessed on 31st March 2008

The Authors would Like to Acknowledge the Support of Ms Monolina Bhattacharyya, (Ex-Research Associate, Globsyn Business School).

CHAPTER 8

INDIAN STRATEGIES FOR GLOBAL COMPETETIVENESS

M. Sumathy

INTRODUCTION

The debate about & the use of the term "Global Competitiveness" is in a state of flux. In the Business World, "Global Competitiveness" has become the fashionable term among CEO's in presentations & annual reports. It resembles, *"A Dialogue of the Deaf."*

Global Competitiveness as "the ability of a country to achieve sustained high rates of growth in GDP per capita" while competing with International Firms.

Global Competitiveness encompasses the following factors that are essential for coping with Global Competition.

- Openness
- Government
- Technology
- Finance
- Infrastructure
- Management
- Labor
- Instituitions

Porter defines Global Competitiveness at the National level, as the ability to export many goods produced with high productivity, which allows the nation to import many goods involving lower productivity.

GLIMPSE OF MODERN GLOBAL BUSINESS

Today's Modern Business is characterized by:

- Goal is to accommodate the demands of diverse stakeholders.
- Networks of Alliances among stakeholders are sophisticated.
- Management is truly professional.
- Ownership is often publicly held, diverse ownership possibly from various countries.
- Structures are varied in nature.
- Systems & Processes are quite complex.
- Not bound to any Nation.
- Root of development is market competition & mechanism.
- Suppose to perform a wide range of activities.
- Taps FDI & follow opportunities wherever they find.
- Required to look upon on Economic & Non-Economic activities.
- Consumer as well as Environment friendly.
- Last but not the least it revolves around "Integrating the World Economy".

The underlying sense of presenting Glimpse of Modern Global Business is to assert that if any Global Corporation follows such modern approach it could touches the star in the sky. The above mentioned aspects are the critical requirement of this evil time for a Firm to be the best out of the best.

INDIAN STRATEGIES FOR GLOBAL COMPETETIVENESS

A realistic approach of Indian Industries is essential for International Business Environment especially making the concept of Liberalization & Globalization more meaningful & understanding in its real essence. The broad areas of Strategies & the important aspect to be considered are:

Consistent Screening of International as well as Indigenous Business Environment

Indian Firm should screen the following 6 broad sectors in order to compete successfully:

- Technological–Emergence of new Technologies, Access to it & Receptiveness.
- Social–Population Trends, Age shifts in the population, Attitude towards consumption & Investment.
- Economic–State of the economy, Overall growth rate, Inflation rate.
- Governmental–Industrial Policy, Tax Framework, Exim Policy.
- Competitor–Firms in Industry, Entry Barriers, Marketing Policies & Practices.
- Geographic–Country, Region, City, Location, Site.
- Supplier–Availability of Raw Material & Sub-Assemblies, Cost of Energy, Cost of Money.

Monitoring Competition Sector

Basically a promising idea that enables a firm (or Entrepreneur) to exploit opportunities in the environment by drawing on its competitive strengths .Hence the firm must systematically monitor the Environment & assess its competitive abilities. Under this sector the aspects to be considered are:

- Number of Firms in the Industry & their Market Share.
- Degree of homogeneity & differentiation among products.
- Entry Barriers.
- Comparison with substitutes in terms of Quality, Price, Appeal & functional performance.

- Marketing Policies & Practices.
- How might they attack in future?
- What are our plans to leapfrog them?

Clout with Governmental & Regulatory Agencies

Indian Firms should abide by the local Norms & Practices. It should oblige Local Government & Local Regulatory Bodies Commands as to enhance smoothing in their all operations & Development.

Strategic Partnerships

Indian Firms should set out to create value through Alliances & Mergers & Acquisitions. This results in minimizing certain deficiencies, enhancing competitive advantage, competing effectively & enhancing flexibility & speed in reacting to certain strategic alerts. & gain of critical mass, access technology & expand distribution channels.

Value Based Management

Firms' primary objective should be to create value to customers, shareholders & Employees. Concepts like Wealth Maximization, Value Added Service, should be practically induced & implemented.

Globalization Through Regionalization

The Global Organization should be flexible in dealing with a wide range of Environment & their peculiarities. Should accommodate business styles prevailing in those surroundings. It should rather mix with its Culture as "Sugar mixes with Milk". Should also look for similarities & understanding differences.

Innovation

The Firm should seek to establish Corporate Environment where everyone is thinking creatively, challenging the way things are done, & connecting people across organizational boundaries. Research is not only enough, there should be coordination between Research & Operations.

Best Cost Producer

This strategy is aimed at improving operating margins, Quality, Customer Service & Asset Utilization. Firm should capitalize the opportunities where it could derive the benefits of *economies of scale.*

Moral Concerns

Indian Firms should always seek to enhance public image & involvement in social activities as necessary conditions for strategically positioning a Firm in the market place. Moral Dimensions encompass issues like People Welfare, Ethical Approach, and Human Rights & Ecology Maintenance. These issues are debated at all societal levels, locally & globally.

Key Success Factor

Firm should identify its Key Success Factor. The factor which is necessary for the firm's survival in the midst of competence & without which their Life is in danger Identification should be followed by Implementation which in turn should follow Maintenance.

Core Competence

Core Competence refers to distinct ability. Similarly Organization should develop such competencies & ca bit the opponents. In short it has to be *"Master of One & Not a Jack of All"*. Ultimately it will lead it to have Competitive Advantage.

Market Image

The firm should try to maintain its market image. They should try to create positive image in the mind of stakeholders. In other words Organization should build Good Public Relations. Even if they do not turn out to be their customers, relations should be such that at the same time, they do not speak ill about them.

E-Concept

New Economy is the Internet Economy. Emerged Economy has made possible linkage with entire World Economy.

Organization that is capable & comfortable in exploiting such Networks & sharing their knowledge can easily outstand their competitors. Joining this Economy will "Beat the Slow" to participate. Hence Firm should introduce Information Technology in all its operation. So that they can easily gather, tap & deploy knowledge to continuously improve their competitive positions.

Tapping FDI

FDI is the most important instrument to tap the Global Business. It offers competitive conditions for Firms to expand & grow. Again one of the most volatile forces has been Capital Flows. It roams the globe searching for better returns & opportunities. World Trade growth gets acceleration due to flow of Capital from different regions.

Collective Endeavour

Team Work should be encouraged. Employees should be motivated to work collectively on Projects.Cututral Differences should also be accommodated. Participative Approach should be adopted with respect to Decision Making. Autocrisim spoils Relations. Hence Free Rein Leadership is more advisable.

CONCLUSION

Several inferences has been drawn & considered for inclusion under Global Competition. The following dimensions define each set of important items that emerged. Indian Industries should conduct Global Business to maximize Firm's benefit without inflicting social damage or violating the rights of people from other cultures.

- Business Organization should care about the development of the host country also & should participate in refinement of business practices & norms across cultures while respecting the integrity & National Sovereignty. Willingness should be there on the part of organization to transpatriate for career & its development. That aspect is of due importance.

- Indian Industries should ensure a flexible Organizational structure & a truly globalized Board of Directors & Executive Management. Should attracts the best personnel globally without prejudice.
- Should develop an explicit statement of corporate "Global Values". Conduct business in a socially & ethically responsible manner. Thus, lead on the basis of character & an ethic of Fairness, Honesty & Integrity & should protect the Consumers around the Globe.
- Should view "Foreigners" simply as people. There should be use of Prepositions "We" instead of "I". Creation of such community feeling among the people of Host country can break down some of the "us" versus "them" barriers. Besides it knowledge & a sense of mutual obligation & belongingness are transmitted & embedded in Organizational Life.

REFERENCES

Franchise Cherunilam, *International Business Environment*, Himalaya Publishing House, Edition 1.

Jean Pierre Jeannette & Hubert D. Hennessey, *Global Marketing Strategies*, Jaico Publishing House, Edition-2.

Abbas J. Ali, *Globalization of Business*, Jaico Publishing House, Edition 1.

Franchise Cherunilam, *International Trade & Export Management*, Himalaya Publishing House, Edition-2003.

P. Subba Rao, *International Business*, Himalaya Publishing House, Edition-2005.

CHAPTER 9

ONSLAUGHT OF GLOBAL BRANDS–INDIAN BRANDS FIGHT BACK!!

M. Sumathy

INTRODUCTION

Indian brands are developing an insight about the survival power of local brand faced with an onslaught from global brands. Indian market is flooded with a variety of foreign goods, and in this scenario, Indian brand are fighting back for survival. This is the major challenge marketer face today. Brands ca survives by delivering value advantage over the new brands. This paper deals with a few Indian Brands that have been groomed on our soil and can take on the world. These are domestic icons that can evoke a feeling of pride in marketers and have enough relevance and charisma to hold the attention of the consumers. Consumers ultimately reach out for them in stores laden with foreign goods. Managing brand is a tricky affair that calls for vigor at one end of the spectrum and maturity of purpose at other. A few homegrown well managed Indian brands that have come up from the sidelines and seized center stage which arouse the unconscious feelings of passion, loyalty and enthusiasm that have stood the test of time and consumer taste and have successfully competed with the world's best.

Brand

Brand as the major enduring asset of a company, outlasting the company's specific products and facilities. If every asset we own, every building, and every piece of equipment were destroyed in a terrible natural disaster, we would be able to borrow all the money to replace it very quickly because of the value of our brand. The brand is more valuable than the totality of all these assets.

Definition

"A name, term, sign, symbol or design or a combination of them, intended to identify the offering of an organization and to differentiate it from a competitive offering". Brands are more than just and symbols. Brads represent consumers' perceptions and feelings about a product and its performance-everything that the product or service means to consumers. As one branding expert suggests, "Ultimately, brands reside in the minds of consumers." Thus, the real value of a strong brand is its power to capture consumer preference and loyalty.

Brand Equity

Brands vary in the amount of power and value they have in the marketplace. A powerful brand has high brand equity. A measure of brands equity is extending to which customers are willing to pay more for the brand. High brand equity provided a company with many competitive advantages. A powerful brand enjoys a high level of consumer brand awareness and loyalty. Because consumers expect stores to carry the brand, the company has more leverage in bargaining with resellers. Because the brad name carries high creditability, the company can more easily launch line and brand extension.

Brand Development

A company has four choices when it comes to developing brands (see figure). It can introduce line extension (existing brand names extended to new forms sizes, and flavors of an existing product category), brand extensions (existing brand names extended to new product categories), multibrands (New brand names introduced in the same product category), or new brands (new brand names in new product categories).

		Product category	
		Existing	New
Brand Name	Existing	Line extension	Brad extension
	New	Multi brands	New brands

Branding the World

Indian is the hottest destination for the world's leading consumer brands. Liberalization was a major milestone in India's market place in terms of the emerging product categories and the number of brands being available to the Indian consumers. These brands came, saw, and conquered.... The scenario was not very different before liberalization, but yes, numbers of brands were less. Table shows major Indian Brads and global brands in Indian Economy.

Can Indian Brands Survive

India with such a rich culture, people have been exposed to variety of brands, but the onset of liberal economy, Indian brands face a lot of threat from global players. The important question arises-'Will Indian brands be able to survive the onslaught of global brands?"

Around 300 respondents in the age group 21-50 were surveyed to find out how many successful Indian brands they could recall, which have emerged strong in fighting the global brands.

The respondents judged the brands on the basis of non-quantifiable emotions, values attached to the brand and the inner strength to survive in spite of attacks from established global players. There is competition, especially hardened battle-scarred competition from overseas; they have started collapsing, as has been the experience in the consumer durable

Sector	Major Brands 1970s and 1980s	New Brads-1990s Onwards Indian Brands	Global Brads
FMCG			
Soaps	Lifebuoy, Cinthol, Liril, Lux, Pears, Rexona, Mysore Sandal, Neem, Margo	Nirma Beauty Soap	Palmolive, Dettol, Dove
Creams and Biotique,	Fair & Lovely, Pond's	Dabur, Himalaya	Oriflame, Avon,
Lotions	Johnson & Johnson		Amway, Garnier
Detergents	Surf, Kissan, Parle, Britannia	Fena, Lakhani	Ariel, Tide, Henkl
Processed foods	Maggie, Kissan, Parle, Britannia	MTR, Aashirwaad, Heinz, Pillsbury	Haldiram, Bikaner
Beverages	Nescafe, Red Label, Campa, Thumsup	Haldiram, Tata Tea, Bisleri, Tajmahal	Pepsi, Coke, Sprite, 7 Up
Cigarettes	Wills, India Kings, Panama		Menthol
Durables			
Automobile	Ambassador, Fiat, Standard, Maruti	Tata Indica, Indigo, Indigo Marina	Honda, Chevrolet, Ford, Benz, Skoda Hyundai, Opel
Computers	IBM, HCL	Zenith, Infosys, Wipro	Compaq, HP, Dell, Microsoft
Scooters/Bikes	Bajaj, Yamaha, Royal Enfield, Java	Kinetic	
Refrigerators	Godrej, Kelvinator, Allwyn	Videocon	LG, Samsung, Whirlpool, Daewoo

Contd.

Sector	Major Brands 1970s and 1980s	New Brads-1990s Onwards	
		Indian Brands	*Global Brads*
Air conditioners	Voltas, Fedder's Lloyd, Blue Star, Carrier	Videocon	LG, Samsung, Hitachi, Haeir
Television	Crown, Videocon, Weston, Dynora, BPL, Onida, Beltex,		Samsung, LG, Philips, Konark, Akai, Sony
Washing Machines		Videocon, BPL	IFB, Samsung, LG, Whirlpool
Tyres	MRF, Goodyear, Ceat, JK	Apollo	Bridgestone
Services			
Banks	State Bank and Government banks, Citibank, Bank of America, Grindlays	HDFC, ICICI, Kotak	HSBC
Insurance	LIC	Kotak, Sun, Bajaj, IFFCO, ICICI	Max
Cellular Services		Airtel, BPL, Idea, BSNL, Dolphin, Reliance	Hutch, Orange
Hotels	Taj, Oberoi, Welcome group, ITDC		Hyatt, Meridian, Best Western, Ramada
Media			
TV	Doordarshan	Aaj Tak, Regional Channels Zee, Siticable, Sorty, NDTV	Star, BBC, CNN ESPN, CNBC
Radio	Vividh Bharti, AIR	FM, Radio Mirchi, Red FM	Radio City

sector. Service brands have the best hope of survival as CK Prahalad pointed out in a recent speech; it takes a genius to be able to replicate the *dabbawalla* system of Bombay- world class and more quality delivered with a modestly educated workforce and cost of consumer of just Rs. 250 per month!

Amul Butter	Onida T.V.,	Raymond Suiting
Asian paints	Parle G.	Nirma
Fevicol	Thumps up,	Bajaj Auto
Godrej Locks	Titan,	Dabur
Lakme	Amruntanjan	Kingfisher
Charminar Cigarettes	Wills	Bombay Dyeing
India Today	Keokarpin	Tortoise Mosquito
Coil		
Parachute Hair Oil	Reliance	Taj Group of Hotels
Videocon	Rasna,	Tata Salt
Tata Tea	Rooh Afza	Airtel

Successful Products Display one or More of the Following Characteristics

- A significant price performance advantage
- Some significant difference from the existing brands
- A new untried idea.
- Strong intangible brand associations.

In conclusion, there are few homegrown brands that have stood the test of time and consumer taste and have successfully competed with the world's best. Size of brands or heritage or history is no protection for Indian brands. Even huge brands can collapse overnight if better value products enter the Indian market.

Brand Battles

How do value brands grow: Typically, value brands don't carve out species for themselves; they fill existing gaps in the market? Once a value brand identifies a slot, it claims it on the price platform. By adopting a low cost business model, offering higher margins to retailers and growing volumes, value lands are able to offer lower prices than the existing players in the market. "Behind a value brand is a business design to give a good quality product at a low price. We have seen them become leaders in several markets. We see some examples of firms; they suffer battles for their brand:

Air Deccan

Indian's first low-cost airline launched operations in 2003 by offering tickets for Rs. 1. Its most expensive ticket was still cheaper than the national carrier Indian Airlines (now Indian) and Jet Airways. Three years on, Air Deccan has a 21.2 per cent market share. Pushing Indian to third place.

Gold Winner

The refined sunflower oil brand was launched in 1995 by Chennai based Kaleesuwari Refinery. When Sundrop was selling at Rs. 40 a liter, Gold Winner offered three liters for Rs. 100. In the past seven-eight years, volumes have trebled and Gold Winners is now the leading sunflower oil brand, with a 24 per cent share of the Rs. 2,000 crore mass packaged sunflower oil markets.

Nirma

Think value brands ad Nirma immediately springs to mind. The Ahmedabad-based detergent brand's growth from a one-man operation to a Rs. 2,500 crore company that employs 14,000 people is the stuff of case studies. In many ways Nirma was India's original value brand-low cost low price and good quality.

Tata Motor

In 2000, losses at Telco (as the company was called until 2003) had crossed Rs. 500 crore and market share had dipped in both light and heavy vehicles. Based on the realization that company's product-centric strategies were probably at fault, Telco initiated a study among customers to discover what they wanted. Customers wanted a vehicle that fulfilled three important criteria: higher levels of safety than the average three-wheeler, comfort ad lower operation costs than most four-wheelers. Based on that research, last year Tata Motors launched the Tata Ace (750 kg. Rs. 2.5 lakh) Ace sold 29,000 units last year and expects to sell 65,000 this year.

Cigaretts

Cigarette major ITC, which ensures it, is present across price points. At Rs. 3.5-4 a stick, Wills Classic Milds and Insignia compete with premium brands like Philip Morris's Marlboro Lights and Indonesian clove cigarette brand Gudarg Garam. In the budget segment Gold Flakc and Wills navy Cut sell for Rs. 2-3 a stick, while Bristol and Capstan (Rs. 1.4 a stick) fight it out with Godfrey Philips' Four Square ad Red & White.

If You Can't Beat 'Em. Buy 'Em

Finally, if nothing else works, analysts believe it makes perfect sense to acquire value-for-money brands. Of course, there is a caveat: study the value brand's business model and ensure you ca leverage the same cost advantage once it is part of your stable. In March 2006, When Hindustan Lever put its hair oil brand Nihar on the block. Marico paid Rs. 216 crore for it. For Marico, the acquisition made immense sense. In one stroke, it was removing Competition for Parachute, its premium hair oil brand and also improving its presence in the astern markets, where Nihar was popular.

Small Indian Brands, Big Global Ambitions

August has been a good month for Delhi-based fashion designer *Manish Arora* designer, he is working on the new *Fish Fry Collection,* set to retail in November, and first collection hit international stores. Sports brands and designer collaborations aren't unusual: Stella McCartney designs for Adidas while Puma has Alexander McQueen. But Fish Fry is the first couture collection from Reebok, and Arora the first designer (Indian or otherwise) to work with the brand.

But this story isn't about just Arora, Fish Fr or even Reebok. It's about not-so-big Indian brands that are making their presence felt in the international arena. There's *Amrut,* a single malt whisky by Bangalore' Amrut Distilleries, that's selling well in *Scotland Or Urvashi,* a sandalwood based perfume that sells in France & is a documented case study on branding success.

Brands like Amrut whisky; Urvashi the perfume brand from Mumbai-based Gandh Sugandh; shoemaker Gaitonde from Chennai and Arora's label, Fish Fry attracting consumer attention in some of the world's toughest markets. Will these brands become global heavyweights and spawn desi versions of Louis Vuitton, Channel and Johni Walker? Ask us again in say, 15 years' time, and we could give you a better answer Building and international brand can be a painfully slow process, unless you are fortunate enough to find an angel investor who pumps in millions of dollars for marketing the brand, or you sell an innovation like the Ipod and polevault into the big league.

But even without these obvious advantages, the little Indian warriors have made an interesting start. At a time where big Indian business houses like the Tata Group, Mahindra & Mahindra and Godrej are trying to make a mark on the global scene either through big-ticket acquisitions or by positioning themselves as value-for –money brands, these much-smaller Indian companies are carving out spaces for themselves in upscale consumer's minds and wallets. That two with a strategy that's different-distinctly different from the bigger Indian companies.

NOTES

1. Principle of Marketing: Philip Kotler & Gary Armstrong.
2. Marketing Master Mind: June 2005.
3. Business Standard January 2007.

CHAPTER 10

GOVERNANCE CHALLENGES IN INDIA– A PERSPECTIVE

K. Seetharama Rao
T. Yadagiri Rao

I

A bird's eye view at the developments that are taking place in India over a period of nearly six decades after independence highlight two main aspects that can be clearly seen; one is the performance of administration, in it's over all political context and another is the study of Public Administration as an academic discipline. The performance of administrative machinery at various levels, especially both at policy formulation and implementation, is continuously dis-appointing and gradually reached to a point of an impasse. More than five decades of experience in our democratic system clearly reveals that the administrative machinery is able to work more effectively and efficiently as a status quo instrument than a change agent. Despite many continuous efforts taken-up by government through various development plans and programmes, and governance reforms still more than forty per cent the population tend to be below the poverty line. The programmes aiming at Social justice are being systematically sabotaged by the manipulative skills of ruling elite and status quo oriented bureaucracy. The National Commission on Agriculture has clearly pointed out in it's report that: "the official machinery ... has been trained and conditioned to function as the guardian of status quo and the defender of existing property relations". Unless we add one more point to the above observation, it would be incomplete, which is related to the dual nature of official machinery. The dual character of administration is: it is more efficient and effective while framing and implementing the programmes related and beneficial to the propertied sections of the Society. But at the same time the bureaucracy tends to be highly ineffective and inefficient while framing and implementing the programmes aiming at social justice that are mainly relevant to the poorer sections.

With regard to the Public Administration as an academic discipline, by and large, it failed to explain the reasons behind the nature and performance of official machinery. In brief, the study of administration has reached to a stage of impasse, which our prestigious institutes and academic departments of different universities are not able to recognize and seem unable to overcome from this situation. While the other social science disciplines are at the stage of being greatly influenced by the latest trends and theories in social philosophies, the study of administration has remained at or tied to the obsolete theoretical frameworks which provide ground work for techniques suited to the exploitation people and manipulation of workers. The main reason for the lagging behind of the discipline is due to the Central Question of the studies in administration being, how to maintain and continue the administrative structure without introducing fundamental changes; rather than how to reorient the administration in order to make it as an effective instrument for the welfare of the poor people. Hence, there is need to examine the theoretical basis of the discipline and reorient the purpose and nature of studies in administration.

II

Keeping above mentioned present situation in view, a moderate attempt is made in this brief note to present the problems, in a lucid and descriptive manner, which is going to be encountered in near future by present Politico-administrative system in India. It is important to note that, the present problems of the society are unresolved problems of the past, neither they are afresh nor they have suddenly erupted. The protracted nature of social contradictions in history and deepening present socio-economic crisis and the public policy and governance dealing with these social issues led to reappearance of these problems with renewed vigour and intensity in the present context on political scenario of India. Another crucial point to note is that the administrative problems cannot be understood devoid of political context. In the final analysis, politics are nothing but "concentrated expression of economic interests of different social classes which are manifested through political conflicts". The complex nature of these contradictions and their dynamic operation need to have a proper attention to understand the nature and resolution of present administrative problems can only be understood in the total societal setting.

In the transitory societies like India, where the old social formation is in dissolution and new one is struggling to take its place, the state acquires certain amount of autonomy. The reason for this situation is, that no single class holds on to the state power. Then naturally bureaucracy, an important organ of the state, is able to subdue all the classes of the society. In this transitory situation, in other words "semi-feudal and semi-capitalist," social relations, the exceptional type of state or 'autonomised state' in the process of resolving contradictions among different social classes and maintaining the existing property relations, i.e., "law and order", the bureaucracy acquires considerably great degree of autonomy. This 'autonomised state' apparatus, i.e., bureaucracy, is being gradually made more powerful and turned out to be a highly repressive instrument in the hands of ruling classes. Apart from this it is necessary to understand hiatus between the structure of governance that is largely stagnant and the society which is constantly changing in the dynamic context of LPG policies persued by government. This theoretical frame work, by and large, provides a suitable approach to understand the nature of political and administrative problems in developing countries like India.

Some of the major challenges identified and discussed here under are: Rural Unrest and Problems of Rural Development, Law Enforcing Agencies and Problems of Civil and Democratic Rights, Rise of Communalism and Problem of National Integrity, Protective Discrimination and Problems of weaker sections.

(a) India continues to be essentially an agrarian economy. The policies pursued by Indian state towards agrarian sector resulted in poverty-development and poverty syndrome. The two major policies aimed at agrarian change, the green revolution and land reforms led to the further intensification of agrarian crisis and regional imbalances. The rural development programmes supported by state owned beauracratic capital, formulated and implemented by unimaginative bureaucracy under the guidance of world bank, resulted in emergence of a peculiar type of 'agrarian bourgeoisie' in rural areas which possessed both feudal and 'capitalistic' characteristics. This neo-rich agrarian class, which is also an upcoming class in politics, neither has respect for democratic values nor concern for the welfare of the agricultural labourers. In the process of enriching itself, this exceptional 'agrarian bourgeoisie', without any benefit of doubt, re-enforced the exploitative semi-feudal relations in the agrarian sector. The net result of this process in the rural areas is, sharpening of contradictions between deprived and disgusted poor peasantry and agricultural labourers and semi-feudal ruling classes finally manifesting into a rural unrest. The problem of rural unrest, manifested in the form of peasant movements, has been viewed by state merely either as law and order problem or as a problem of 'internal security' rather than a socially justified demand of poor peasantry. The outcome of this attitude of official machinery led to unleashing of severe repression on socially justified demands of peasant movements of different parts in the country. Hence, agrarian change oriented rural development in India is still one of an unresolved social problems.

(b) Recently, the feeling of the 'soft' state being replaced by 'hard' one in India is constantly haunting the minds of some of the social scientists. This idea originated from the idealist view of state. According to them, the 'modern state' in India should be, "the developer, the modernizer, the reformer, and it should stand above the sectional conflicts to democratically mediate difference of interests". Whether this type of 'ideal state' or 'modern state' had existed or not in India is a debatable point. The existence of ideal state, in India since independence was highly doubtful reality. But, there used to be a peculiar idealistic ideology with regard to the state and development in India during the early years of independence. The tragedy is this ideology is increasingly withering away in the recent Indian politics. Since independence there has been increasing tendency to tackle civilian problems by employing the police, para-military and the military. To explain this phenomena in the words of Rajani Kothari: in India the 'populistic' state of initial stages has been gradually transformed into a 'managerialistic' one. This fact can be proved with the evidence of growing importance to the civil and democratic rights movement during 70's and especially after emergency. The law enforcing agencies, especially the police, are increasingly taking the side of propertied sections of the society rather than defending the constitutionally accepted democratic rights of the poor people. In the recent years, in some of the states, the existence and functioning of civil rights groups has become a great threat to the illegal activities of the law enforcing agencies. The state increasingly tends to be more authoritarian without invoking the emergency provisions merely depending upon a number of black Acts. Some of these black laws can be compared with draconian Acts of Colonial period. In the name of 'law and order', 'public order', 'security of the state' and 'National integrity', etc. without defining these terms properly, the state is unleashing violence against the political dissidents. In these circumstances, the 'progressive' laws may at best may mitigate but can never abrogate social disequilibrium. The increasing harassment faced by the civil liberties organizations, setting up a national human rights commission clearly indicates the significance of protecting the civil and democratic rights in India. Even after the more than five decades of independence, the civil and democratic rights are considered to be major public concern. In this context, the real opposition in India is only civil and democratic rights movement.

(c) "Communialism is the most intractable problem of the Indian Polity and society. It is a multi-faceted phenomenon with variety of causes and reveals itself in difficult forms under different set of circumstances". Many a time the revealing fact is that, in Communalism and Communal Politics, before and after independence, the determining role has been played by non-religious and non-cultural forces operating in the society. The recent communalist politics in India is a direct outcome of the decline of democratic politics. The economic and political interests of the lower middle classes and urban intelligentsia is being protected under the mask of religion. This can be understood through the demands put forward by the religious leaders. In this sense in Indian Communalism is a middle class phenomenon. An enormous amount of violence erupted, beyond the reasons, during the communal riots of Bhiwandi, Hyderabad, Gujarath, and Delhi and the growing Hindu, Muslim and Sikh fundamentalism clearly reveals the virus of Communal conflict spreading into the Indian body politic. The Communalism and Communal politics has become an instrument in the hands of ruling as well as parliamentary opposition parties to create vote banks for the purposes of their electoral politics. The abstract ideal secularism could not control effectively the cancerous communal politics in India. The secularist ideology could not contain the spread of communalist politics. One can find the emerging new variety of festivals becoming larger and longer also undergoing profound change in their nature. Local deities and rituals are gradually either replaced or grabbed by universalized Hinduism. The electoral compulsions and the growing pre-occupation of survival in office are major responsible factors for a shift from an 'open democratic' political process to a 'techno-bureaucratic' military order mainly committed to the status quo. In the economy the lumpen sector thriving on bureaucratic capital supported by state and built by a new genre of leadership is mainly responsible for spread of Communalism. The lumpenisation of the economy leads to neo-rich vulgarity both in culture and politics. The compromise between India 'bourgeoisie' and the pre-capitalist institutions and ideologies provided a fertile ground for the growth of communalism. In a way religion has become an instrument in the hands of ruling classes for legitimizing the exploitative social order. The ruling class has a vested interest in dividing the masses on communal and caste lines, in order to maintain disunity among the people on these lines the ruling class even will not hesitate to go back to make shrewd and cold blooded calculations, often forgetting the social costs of such ventures. This entire process of consistent growth of communalism and continuous spread of religious fundamentalism over a period of time in India finally proved to be a big threat to the national integrity and security. At present the communalism has become part and parcel of the existing socio-economic reality, neither the secular rhetoric nor the constitutional guarantees could not make the communalism ineffective and inoperative.

(c) After witnessing the anti-reservation movements of 1990s in Gujarat and Andhra, it can be observed that the major protective discrimination policy of state aimed at social justice of weaker sections – backward and scheduled caste and scheduled tribes – also reached to a point of open attack by the propertied sections of the society. The growing tendency of antagonism of propertied sections against the development and welfare schemes clearly manifested in the anti-reservation movements organized by children of these classes both in Andhra and Gujarat States. This sort of anti-reservation tendency, at present which is confined to only two states, has a possibility of becoming a national wide phenomenon. The most essential points in the arguments of anti-reservationists are: one, the reservations are a major threat to the merit and its' flourish since the meritorious candidates are undermined due to the reservations; two, caste based reservations are anti-constitutional and anti-secular since they encourage the communal and caste based tendencies in the society. Both these arguments, can be effectively countered through attacking the concept of merit which is based upon the arrogance and false notions of the upper castes and analyzing the history and dynamics of communal politics in India. The caste based reservations was aimed at countering and removing social injustice and not mere economic backwardness, but in reality the ruling political parties used this as an instrument to create vote banks for their electoral purposes. Another important argument of anti-reservationists is economic factor should be taken as criteria to provide reservations than on the basis of caste. In a pre-capitalist social formation like India, where caste is an important social indicator for backwardness and as well as for advancement of particular class providing reservations purely on economic factors is not possible and in reality it will defeat the very purpose of the protective discrimination policy. In India, if one can understand the social history in a correct perspective, one can see through clear cut correlation between class and caste. In other words, by and large, the upper castes are ruling and exploiting classes and lower and backward castes are ruled and exploited. However, the reservations to weaker sections do not provide an ultimate solution to the problem of un-employment and to introduce fundamental changes in the society. The Central question here is, how best one arrives at a policy of distributive justice with regard to the providing of equal opportunities to all in government employment keeping in view existing social inequalities. Hence, as long as socio-economic inequalities continue, it is essential to continue the policy of protective discrimination for the welfare of the weaker sections.

Finally, keeping above brief descriptive analysis in view, it can be concluded that, the present politico-administrative challenges which are going to be further intensified in near future are unresolved social contradictions of the past. The resolution of these contradictions is possible only through mass oriented politics but not merely through administration. At the same time, unless bureaucracy becomes an effective instrument in the hands of powerful mass oriented political organization, it cannot become a real change agent. The final question is, can the Indian political and administrative systems reorient and reorganize themselves to become real change agents of society? The answer is that the changes seem to be very bleak.

REFERENCES

—(1976), National Commission on Agriculture, Vol-I, Government of India, New Delhi, .

—(1997), Research and Teaching in Public Administration in Restructuring Public Administration, (Ed) Mohit Bhattacharya, Jawahar Publishers, New Delhi.

—(2003), Op. Dwivedi, William Graf and J. Nef, Marxist Contribution to the Theory of the Administrative State, in Public Administration, A Reader (Eds) Bidyut Chakravarthy and Mohit Bhattacharya, Oxford University Press, OU, New Delhi .

Nirmal Mukarji, Changeful Society and Changeless Governance in Public Administration: A Reader, *Op.cit.*

Dolly Arora (2007), Internal Security in India, 51st IIPA Members' Annual Conference Theme Paper, IIPA, New Delhi.

K. S. Subramanian (2005), Naxalite Movement and the Union Home Ministry, Economic Political Weekly, Vol. XI, No. 7, (February 19, pp. 728-29.

Rajani Kothari ((1988)), State against Democracy, In Search of Human Governance, Ajantha Publishers, New Delhi.

Jaya Tilak Guha Roy, Human Rights Dimensions of Public Administration in India, In Public Administration, A Reader, Op.vit.

—(2002), National Human Rights Commission, Proceedings of the Commission on Gujarat, New Delhi, 2002, and also please see People's Union for Civil Liberties (PUCL), An Interim Report to NHRC, New Delhi.

Marx Galanter (1963), Law and Caste in Modern India, Asian Survey, Vol. 3, No. 11, Nov. pp. 544-559.

Shishram Sharma (2002), Protective Discrimination; Other Backward Classes in India, Raj Publishers, Delhi.

CHAPTER 11

A STUDY ON THE RENDITION AND CONTENT DISCERNED BY THE FREIGHT FORWARDERS IN LOGISTIC OPERATIONS

J. Paul Sundar Kirubakaran

INTRODUCTION

Freight forwarding agents are one who specializes in arranging of shipping, insurance, and many of them today arrange land, sea and air transportation for goods. They take a major portion of the exporters work and their risks. On behalf of the shippers, they do all procedural and documentation formalities involved in the customs and port clearance. They also look after the warehousing and transshipment of cargoes before shipment of export consignments and after discharge of import cargoes, by the sea carriers.

There is another important aspect of their work-consolidation of shipments. A forwarding agent receives a large number of consignments and often group together a number of small ones and, by putting them into one large consignment, obtain preferential freight rates from the shipping line or the airline. Otherwise the shipper of a small quantity of goods may pay a rather high freight charge.

Freight forwarding agents are licensed by the customs. The name and address of the freight forwarding agents operating from different ports can be obtained from customs house or from there local association. However selection of suitable forwarding agents is very important. The exporter should due care in various selecting criteria of fixing freight/forwarder Viz., location, facilities rates, services, flexibilities and efficiency.

Role of Freight Forwarders

A present Day Freight Forwarder carries out the following duties:

On Behalf of Consignor

- Selection of route
- Determination of shipping documents
- Arrangement for packing, marking, etc, if required preparation of regulatory documents.
- Delivery to carriers and if required consignee, informed
- Keeping the consignor and if required consignee, informed
- Assists in preparation of shipping documents for negotiations.

On Behalf of Consignee

- Receives shipping documents
- Prepares and processes documents through customs and port, octroi, authorities, payment of duty fees, etc.
- Arranges delivery

For Both, If Required

- Arranges insurance and process claims
- Offers warehousing
- Offers distribution services
- Offers consolidation services

Preparing Price Quotations

Freight Forwarder plays a vital role in assisting the exporter to fix cost and logistic operations. The following are the freight forwarders areas of assistance:

- Act as shipper's agent under a power of attorney.
- Finalizing the methods of transport.
- Advice on best packaging for the exporter's product.
- Taking care for packing, marking, and containerizing goods at the port.
- Finalizing the best prices.
- Arrange for loading and unloading of shipment at the port.
- Overseas On-loading procedures.
- Issue delivery orders
- Arrange for insurance.
- Arrange for receipt of bill of lading or airway bill.
- Finalizing CFS and delivery.
- File damage claims with carriers or insurance companies.
- Prepare documents for collection of payment under the letter of credit.
- Provide messenger services.

Freight Forwarders facilitate the exporters, to know the pertinent laws and regulations of foreign licensing.

NEED FOR THE STUDY

Freight Forwarders play a vital role in transacting the goods along with doing all the documentation work on behalf of the Exporters/Importers. Freight Forwarders are applying different formula for the effective Logistics business transaction.

The study aims at analyzing the functioning of the Freight Forwarders in Tamil Nadu and giving suggestions for improving their services. It throws light on container handling at the Tamil Nadu ports and also the problems faced by Freight Forwarders with regard to the container handling.

SCOPE OF THE STUDY

The present study covers the various aspects of functioning of Freight Forwarders (CHA's) in Indian marine cargo industry.

It highlights the Freight Forwarding operations, opinion perceived by them and the problems faced by them. Among all these aspects of freight forwarding operations, containerization is essential for speedy and safety reach. Hence, the study encompasses the role of freight forwarders in containerization.

OBJECTIVES OF THE STUDY

The present study is aimed to analyze the following objectives empirically.

1. To give an overview about the Freight Forwarders (CHA's) and their effective operations of marine trade.
2. To study the contributions of Freight Forwarders in promoting port performance.
3. To identify the level of satisfaction perceived by the Freight Forwarders.
4. To limelight the various problems faced by the Freight Forwarders.
5. To suggest ways and means for effective Freight Forwarding Operations to enrich India's Maritime Trade.

METHODOLOGY OF THE STUDY

In the present study, an extensive use of both primary and secondary data was made. The study has been made in a descriptive and analytical way.

Sampling Design

Judgment sampling was followed to select the sample respondent for the study. To obtain primary data, the researcher approached 300 respondents out of 640 registered freight forwarders in the area of Chennai, Tuticorin, Tirupur, Coimbatore and Karur. The data collected from the sample respondents has been subdued in to suitable tabulated forms.

Collection of Data

The study has been used both primary and secondary data.

Primary Data

The primary data collected from the selected respondents, viz., Logistics operators, freight forwarding agents and multi model transport operators in the study area. Field survey techniques were used to collect the first hand information from the respondents. A well structured interview schedule was prepared to collect data from the freight forwarders. Pilot study has been conducted with the help of the few sample schedules and necessary modification was carried down as and when required.

Secondary Data

The Secondary data was gathered from the records of freight forwarders association, internet sources, libraries in Bangalore, Tuticorin, Chennai and Coimbatore.

FRAME WORK OF ANALYSIS

The data collected were analyzed by applying the tools viz:

- Chi-square analysis, Percentage analysis, Multiple Regression analysis, and Factor analysis has been used to identify the factors influencing the Freight Forwarders/logistic operations.
- Garrett Ranking was used to rank the problems faced by the Freight Forwarders.

MAJOR FINDINGS OF THE STUDY

Major Findings of the study has been given in the following five broad heads:

Factors Influencing Freight Forwarding Operations

Chi-square Analysis

The factors that influence the freight forwarders in logistic operations was studied by selecting a variables such as Year of Establishment, Nature of Organisation, Experience, Income Generated Per Annum, Wealth Position, Source of Information about the Exporters, Annual Turn Over, Countries which undertake operations along with Modes of operation undertaken. It is divulged from the analysis that out of 9 variables 6 variables are significant at 1 % level they are Year of Experience in freight forwarding operations, Income generated per annum, wealth position, annual turn over and modes of operations undertaken. The results of chi-square test shows the factors Nature of organization, Sources of information about the exporters and Countries which undertaking freight forwarding operation are statistically not significant at 1 % level and 5 % level. This shows that the six factors such as Year of Experience in freight forwarding operations, Income generated per annum, wealth position, annual turn over and modes of operations undertaken are closely associated with the level of satisfaction of the freight forwarders which motivates them to be active in the Logistic operations.

Percentage Analysis

- The percentage analysis reveals that 51.7 % of the respondent are having below 10 branches for their logistic operations in India.
- While analyzing the branches in abroad, it is noted 33.6 of the respondents are having less than 5 branches for their logistics operation in abroad.
- 81.3% of the respondents are having agents for their effective operation where they are not having their own office of operation.
- Container Freight Stations are the most important in the logistic operations but nearly 71.3% of the respondents are not having Container Freight Stations (CFS) for their effective operations. The freight forwarders are depending on the private owned CFS; ultimately it increases the logistics costs. Further, 74.4% of the respondents are having below 5 Container Freight Stations (CFS) for their effective and safe Logistic Operations.
- The percentage analysis shows that 86 3% of the respondents have rated their service quality as Excellent by their clients.

- The shippers should have a specialized facility to see the status of goods when the goods are in transit, the percentage analysis shows that 92% of the respondents are having the specialized facility to see the status of goods by their clients when the goods are in transit.
- From the analysis, it is identified that 97% of the respondents are having the specialized facility to ensure the arrival of goods at buyer agents destination.
- The percentage analysis reveals that 97.3% of the respondents are informing their clients relating to delivery of goods at the buyer agents destination.
- While analyzing the problem faced by the freight forwarders with regard to the financial in nature that 78.3% of the respondents are facing problem related to non payment by their clients for their invaluable quality of service in the Logistics Operations.

Multiple Regression Analysis

The analysis made is Multiple Regression in this study. This helps to find out the correlation between the dependent variable and independent variables. The relationship between the Level of satisfaction perceived by the freight forwarders on logistic operations Nine independent variables were selected and it was found that out off Nine variable Six factors were closely associated and Three factors were not significant. The factor like nature of organization, annual income, wealth position, source of information about exporters, logistic operational countries and mode of operations are positively associated, this shows that the volume of business can be operated through the freight forwarders only when they have perceived the maximum level of satisfaction.

The multiple regression analysis reveals that the satisfaction perceived by the Freight Forwarders on logistic operations is positively associated with the factors like nature of organization, annual income, wealth position, source of information about exporters, and the logistic operational countries of the respondents. It will generate more business for the Freight Forwarders when they implement the Supply Chain Management Concept, is practiced with the highest level of satisfaction.

Multiple Regression Analysis of Logistic Operations (Coefficient Table)

Variables	Non-standardized Coefficients B	Std. Error	Standardized Coefficients Beta	t	Sig.
(Constant)	1.865	0.247		7.558	
Year of Establishment	4.713E–02	0.061	0.066	0.777	NS
Nature of organization	0.171	0.058	0.246	2.960	1%
Experience in Logistics operations	–4.594E–02	0.050	–0.079	–0.920	NS
Annual Income	6.509E–02	0.029	0.121	2.267	5%
Wealth Position	0.195	0.056	0.249	3.499	1%
Source of information about exporters	–5.607E-02	0.017	–0.203	–3.288	1%
Annual turnover	–3.652E-02	0.035	–0.062	–1.055	NS
Logistic operational Countries	–0.162	0.045	–0.209	–3.622	1%
Mode of operations	9.031E–02	0.046	0.111	1.983	5%

R-Value	R^2-Value	Degree of Freedom – V_1	Degree of Freedom – V_2	F Value	Significance
0.861	0.741	10	289	84.54	1% Level

Component Matrix[A]

Factor	Component 1	2	3	4	5
Authorised agent	0.247	7.840E-02	–0.282	–0.213	0.846
Complaints Redressal	0.114	-5.203E-02	0.592	0.523	0.343
Own CFS	0.681	-9.253E-02	-9.831E-02	–0.318	0.138
Own Website	0.611	–0.112	-2.077E-02	0.176	5.514E-02
Status of goods	0.307	0.811	–0.143	-0.121	-2.593E-02
Arrival of goods	0.282	0.722	–0.303	0.173	–0.173
Delivery time	–0.188	0.382	-8.368E-02	0.677	0.109
Meeting with exporters	0.603	–0.367	–0.201	0.346	–0.119
High risk	7.058E-02	0.499	0.649	–0.267	1.480E-02
Registered claims	0.477	–0.115	0.381	–0.176	–0.227
Awareness on SCM	0.642	–0.183	0.120	7.862E-02	8.866E-02
Additional Benefits by SCM	0.647	0.232	0.256	2.965E-02	-1.599E-02
Providing Knowledge on SCM	0.716	-7.691E-02	–0.214	5.897E-02	–0.232

The multiple linear regression component (dependent variable) is found statistically a good fit as R^2 is 0.741. It shows that six independent variables contribute about 74% on the variations in level of satisfaction on logistic operations practiced by the Freight Forwarders and this is statistically significant at 1% and 5% level respectively.

This Component Matrix indicates the relationship between the factors and individual variables, and it is seen that several factors are having high correlation with the same component. For better interpretability, we move on to the next step.

Factor Analysis

Factor analysis helps to mark the major component considered important by the respondents. The research takes in to account the following thirteen important and enhance the effective logistic operational factors namely Authorization of agents for their operations where they do not have their own office, Shippers/clients/exporters complaints redressal, having own CFS, Owning web sites, additional facility to see and ensure the status of goods, arrival of goods and delivery time by their clients, periodical meeting with their clients, riskness in their operations, Cliams with insurers, awareness on Supply Chain Management, obtained additional benefits from the effective implementation of the SCM concept and efforts has been taken to provide knowledge on SCM which are determinants the effective logistic operations and to the level of Shippers/ Clients/ Exporters.

From the analysis, it is evident that the respondents agreed to the fact that they intended to have the services of the freight forwarding and have considered these thirteen factors namely authorization of agents for their operations where they do not have their own office, Shippers/clients/exporters complaints redressal, having own CFS, Owning web sites, additional facility to see and ensure the status of goods, arrival of goods and delivery time by their clients, periodical meeting with their clients, riskness in their operations, Claims with insurers, awareness on Supply Chain Management, obtained additional benefits from the effective implementation of the SCM concept and efforts has been taken to provide knowledge on SCM to be determinants of good service quality levels and the key for efficient and effective logistic operations by the freight forwarders in the study area.

Problems Faced by the Freight Forwarders

Extensive research and observations during the course of the study revealed overall twenty five unique problems faced by the freight forwarders/CHS's. These problems are organized in to five major headings such as problems related to exporters, problems related to insurance company, problems related to financial aspects, problems related with operations and problems related to the port authorities.

1. While analyzing the problems faced by the freight forwarders with their exporters/clients are indifferent product, over expectation, lack of cooperation, terms of contracts and lack of export knowledge. The most burning issue was over expectation on prompt service, and it is followed by terms of contracts.
2. The problems faced by the freight forwarders with the insurance company are, want of unnecessary documents, delay in settlement, indifferent attitude, lack of co-operation and redtapism. The most burning issue is delay in settlement, and it is followed by redtapism.
3. While analyzing the freight forwarders problems related to operations are higher operating cost, a more of government policies, elaborate documentary works, delay in operation and natural calamity. The most burning problem was government policies (legal restriction) and it is followed by delay in operation due to some reasons.

SUGGESTIONS

1. All activities, communications and promotions of the freight forwarders should focus on maintaining long term customer relationships to retain existing customers, create customer loyalty and attract new customers.
2. The reception of the Custom officers by the freight forwarders must be friendly and courteous which would create a long lasting relationship between the freight forwarders and the custom officers.

3. Better connectivity should be developed between the road, rail and the sea.
4. Chennai and Tuticorin ports should be equipped with advanced equipments to improve the turn around time.
5. Proximity to the Container Freight Station (CFS) and Inland Container Depot (ICD) from the Chennai and Tuticorin ports to be facilitated.
6. Online Customs connectivity to port and Container Freight Station should be created.
7. Government of India should offer more attractive packages for the transshipment containers.
8. Agents acting on behalf of the freight forwarders should avoid making false promises and misleading the customers in terms of time, cost and delivery of the product.

CONCLUSION

The freight forwarders prove the great poet Mr. Bharathiyar's saying of "Thirai Kadal Odiyum Thiraviyam theadu" through efficient logistic operations to various countries with limited infrastructural facilities particularly in the study area. Though various problems are studied and highlighted in this research, the researcher specially notes that the freight forwarders in Chennai and Tuticorin are performing in an excellent manner. They are also very much enthusiastic and most dynamic personalities and have the willpower and courage to dominate the Germans container vessels operations.

Further, it is observed that, a very meager percentage of freight forwarders are applying supply chain management concept while a good majority of freight forwarders are not at all following the concept of supply chain management because most of them following sub agency system. In order to utilize the supply chain management concept at the optimal level a proper initiation should be made to encourage the freight forwarders this can be very easily achieved by the freight forwarders association, CII and government of India. Adequate training should be given to the freight forwarders on supply chain management concepts and also to avert the common problems faced by the freight forwarders.

REFERENCES

Text References

Aljian, G. W. (1984), *Purchasing Handbook*, McGraw Hill, New York,

Anderson, J. & Narus, J. (1998), *Business Market Management, Understanding, Creating and Delivering Value*, Prentice Hall, New Jersey.

Ballou, Ronald H. (1999), *Business Logistics Management: Planning, Organizing, and Controlling the Supply Chain*, 4th Edition, New Jersey: Prentice Hall, ISBN: 0-13-081262-5.

Bowersox, Donald J. (1996), *Logistical Management: The Integrated Supply Chain Process*, New York: McGraw-Hill, ISBN 0-07-11407.

Mercer, James L. & Koester Edwin H., Public Management Systems: American Management Association.

Seturam, Shobha (1999), Corporate Profitability and Supply Chain, *Supply Chain Management for Global Competitiveness*, Macmillan, New Delhi, pp. 77-93.

Taff, Charles A., Management of Physical Distribution and Transportation: Irwin.

Thomson, A. W. J., & Hunter L.C., *The Nationalised Transport Industries: London*, Heinemann Educational Books.

Williams, H. (1992), "Building a Data Warehouse", QED, Wellesly, MA.

Womack, J. P., Jones D. T. & Roos D. (1990), *The Machine that Changed the World*, MacMillan, New York.

Willis, Roger, Physical Distribution Management, An Analytical Approach to Cutting Costs, Noyes.

Journal–Research Paper References

Anderson, D. L. & Lee Han, (1999), "Synchronized Supply Chains: The New Frontiers, Achieving Supply Chain Excellence Through Technology", *Montgomery Research Inc.*, san Francisco, pp 12-21.

Ansari, A. & Modarress B. (1990), "Just-in-Time Purchasing", The Free Press.

Hines, Peter & Nick Rich (1997), "The Seven Value Stream Mapping Tools", *International Journal of Operations & Production Management*, Vol. 17, Number 1, pp. 46-64.

Mason, J. (1999). "Total Cycle Time Compression and the Agile Supply Chain", *International Journal of Production Economics*, p. 62.

Sheth, J. N. (1973), "A Model of Industrial Buyer Behavior", *Journal of Marketing*.

Reports References

Freight Forwarders Association Reports.

Indian Ports Associations Annual Reports.

Imaritime Research Report 2003.

The Economic Times – ET Knowledge Series 2002.

Websites

http://www.imaritime.com

http://www.atlaslogistics.co.in

http://www.tradeport.org

http://www.ais.misstate.edu

http://www.supplychainaccess.com/pubs/ERA-isource.htm

http://www.intel.com/internetservices/intelsolutionservices/downloads/ariba.pdf

http://www.cio.com/summaries/enterprise/scm/

http://www.infochain.org/quarterly/Spring98/Practitioner.html

http://www.apldirectlogistics.com

http://www.clml.org/

CHAPTER 12

CORPORATE GOVERNANCE AND ITS POSSIBILITY FOR BUSINESS PRACTICES

M. Sumathy
K. N. Kalaivani

PROLOGUE

Corporate Governance (CG) has emerged as one of the key elements of public policy reforms individuals. It is still in its infancy; it has been around only for the last three to four years. It is however not a foolproof concept as it relies heavily on data available from insiders. But it has specific and special role to play to enhance the strength of a particular unit and of the entire corporate sector. Corporate Governance is to be maintained or observed as effective tool to assure the stakeholders of their long-term interests without prejudice to public interest.

Corporate Governance is the term given to the management practices followed by the business organization. At flour, we believe that good business practices, transparency in corporate financial reporting and the highest levels of corporate governance must be maintained. This section includes documents regarding flour's corporate governance practices that keep flour accountable to its shareholders. These channels in turn are activated through several structural and institutional factors pertaining to the corporation. They are as follows:

1. The ownership structure of the organization.
2. The financial structure of the corporation.
3. The structure and functioning of the company boards and the associated internal control systems.
4. The legal, political and regulatory environment within which the corporate functions.

Thus Corporate Governance (CG) is the way the firm ought to be run, managed and controlled. It is related with supervision and holding the responsibility of those who direct and control the management. It also includes framing rules and procedures to run the unit. It directly refers to the induction of checks and balances in the system to prevent abuse of authority. Corporate Governance also hints at ethical and integrated behavior to maintain the financial results.

CORPORATE GOVERNANCE AT UNIVERSAL LEVEL

Traditionally the matters with corporate sector were involved with esoteric branch of commercial law. Limited generally to a narrow view of how to ensure the managers follow the interests of shareholders. Basic standards of Corporate Governance structure and processes have been slowly evolving over last two decades. Traditionally it was observed only in respect of the operation of market pressure.

Looking beyond India the scenario in general is different. In the country like U.S. and U.K. there is an active market for corporate control to discipline managers, if they fail to maximize shareholders wealth. They largely adopted three main instruments they are– "Proxy Contests". Friendly mergers and Hostile take over. The first among the above said there is considered more effective Friendly mergers have hardly succeeded to solve the "agency problem". While take over is not appealing strongly on the ground of heavy cost incurred in it and also for want of political will conducive to the policy. In Germany and Japan the system that prevails in U.K. and U.S. is absent. Unlike that system there is "Banking

Supervision". The main bank financing the corporate unit acts as an external control mechanism. In such case very least intervention is found and that only when financial problem arises. It is in light of these experiences that innovative approach to the concept is formed. Several credit rating agencies have stepped in the market and they are offering services of the kind, which meets with the Quality of Governance in corporate entities.

INDISPENSABLE PRINCIPLES OF CG

There are certain indispensable Principles envisaged in the concept. These mainly include the following;

Discipline in Operations

Operational discipline refers to healthy manufacturing practices; Full utilization of installed capacity in accordance with financial viability and demand pressures must be practiced. Operational discipline asks for quality approval at every stage of predictor services. It refers to the effective and optimum application of the technology available at times. Integration and coordination in the entire system is but the prime requirement for the operational efficiency.

Transparency in Dealings and Disclosures

Transparency here means "perfection" with "holistic approach". It means that dealings with clients, customers, suppliers, distributors to whomsoever, must be fair and healthy. Legitimate grounds for differentiation should be can be maintained in consideration of the relationship. Transparency includes fairness with purchasers and sellers. Disclosure pertaining to the balance sheet must be perfect in tune with the standardized accounting practices. Besides observance of legal norms, commitment to the moral standards must be reflected in accounting procedures. "Hidden charging", "Secrecy" which violate the fundamentals of accounting in theory and practice be not allowed. Disclosures through the balance sheet must be in tune with prevailing taxation norms.

Accountability to Shareholders

Let the company perform in a manner through which shareholders long term economic interest may remain intact. Accountability includes taking shareholders into confidence. This is legal binding also. Let there be healthy democratic practices to be followed by the company, convening anneal general meeting, minimum time in advance notice to be saved comprising all technical adequacies, free and fair election of board of directors. Chartered Accountant, these are the prime requirements. Dividend, bonus all other legitimate interests to be performed in adequate manner. Shareholders are virtual partners; hence their trust in the company and their goodwill for the company does work as an asset. This must be considered as part of accountability.

Responsibility of Company's Action

Company's all actions must be well planned and thoughtful. Any action of haste may prove boomerang. In event of any failure or poor performance company must done to share the responsibilities. Strategic actions may some time not sound well. Human resource practices adopted may at times affect to the growth of the company. All such results must be treated positively and corrections over period of time be made without any kind of bias or prejudices. What may apparently seem too little as action or result may sometimes turn into too big impacts.

Social Responsibility

To think strictly in respect of shareholders' interest is considered too narrow view. There are many stakeholders beyond the shareholders. The society in general is the largest stakeholders. There fore observance of social responsibility must be reflected in Toro, prudence in environmental norms, adding to the societal value, sharing with Government or other agencies in social uplift men's tasks these are to be considered as "Investments" rather than more "cost", social health if cared for a long period may enhance "wealth" of the company over a period of time.

RANKING THE CORPORATE GOVERNANCE

It is expected that Corporate Governance aim to ensure that investors should get an appropriate return on their money. The modern approach of Corporate Governance includes stakeholders namely employees, customers, suppliers, community and Government. In the early 1990's recommendations on institutional codes of Cadbury committee were published in UK. Stock exchanges and regulators around the world have already begun to set standards or codes of best practices for Corporate Governance. Elite group of investors irrespective of nation or occupation have also begun to review more systematically company's Corporate Governance practices as part of their investment and under writing decision-making process.

There are different perspectives applied in rating Corporate Governance. Leading global agencies, standard and poor, and moody has adopted "Financial Perspective" to rate Corporate Governance. They mainly stick to the interests of "Financial stakeholders". This particular term includes both shareholders and creditors. Their interests are closely interred linked. It depends on company's ability to honor contractual financial obligations to creditors and to maximize the value of its equity and distribution for its shareholders. In consideration of these criterions rating agencies tend to review the process of interaction among managers, directors and shareholders to direct and control the affairs of the company and to ensure that all financial stakeholders receive their fair share of earnings and assets.

INTER RELATED APPREHENSIONS

Some important issues carry interrelation significance in the whole task of Corporate Governance. It is important to understand the relationship and mark of difference that is found existing between Corporate Governance and credit rating. There is no positive correlation always found between the two.

Second very important component is to understand and examine the relationship between Corporate Governance assessments and share holder value creation. Here most notes worthy illustrations are available from ICRA and CRISIL. These two Indian agencies involved in credit rating have tried to factor in value creation in their assessment. There are legitimate doubts being raised regarding applicability of any realistic model in which entrepreneurial ability and value creation can be covered to gather. It is because that the factors, which determine and measure entrepreneurial ability and that influences value creation, are basically different. These two-intact demand extensive empirical researches, over a period of time to developed and validate any model.

Third critical issue is related with share price performance. Through in some cases it is observed that operating and share price performance is having positive relationship with governance measures, there are no fact-finding studies deriving conclusion where in strong causality is found.

NECESSITIES FOR INFLUENTIAL CORPORATE GOVERNANCE

A climate of Trust, a culture of open dissent, a fluid portfolio of roles that ensures individual accountability and self-evaluation by the board engenders the foundation of good Corporate Governance. Second important requirement for sound Corporate Governance is to understand the precise pattern of ownership.

Affiliation amongst shareholders or the type of collusion may prove sometimes more effective. It is equally important to know the adverse impact of expropriation on efficiency through effects on the incentives of managers and employees. Some important board decisions are equally important. Incentive contracts decision is recently found more effective as far as the opportunities are concerned. Managers are found more comfortable and in more commanding positions to successfully negotiate such contracts when they enjoy the autonomy for such contracts.

Another important area is of ethical practices. It depends on company's ability to promote corporate fairness and transparency. It demands company's commitment to maintain the highest standard of ethical practices in all its transactions. Financial transparency is a must in the form of "Disclosures".

All information's must adequately disclose regarding modes operandi of company, Prospects of the company and risk factor involved in the same. Transparency primarily must focus on "Access", "Comprehensiveness", "Relevance, Quality and Reliability". These must be followed appropriately.

REIMBURSEMENT OF UNASSAILABLE GOVERNANCE

There is certain reimbursement of Corporate Governance. These can be outlined as under;

(a) It strengthens operational efficiency and financial performance of the firm.

(b) It improves customer satisfaction and results into an excellent internal environment.

(c) It adds to the integrity of the business and there by becomes helpful in extending the Market base and share.

(d) It works as most effective tool to diversify and or to acquire the new company or other company.

TRIBULATIONS

The entire task of Corporate Governance is having a mechanism where in some inbuilt problems are found. These problems can be summed up as under;

Effectiveness of the Board

The board may not in all cases may all-time be having an entity independent of management. No outsider can inquire into this from inside. Some external procedures followed as part of the rules can well be checked but that alone does not suffice the purpose to justify independent entity, Appointment of committees and sub committees may in many cases be preplanned with certain determined goals.

Balanced Board

Board of directors of the company may not be found appropriately balanced. Many a times it is found in many cases the board is not having an appropriate mix of business experience and functional discipline.

Directors Turnover

It is well known fact that in some companies Directors turnover is not supported with strong director evaluation procedure. Directors appointed may not be having strategic planning or risk management experience. And or sometimes against expectations traditional director may tend to stick with the company by certain practices not prescribed in the norms.

Cultural Behavioral Element

In any company, irrespective of size or nature of product or services, it is clearly found that ultimately it is the behavioral culture inbuilt in the members who play major role in governing the unit. This behavioral part plays more important role when CEOs in the respective companies perform better and enjoy commanding height as functionaries. Behavioral segment is important in context of conflict resolution, reengineering the growth, reinvesting the assets etc. In such case problem is to anticipate and identify behavioral norms in respect of the cultural lag that precisely exists within the board between the boards of directors.

EPILOGUE

Corporate Governance is wrongly interpreted to nurture the interest of the shareholders only. It is beyond that which promotes the integrity in business. Besides it is also equally important that effective Corporate Governance is not suited only to large-scale players, on the contrary it creates better image, more market potentials for small-scale sector too. Good Governance is a key to successful business. Today's small units can well begin their journey towards large scale through achieving the norms of Corporate Governance.

REFERENCES

D. N. Ghosh (2005), "Corporate Governance Rating: Objective, Scope and Limitations," *Economic & Political Weekly*, Vol. 40, No. 42 pp. 4539-4544.

Sanjay Chaugale (2006), "Corporate Governance and SMES," *Economic Times*, p. 4, 24th January.

CHAPTER 13

AN ALTERNATIVE ENERGY– A COMPARATIVE STUDY OF E-BIKES WITH PETROL BIKES

A. Saradha

INTRODUCTION

Bicycles are the primary transportation for billions of people around the world. In early 1990s as pushed by the trend of energy saving, one peak for the E-Bike development was brewed, but it was quickly wiped out by the emerging automotive vehicle. However, after the mid 1990s, the rapid development of automotive and other fuel-assistant brought problems like pollution, safety and resource water, the air pollution problem became serious in major cities. Since 2003, the E-Bike development is supported by the government because it matches with the national policy of energy saving and environmental friendly.

Electric Cycles as a Sustainable Element in Urban Transportation System

Government in city areas makes it as an important part of their responsibilities to improve mobility. The constraints they face are more general than just reducing emissions or oil consumption, because in most cities the limited amount of space available for vehicles, traffic safety and noise reduction–

key issues. Generally, city governments have to take a wide range of measures including the improvement of public transit facilities of non-motorized transport (walking and cycling) and improvement of roads and parking facilities for vehicles. Many solutions have to be adopted, and the interface among these solutions has to be convenient and smooth, so that overall the inhabitants can confidently reach all their many destinations within a city. Within this context, electric two wheelers can be an important component of an overall programme to improve mobility. They require very little space, they cause no pollution and they make no noise. They can replace not only bicycle trips, but more importantly some specific short vehicle trips.

Energy Issues are Concerned in Two Ways by Electric Two Wheelers

- They reduce energy consumption generally.
- They can run on renewable energies.

The Public Awareness of Electric Two Wheelers

In recent times the public awareness of electric two wheelers is still poor. And even if people know about them, they often have a bad and wrong image, especially of E-Bikes. They think that they are only useful for old and handicapped people and they imagine the "fun-to-drive" factor of power assistance.

Salient Features

- Aerodynamic Shape
- Eco-Friendly
- Travels100-110 kms per charge
- Strong Shack Absorbers
- Easy Charging
- No Pollution
- No Fuel Required
- No Maintenance Problem
- Comfortable and Easy to Drive
- No Hassle of Changing Gears

Advantages of E-bikes

- Zero Fuel Consumption
- Lower Maintenance Costs
- Environment Friendly (Zero Emission)
- They can run for 10 to 15 paise per km in comparison to petrol bikes

HOW DOES IT WORK

The Electric Vehicle (EV) technology comes with a complete power pack, which consists of ultra motor, electronic controller, specialized battery and charger. The technology is provided by Ultra Motor who has already tested this technology. The "Impulse Inertia" technology used in it provides higher torque to the bike. Thus, the driver's part is only controlling it. This electronic vehicle is coupled with the advantage of windings and water proofing.[1]

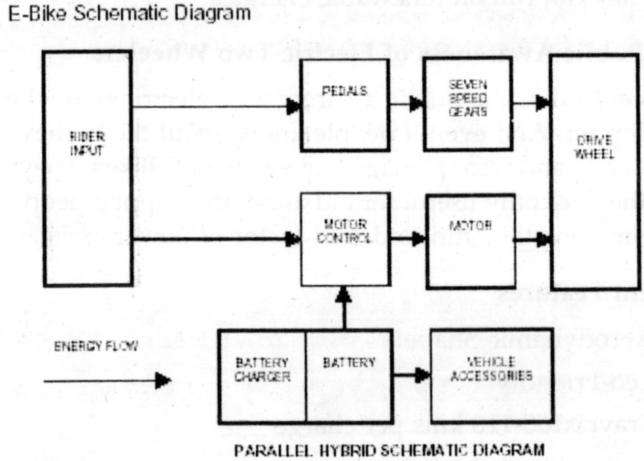

Figure 1

Source: NASA/TM-2001-210569

Maximum Speed

The maximum speed of the vehicle was measured to be 12.1 mph with no grade under full power. The figure below indicates the maximum speed achieved at various grades, as well as the various powers that were obtained.[2]

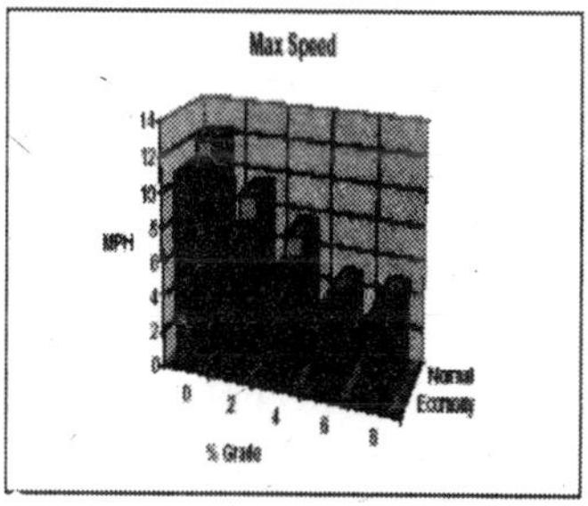

Chart 1

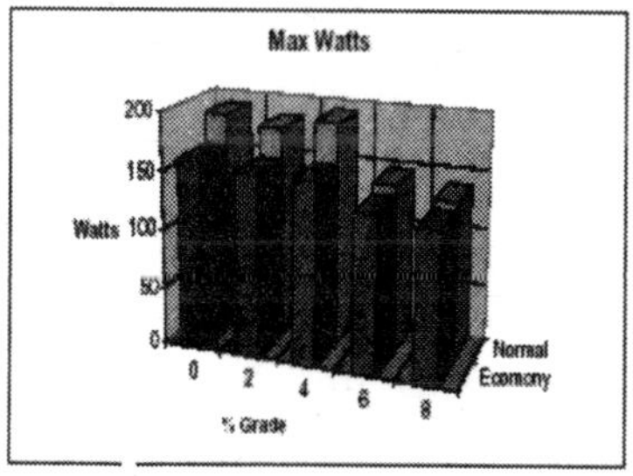

Chart 2

Vehicle Instrumentation System – Description of the Instrumentation System

A Block Diagram of the instrumentation system is shown in Fig. 2.

The Vehicle dynamometer has an integral instrumentation system that monitors vehicle speed, distance and power. These data are sampled at 3Hz and transmitted to the desktop PC via a serial interface. The PC logs the dynamometer data. All other measurements were obtained with a Hewlett Packard Data acquisition systems, sampling at 100 Hz. Type K thermocouples were used for all temperature measurements. Hall Effect transducers were used for all current measurements. These data are transmitted to the laptop PC via a serial interface. The PC logs the data.

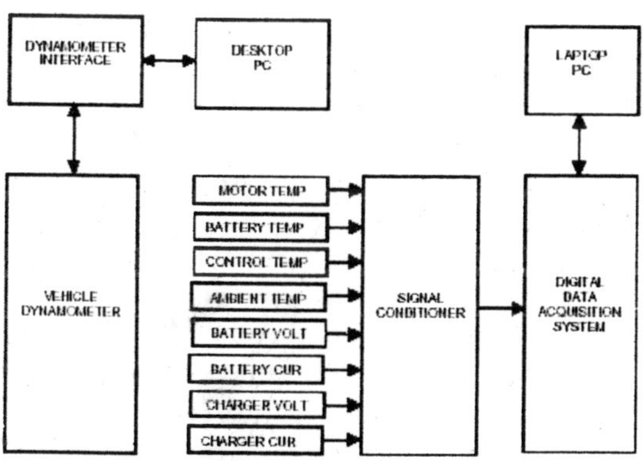

Figure 2: Vehicle Instrumentation System

Source: NASA/TM-2001-210569[3]

E-BIKE MARKET IN INDIA

Especially for a fossil deficient country like India, Hybrid, Fuel Cell Powered and Bio-Diesel Powered Vehicles seem to be a good alternative. Bio-Diesel Electric Vehicle (EV), Hybrid Vehicles and Fuel Cell Vehicles will replace the Petrol-Diesel Vehicle in coming years. Electric Vehicles are virtually maintenance free. It has no gears; no engine; no belt; or chain; drive Zero Emission; no pollution; electronic start and accelerator besides it is exempted from the Central Vehicles Registration Act by the Automotive Research Association of India (ARAI) and does not require any registration or license. These bikes are usually chargeable at 220v. For charging E-Bikes, it requires special adapter. Electric bikes targets are School Students, Women and who less than 18 years of age. According to a recent 10-city study by *A.C. Nielsen*, it is assumed that the nascent electric two-wheeler (E-Bike) market in India is at nearly *5 Lakh* Units. It is not a small market for a comparatively new technology and obviously many companies want to launch their models in India. According to ARAI, since January this year at least 12 companies have applied for certification to launch their E-Bikes in the Indian Market.[4]

The Well-Known E-Bike Manufacturers in India were

- Electrotherm India (Ahmedabad)
- Ace Motors (Maharashtra)
- Hero Electric (Joint Venture between the Hero Group (India) and Ultra Motors (UK))[5]
- Atlas (Haryana)

PRODUCTION OF BATTERIES

The energy storage source of an electric bicycle is the rechargeable battery. At present, there are 4 battery chemistries that are observed in use. The Lead Acid (PbA) battery is by far the most common, while Nickel Cadmium (NiCad) is occasionally seen, and Nickel Metal-Hydride (NiMH) and Lithium Ion (Li-ion) batteries are both making headway as the choice for the future. The task of choosing battery chemistry typically comes down to weighing the high energy density advantages lithium and NiMH over the considerably lower cost of Lead Acid and the long cycle life if NiCad. Rarely is the total environmental impact of each choice considered.

Battery Life-cycle

The total energy that can be extracted from a battery is equal to its capacity in watt-hours times the number of complete charge and discharge cycles it can deliver. The mechanical energy delivered to a bike is simply this total energy multiplied by the motor efficiency. The total energy consumed by the battery pack through the recharging process is higher than the energy delivered to the motor because of various inefficiencies at each conversion stage from the utility grid to the pack.

The Main Drivers for The E-bike Battery Market Are

- The Economic development with a GDP growth rate of 8-9% on average
- The Substantial demand for E-Bike
- The increasing E-Bike Population

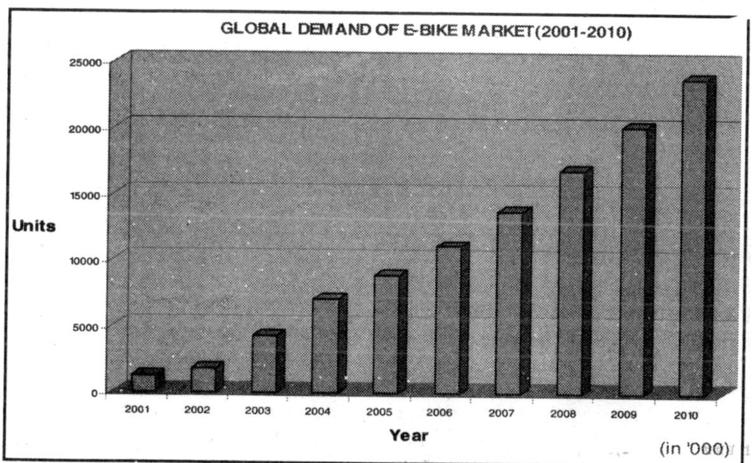

Chart 3: Demand for E-bike Market (World), 2001-2010
Source: Frost & Survillan

- Environment Concern for the lead recycling comparatively higher price of other rechargeable battery
- The cost pressure from the raw material
- Product quality restrain the development
- The commercial development of other kinds of rechargeable batteries.

On the Whole, the overall view of the present E-Bike market is estimated to grow. The forecast for the industry is good while other relevant factors including the economic outlook, government regulations and market trends are all favorable towards the E-Bike battery industry.

During the period from 2001 to 2005, the global E-Bike market increased by around 7 million units. In 2001, global E-Bike market totaled *1,200* thousand units. Up to 2006, the number of units is 10 times than the units in 2001, and the overall global E-Bike demand in 2006 is *11,053* thousand units. It has been forecasted that the total global demand of E-Bike in 2010 is expected to reach over *20 million* units.[6]

PETROL BIKE MARKET IN INDIA

The Indian two-wheelers Industry can be broadly classified as scooters, motorcycles and mopeds. The domestic two wheeler sales of 3.4 mn in FY99 is constituted by these segments as shown below.

Table 1
Petrol Bike Market in India (1992-2000)

Year	*Scooter*	*Motorcycle*	*Moped*	*Total*	*Growth %*
FY92	769,955	428,118	408,022	1,606,095	–
FY93	709,725	379,060	414,567	1,503,352	6.40
FY94	840,173	472,582	457,471	1,770,226	17.75
FY95	1,033,524	652,012	523,700	2,209,236	24.80
FY96	1,223,425	809,527	627,079	2,660,031	20.41
FY97	1,301,051	978,682	683,756	2,963,489	11.41
FY98	1,262,699	1,131,314	648,842	3,042,855	2.68
FY99	1,325,868	1,395,657	681,902	3,403,427	11.85
FY2000	1,253,969	1,796,734	726,075	3,776,778	10.97

Source: SIAM

Table 2
Comparative Study of E-bike with Petrol Bike

Particulars	*Petrol Bikes*	*E-Bikes*
Weight	84 Kgs Battery Weight : 11 Kgs Kerb Weight : 60 Kgs	Vehicle Weight : 49 Kgs
Range (Kms)/Litre of Petrol	50/Ltr	100/Charge
Cost/100 Kms	Rs.105.00 (2 Ltrs)	Rs.7.00
Cost of Fuel : Rs/Km	Rs.1.05	Rs.0.07
Cost of Fuel – Power over 30,000 Kms in Rs	31500	2,100.00
Service and Maintenance over 30,000 Kms(in Rs)	9,000.00	1,000.00
Battery Replacement over 30,000 Kms (in Rs)	N.A.	3,000.00
Total Expenses towards fuel for 30,000 Kms (in Rs)	40,500.00	6,100.00
Cost of Bike (Scooter in Rs)	28,534.00	24,500.00 (approx)
Registeration (Rs)	620.00	N.A
Registeration Tax (Rs)	2,480.00	N.A
Insurance (Rs)	809.00	573
Handling (Rs)	100.00	80
Total Investment (Scooter)	32,543.00	25,153.00
Total Investment + Running Cost for 30,000 Kms	Rs.73,043.00	Rs.31,253.00

Source: Compiled from Primary Data

From the above table, it is clear that there has been an increase in the purchase of two wheelers (Petrol Bikes) over the years. In the year 1992 the total two wheelers on road were 1,606,095, whereas in 2000 it has been increased to 3,776,778.[7]

Petrol Bike users revealed that the cost of the bike is Rs. 28,534 and the mileage it gives is 50 km per litre. They also spend for the maintenance and service over 30,000 kms which is Rs .9000. Whereas on the other hand the E-Bike users responded that the cost of the bike is Rs. 24500/- and they spends Rs.1,000/- only towards the maintenance and service cost over 30,000 kms. The total investment made on Petrol Bikes is Rs. 73,043 whereas the total investment for E-Bike is only Rs. 31,253.

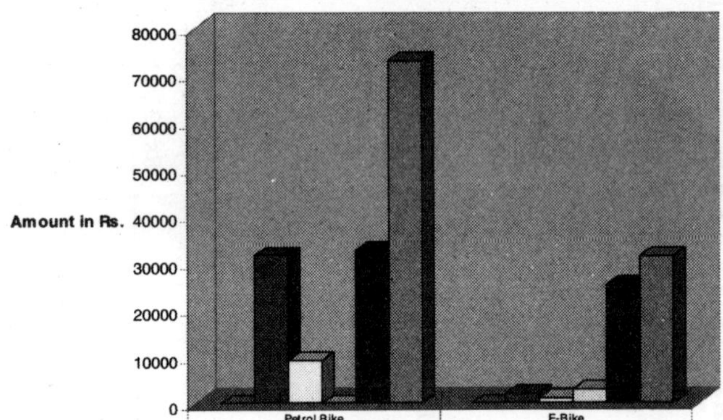

	Petrol Bike	E-Bike
Cost of Fuel : Rs/Km	1.05	0.07
Cost of Fuel - Power over 30,000 Kms in Rs	31500	2100
Service and Maintainance over 30,000 Kms, Rs	9000	1000
Battery Replacement over 30,000 Kms, Rs	0	3000
Total Investment on Scooter (Rs)	32543	25153
Total Investment + Running cost for 30,000 Kms (Rs)	73043	31253

Chart 4: Comparison of Petrol Bike with E-Bike

Source: Compiled from Primary Data

Table 3

Money Comparison of Petrol Bike with E-bike in Terms of Money

Type of Bike	*Mileage*	*Fuel/Charge*	*Cost of Fuel/ Charge (in Rs.)*
Petrol Bike	50 Kms	1 Litre Petrol	50
E-Bike	50 Kms	1 Charge	12.00 (Power Consumption)
Savings	50 Kms	1 Ltr Petrol/Charge	38.00

Source: Compiled from Primary Data

From the above table, it has been found that for a Petrol Bike the cost of fuel is Rs. 50.00 per Kilo Meter. But for E-Bike the cost of one full charge of the battery is only Rs. 12.00 which is spent towards power consumption. Therefore, we can save a reasonable amount of Rs. 38.00 towards the cost of fuel/ battery charge. This can be depicted with the help of a chart. The following chart explains the comparative study of E-Bike with Petrol Bike in terms of savings.

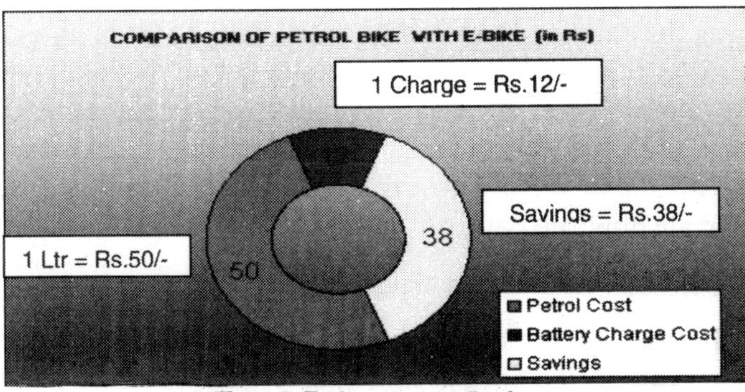

Chart 5: Estimation of Savings

Source: Primary Data

FINDINGS

From the study conducted it has been found that if Petrol Bikes has been replaced with E-Bikes, an individual can save Rs. 38/- per day and the savings of a city is Rs. 256,512,464 per day and for a year it can save nearly nine thousand crores of rupees towards consumption of petrol.

Table 4

Estimation of Savings in Terms of Money

Vehicles on road in Chennai	6,750,328.00
Savings of 1 bike (for an individual)	Rs. 38.00
Savings of total two-wheelers (if replaced with E-Bike)	Rs. 256,512,464.00
1 day savings (for a city)	Rs. 256,512,464.00
1 year savings (for the government)	Rs. 93,627,049,360.00

Source: Compiled from Primary Data

It is also estimated that India's fossil fuel dependency on other countries currently is 70%. It can be increased to 82% in

2012. If we can have just three lakh electric vehicles on the roads by 2020, including three-wheelers, cars and scooters, this could result in a reduction of over 16 lakh metric tons of petrol, with a savings of over Rs. 3700 crores in foreign exchange and significant health cost savings.[8]

Reasons to Ride in Electric Bike

Health

An electric bike is an incredibly seductive form of exercise. One never needs to force themselves to get on the bike. It will make one feel good. Physical disabilities or encumbrances, an electric bike can mean all the difference in the world. An electric bike can mean feeling healthier day in and day out, and appreciate how "no pain, no gain" becomes "all gain, no pain."

Convenience

An electric bike is an exceptionally convenient form of transportation. It's simple and quick. One can easily move around the town and can also carry two big bags. An electric bike can easily carry a child-seat. By removing the hassles of parking and adding the endorphins of an easy bike ride, an electric bike can replace a car for neighborhood errands.

Money

An electric bike can be cheaper than a gym membership, car insurance, or car payments. For many people, an electric bike will replace the car for neighborhood errands, enable them to drive a car significantly less, or replace a car altogether. It's one of the most convenient and cost effective form of transportation.

Time

An electric bike saves time. It eliminates the time spent looking for parking. It eliminates time waiting for the bus. It's often faster ride than the bus! Traffic jams can be avoided via side streets.

Hills

It's actually easy to ride up hills on an electric bike. With the power of the motor supplementing pedaling, one can able to comfortably ride up hills and might not even attempt on a traditional bike.

Parking

On an electric bike, parking ceases to be a hassle since bikes easily finds parking where cars drive around the neighborhood searching. An electric bike can pay for itself just with what one pay in parking tickets.

The Environment

Our choice of transportation has a direct and significant impact upon both our lives and the world around us. An Electric Bike is high-utility, low-impact transportation. In many parts of the country, the automobile is the top contributor to local air, water, and noise pollution. A large percentage of cars are driven used for short trips (often miles or less) with only one person in the car.[9]

Replacing the high impact of a single passenger car with the low impact of an Electric Bike will make a positive difference for both the individual and environment. The choices have an impact on the future. An Electric Bike is healthy step in the right direction.

SUGGESTIONS

- The Government of India should waive all duties on the import of foreign E-Bikes or spares to encourage use of the vehicles simply because it will reduce India's dependence on crude oil.
- Discount in the price of E-Bike should be given.
- Funds should be collected for Research.
- The gap between petrol bikes and E-Bikes relating to speed, mileage and cost should be reduced.
- To support the E-Bike market in India, we need electricity backup. For that either we have to develop the

infrastructure in electricity generation or enhance the production capacity of existing power plants.

- India has to set up more battery manufacturing plants to support E-Bikes manufacturers, so that the country can control foreign exchange outflow in importing the batteries.
- It will also help to promote employment opportunities in India.

CONCLUSION

EkoVehicles is the name which is associated with non polluting powered transportation. EkoVehicles produces the wonder of conveyance of today's robust and distinct line of silent emission-free powered vehicles which are supreme, delightful and economic. The E-Bikes run at $1/10^{th}$ of the running cost of conventional petrol driven two wheelers with a maintenance cost of $1/3^{rd}$ of a conventional two wheeler. The price of running an Electric Two Wheeler works out to be an unbelievable 10 Paise per Km, which is the cost of charging the battery. Due to its convenience, environmental-friendliness and high performance-cost ratio, E-Bikes have received an increasing demand around the world.

REFERENCES

http://www.thebikegeek.com

www.alibaba.com

Center for Electric Bicycle Quality Inspection Quality of Electric Bicycle Analysis Report, (2006), Beijing.

Business & Industry, Environment, India, Science and Technology.

—(2007), Hero Introduces E-Vehicles in Collaboration with Ultra on October 11.

www.Frost & Survillan.com

www.siam.com

—(2006), Business Daily from *"The Hindu"*, Group of Publications, Thursday, Dec 14.

—(2006), Business Daily from *"The Hindu"*, Group of Publications Saturday, Nov 11.

WEB SITES REFERRED

www.ebikes.org

www.myebike.com

www.evfuture.com

www.indiafirstfoundation.org

www.evehicles.com

CHAPTER 14

STRATEGIC MANAGEMENT OF MANUFACTURING & SOME ISSUES

Mahender Singh
P. C. Basak
Rajbir Singh

INTRODUCTION

The literary meaning of strategy is the imposition upon an enemy of a place and time and conditions for fighting preferred by one. There is a clear similarly in competition between manufacturing organization and competition between armed forces. The business of manufacturing has to choose the best course of action for marching forward with the given availability of resources under the present and anticipated uncertain future environmental conditions. Manufacturing strategy has increasingly been regarded by the researchers, academicians and practitioners as having an important contribution to make for enhancing the competitiveness of the firm.

Manufacturing Strategy can be defined as a framework of integrated decision process for enhancing competitiveness of the organization in a dynamic environment. This pious objective can be achieved only by designing, organizing, managing and developing the company's manufacturing resources and shape a consistent pattern of manufacturing decisions in order that they can result in an adequate mix of performance characteristics which will allow the company to compete effectively in future. To be most effective the manufacturing strategy should act in support of the overall strategic directions of the business and provide for competitive advantages. Thus, it is quite evident that the manufacturing strategy has significant role to play and need critical attention in the corporate setting of manufacturing organization.

Hill (1995) argued that the need for a manufacturing strategy to be developed and shared by the business has to do not only with the critical nature of manufacturing within the corporate strategy but also with the realization that many of decisions in manufacturing are structured in nature. It is also suggested that resource based view of strategic management should play an important role in the development of manufacturing strategy. The resource-based view would help manufacturing strategies to be more difficult to imitate resulting in more sustainable competitive advantages.

Today's manufacturing activity is not only confined to domestic production by a manufacturing firm in its native country; rather manufacturing has been conducted internationally, by realizing the optimum combination of resources of production available throughout the world. This international business activity unhampered by the boundaries of a country is the movement towards globalization. As a matter of fact, the movement towards International Corporation in a limited sense started in 1950s, seeking to capitalize on the low wage rate of developing countries. An essential characteristic of global manufacturing is the transfer of internal management resources to foreign countries with low labour cost or those exporting a great amount of products in order to win competition internationally. The performance of global manufacturing is important in the age of globalization.

HISTORICAL PERSPECTIVE

Professor Skinner (1969) of Harvard Business School was first to recognize that manufacturing is the missing link in corporate strategy. He observed that many senior managers were delegating policy decisions to manufacturing that could have strategic consequences on competitiveness of the firm as a whole. Skinner specifically noted that there is strategic implication for manufacturing decision and therefore, strategic manufacturing issues should be incorporated within corporate strategy. To sort out these problems, Skinner proposed a holistic framework for manufacturing strategy development. Skinner's observations motivate the academicians and practitioners to initiate the process for bridging the gap between manufacturing and corporate strategy. The growth of literature in manufacturing strategy has matched with the growth of interest in the area of industrial engineering, manufacturing management and the philosophy of systems approach. The following four factors can be attributed for the rapid growth of this area.

(a) invasion of electronics and computer technology in the mechanical goods as well as in the advanced manufacturing technology. It facilitates the integration of the management of design and manufacturing that result in the drastic reduction in product life cycle and eventually accelerates the product proliferation.

(b) the new competition is in terms of reduced cost, improved quality, and products with higher performance, a wide range of product and better service, and moreover all delivered simultaneously within a shortest span of time.

(c) Increased potential to be gained from the development of new manufacturing technology, the potential of which grows much faster than our ability to use it for competitive benefits.

(d) with the advent of liberalization, privatization and globalization the industries are facing intense domestic and global competition.

The second stage followed with the framework proposed by Wheelwright (1978) that showed how manufacturing strategy could be linked to corporate strategy. The third stage was provided by Hayes and Wheelwright (1985) who suggested that the strategic manufacturing effectiveness is developed along a continuum. Various researchers (Skinner, 1969; Hill, 1987; Hayes and Pisano, 1994) elaborated on customer expectations, *i.e.*, cost, quality, delivery, flexibility and innovation which are popularly termed as competitive priorities or manufacturing performance objectives. These competitive priorities can be stated as follows:

- *Cost:* Production and distribution of product at low cost.
- *Quality:* Manufacture of products for conformance to some specific standard to fulfill the customer desired performance.
- *Delivery dependability:* Meet delivery schedules.
- *Delivery speed:* Respond quickly to customer orders.
- *Flexibility:* React to changes in production, changes in product mix, production volume, modifications in design, fluctuations in materials, changes in sequence.
- *Innovation:* Introduction of new product and processes.

Hill (1987) introduced the concept of qualifying criteria and order winning criteria. Order qualifiers are those criteria that a company must meet for a customer even to consider it as a competitor. Order winners are those criteria that win the order. To provide qualifiers companies need only to be as good as competitors but to provide order winners they need to be better than competitors. Similar to competitive priorities he identified various order winners and qualifiers, which are market and time specific. He categorized them into manufacturing related and non-manufacturing related criteria. Manufacturing related criteria includes price, delivery reliability, delivery speed, quality, demand increases, product range, design and distribution. Non-manufacturing related criteria may include design leadership, marketing and sales, brand name, technical liaison and support, and after sales support. It is recognized that the strategic manufacturing effectiveness can be operationalized only through a set of coordinated decision for improving the factors that affect strategic manufacturing effectiveness. These factors are:

(i) the attitude of top managers towards manufacturing;
(ii) involvement of manufacturing managers in setting the strategic direction of the firm;
(iii) the emphasis on formulating manufacturing strategy;
(iv) proactive approach to manufacturing function;
(v) coordination between manufacturing and other function.

WORLD CLASS MANUFACTURING STRATEGY

Manufacturing strategy has started to be considered as an integral part of the corporate strategy, dealing with production function for world-class manufacturing enterprise. This terminology started emerging at the end of the1970s in the wake of stiff competition faced by the goods manufactured in English speaking developed countries from the goods of the war ravaged non-English speaking countries like Japan and Germany. Schonberger (1986) was first to coined the term of World class Manufacturing (WCM) based on the Organizational and Managerial approach for the global success of Japanese manufacturing. The great success story of the manufacturing organization of Japan, in particular, has forced others in developed as well as in developing countries to have a serious rethinking into the matters of manufacturing. Manufacturing has now been considered in developed countries as an important part of management strategy for each individual manufacturing firm. The following key changes have been observed during the last two decades:

(a) Significant reductions in all forms of wastes through manufacturing system integration.
(b) Manufacturing is integrated with the market
(c) Drastic compression of product and process development time
(d) Shorter product life cycles
(e) Decentralized production and innovative inventory control

(f) Improved distribution facilities

(g) Global market place

(h) Automated material tracking and control

(i) Integration of various manufacturing technologies with business process activities due to rapid advances in electronics and computing technologies

The role of global strategy is to focus the firm's decisions for creating sustainable competitive advantages over the other in global market environment. The issues of competitive manufacturing strategy which potentially differentiate a firm from its competitors include specialization, brand identification, technological leadership, customer service, speed of delivery, and pricing policy. Some researchers suggest that each of the various manufacturing strategy issues which affect competitive position can be classified into five major areas – cost, quality, delivery dependability, flexibility and innovation. These five areas all fall within the domain of the value-added processes represented by manufacturing. Thus, competitive success in the 21st century will depend greatly on how the firm manages its manufacturing activities. However, in today's global manufacturing environment, all firms, regardless of whether they operate globally, face the task of establishing competitive position in the minds of customers who expect world-class product performance. Competing at very high levels represents the major challenge in global manufacturing. Thus to build a sustainable competitive advantage based on firm's value-added capabilities, and careful management of a firm's production operation is required to assure that value is created throughout its global channel system. Coordinated global manufacturing strategies attempt to do this by linking the value-added capabilities of manufacturing within a cohesive conversion system. Competitive economies arise not only through rationalization but also as firms locate productive activities in different areas of the world to increase global market share.

The decisions of manufacturing in foreign lands have been based on accessing lower production costs. However, given the increasing importance of coordinating activities and decreasing and more transitory nature of factor input savings, it is clear that the manufacturing issues of value chain must be viewed as vital for the creation of sustained competitive advantage. Therefore, in order to take advantage of opportunities in traditional low cost locations (*e.g.*, pacific Basin countries) as well as emerging locations (*e.g.*, Mexico, South America and Central Europe) the firm should acquire and evaluate information regarding the impact of manufacturing issues. Only when, all the value added areas are considered concurrently a firm will be able effectively to utilize global manufacturing to built and sustain a strategic competitive advantage.

MANUFACTURING STRATEGY SCENARIO IN INDIA

Manufacturing always remains an important activity for India in terms of its contribution to GDP, employment opportunities and export amount. The share of manufacturing in India s GDP has moved slowly from 25.38 per cent in 1991s to 27 per cent in 2004s. The share of manufacturing in its export is also on the rise. The contribution of manufacturing to export has increased from 71 per cent in 1991s to 77 per cent in 2004s. India currently exports manufactured goods worth about $ 50 billion. Manufacturing exports accounted around 5 per cent value of output in 1990s. It is now close to 10 per cent.

Manufacturing up till now, has always been considered merely as a pure technical activity for the conversion of raw materials into finished products by employing various standardized manufacturing processes. From the dawn of independence, the Indian manufactures were heavily relied upon the foreign collaboration for the design of both product and process. In most of the cases these foreign collaborated products were in the declining phase of product life cycle in their parent countries. Two such important products are ambassador car and Jaguar aircraft. This result is lack of innovation in the field of product and process development on the part of the Indian manufacturing industries. The protected market environment till the end of 1980s has also contributed to some extent towards the development of lackadaisical approach for the improvement of management of manufacturing from strategic consideration. The habit of giving overemphasis on finance and marketing is also the reason for lack of development of the concept of manufacturing strategy among the Indian manufacturing organization in general. Due to recent developments towards the formation of borderless world such as the passage of the General agreement on Tariff and Trade (GATT) in 1994, the World Trade Organization (WTO) in 1995 and other international trade agreements, the companies world-wide are facing a new era of intense global competition. To achieve competitive advantage the industry will have to search new methods for managing manufacturing technology effectively and efficiently for the survival in the turbulent market environment.

Several studies have been reported regarding the status of manufacturing strategy research and practice in Indian industries (Chandra and Sastry 1998, Sharma and Upadhayaya 1998, Nagabhushana and Shah 1999, Yadav et al 1999, Dangayach and Deshmukh 2000, 2001). Chandra and Sastry (1998) reported in their survey of manufacturing Industries that Indian firms are competing on quality. No focus is on the identification of improvement plans. They observed that the focus of Indian firm is on the competitive priorities. Sharma and Upadhayay (1998) studied manufacturing strategy issues in 20 manufacturing Industries. They observed the prescriptive categorization of manufacturing strategy. Nagabhushana and Shah (1999) have identified manufacturing Priorities and action programs in their study of thirty eight manufacturing industries from the electronics and machine tool sector. They did not mention the linkages of manufacturing priorities and action programs with manufacturing strategy. Yadav *et al.*, (1999) describe about level of competence in 80 manufacturing firms. Dangauach and Deshmukh (2000) observed manufacturing strategy practices in three different companies from automotive and electronics sector. Dangauach and Deshmukh (2001) have also studied process industries situated all over country and concluded that Indian process companies are investing in advanced management systems to manage the competition.

From all these studies we observe that manufacturing in India is at a critical juncture. Manufacturing is treated as a supporting activity for marketing and finance in most of the Indian organization. Thus, till very recently, manufacturing have got little attention from top management. The Indian firms are still very far from world class practices. Many firms are not even practicing well tested efficiency methodologies of scientific School of management that provides the foundation for further development as it happens in western industrialized countries. Indian firm are facing a very different competitive scenario compared with past. The competition is in terms of reduced cost, improved quality, product with higher performance, flexibility better service, innovation and all these have to be delivered simultaneously. So, to compete effectively and to survive in turbulent competitive environment the Indian firm has a real need to evolve an effective manufacturing strategy by adopting new manufacturing management philosophies from holistic view point.

CONCLUSION

The manufacturing function can be a formidable weapon to achieve competitive advantages. Manufacturing was never managed in Indian firm from strategic consideration. As a consequence, the manufacturing remains always a missing link in corporate strategy for Indian manufacturing firms. In this paper, we have discussed the influence of various issues of manufacturing strategy which are helpful for making the framework of manufacturing strategy. The business of manufacturing survives only when customers support the products in various ways. Manufacturing strategy issues have been elaborated from the view point of customer expectations. These issues are identified as cost, quality, deliverability, flexibility and innovation which are also known as manufacturing performance objectives. Even to be just qualified for consideration by the customers, any Indian manufacturing firm has to achieve a minimum critical value on these issues either individually or in a certain combination of all. It is obviously a stupendous task for any firm to compete on all the manufacturing objectives concurrently.

In this paper the various aspects of manufacturing strategy have been discussed in the Indian as well as in global context. There is an urgent need for the Indian firm to evolve the manufacturing strategy framework for its survival in the domestic competition provided by the both Indian as well as foreign multinational firms. Indian firms also need to explore the possibility of competing with the firms from TRIAD (Japan Europe and America) countries and also with the firms from newly industrialized south East Asian countries like Korea, Taiwan, Malaysia, Thailand, and Singapore in the international market. The method of doing business is also rapidly changing. Outsourcing is fast emerging as a business and manufacturing strategy for many large firms. India has a great potential to play a significant role in this new strategy of manufacturing business. India has already been identified by the several multinational firms as an important market place for the purpose of outsourcing of auto components, defense components, components of electronic entertainment products apparel, special chemical and pharmaceutical. The critical success factor for all these potentialities depends upon the abilities of the Indian firms to link manufacturing strategy with the corporate business strategy through the achievements on various manufacturing performance objectives.

The seriousness of the manufacturing sector can easily be understood by the fact of establishing a National Manufacturing Competitiveness Council (NMCC) by the government of India. The recent survey conducted jointly by the Confederation of Indian Industries (CII) and Mckinsey has predicted the possibility of annual growth of the export of 17 per cent to reach at $ 300 billion mark by 2015. However, this is not going to happen automatically without drastic improvement in the factors for internal competitive environment. The condition of internal manufacturing environment of Indian industries is quite different when compared with its counterpart in advanced countries as well as in newly industrialized countries. Indian firms in general suffer from the shortages of the various kinds of resources in comparison to its counterparts from foreign lands. In view of the resource constraints, the Indian firms needs to find out appropriate methodologies for assigning priorities among the various performance objectives. This roadmap of incremental development for continuous strategic improvement will certainly help any Indian firm to retain atleast its existing market share in domestic market. Indian manufacturing industry will be able to reap the full benefit of outsourcing only when the status of the functional area of manufacturing will be upgraded equal to the other functional areas like marketing & finance. The manufacturing philosophies and methodologies developed by the Japanese such as TQM, Kaizen and 5s programmed need to be adopted widely by the Indian industries. There is also an urgent need in the academic field of integrating the discipline of manufacturing process technology with manufacturing management and Industrial Engineering. It is also imperative for successfully absorption and implementation of this logically incremental strategy, the manufacturing organization has to be converted into a really learning organization by adopting the system philosophy.

REFERENCES

Bowonder, B. (1998), "Industrialization and Economic Growth of India: Interactions of Indigenous and Foreign Technology", *International Journal of Technology Management*, 15(6), 622-645.

Chandra, P. and Sastry T. (1998), "Competitiveness of Indian Manufacturing", *Vikalpa*, 23(3), 25-36.

Dangayach, G. S. and Deshmukh, S. G. (2000), "Manufacturing Strategy: Experiences from Select Indian Organizations", *Journal of Manufacturing Systems*, 19(2), 134-148.

Dangayach, G. S. and Deshmukh, S. G. (2001), "Manufacturing Strategy Literature Review and Some Issues", *International Journal of Operations and Production Management*, 21(7), 884-932.

Englyst, L. N. (2003), "Operations Strategy Formation–A Continuous Process", *Integrated Manufacturing System*, 14(8), 677-685.

Hayes, R. H. and Pisano, G. P. (1994), "Beyond World Class, The New Manufacturing Strategy", *Harvard Business Review*, 79(10), 77-86.

Hayes, R. H. and Wheelwright, S. C. (1985), "Competing Through Manufacturing", *Harvard Business Review*, January-February, 99-108.

Hill, T. (1987/1995), *Manufacturing Strategy*-Text and Cases, Irwin.

Kakati, R. P. and Dhar, U. R. (2002), "Competitive Strategies and New Venture Performance", *Vikalpa*, 27(3), 13-26.

Ketokivi, M. and Heikkila, J. (2003), "A Strategic Management System for Manufacturing: Linking Action to Performance", *Production Planning & Control*, 14(6), 487-496.

Mohanty, R. P. and Deshmukh, S. G. (1999), "Evaluation Manufacturing Strategy for a Learning Organization: A Case", *International Journal of Operations and Production Management*, 19(3), 308-327.

Nagabhushana, T. S. and Shah, J. (1999), "Manufacturing Priorities and Action Programmes in the Changing Environment: an Empirical Study of Indian Industries", *International Journal of Operations and Production Management*, 19(4), 389-398.

Schonberger, R. J. (1986), "World Class Manufacturing: The Lessons of Simplicity Applied", Free Press, New York.

Sharma, R. R. K. and Upadhyay S. (1998), "Manufacturing Strategy: Relating Process to Contents", *Productivity*, 16(2), 272-279.

Skinner, W. (1969), "Manufacturing-Missing Link in Corporate Strategy", *Harvard Business Review*, 47(3), 136-44.

Skinner W. (1985), *Manufacturing: The Formidable Competitive* Weapon, Johan Wiley.

Wheelwright, S. C. (1978), "Reflecting Corporate Strategy in Manufacturing Decisions", *Business Horizons*, 57-66.

Wheelwright S. C. (1984), "Manufacturing Strategy: Defining the Missing Link", *Strategic Management Journal*, 5(1), 77-87.

Yadav O. P., Bhandari R., and Mohanty R. P. (1999), "Level of Manufacturing Competence in Indian Companies", *POMS-99 New Delhi*, India, 3-12.

Chapter 15

COMMERCIAL MORTGAGE MARKET OF THE UNITED STATES: FINANCIAL INSTITUTIONS . PARTICIPATION. DOES BANK SIZE MATTER? AN ANALYSIS OF COMPARATIVE LENDING

INTRODUCTION

Commercial realestate lending (commercial mortgages) is an important factor in the United States real estate/total mortgages market. There has been phenomenonal growth in the commercial real estate market. Commercial realestate lending has flourished since the 1980s. In 1986, the commercial and multifamily mortgage flow was $112 billion. In 2005, total commercial mortgages (commercial realestate lending) was $233.3 billion and 18 per cent of the total mortgages $1269.6 billion. They are second only to one-to-four family mortgages (home mortgages)[1].

A study of commercial real estate financing and the character of institutional financiers are important for several reasons, including:

The mortgage market occupies an important position in the U.S. economy. Housing sectors alone contribute approximately 20 per cent to the GDP1.

The housing and commercial real estate market in past decades witnessed an unprecedented expansion. For example, homeownership rate increased from 64 per cent in 1994 to 68 per cent in 2003 (Liang and McLemore, 2004). At the center of the mortgage market boom the most important contributors are institutional financial investors–savings and life associations, commercial banks, and life insurances.

More recently, improved risk management tools, along with appealing income generation opportunities, have attracted institutional investors into private equity financing in commercial real estates. Institutional investing (financing) in real estate began with mortgages and directly property and then gradually moved into public securities (Conner and Liang, 2003). The institutional real estate financing (mortgage) industry has undergone profound changes since investors made their first commitment to equity financing nearly four decades ago, with the structure and composition of institutional investors in real estate (home) financing experiencing the most changes. Savings and loan associations (S&Ls), once were a dominant player in home mortgage market in the 1960s, but no longer continue to be a dominant player.

Commercial banks among institutional investors have become a significant source of financing real estate (home) mortgages. Within the sphere of real estate financing, the share of small vis-à-vis large commercial banks is not similar. The development of market shares is highly asymmetric and skewed. Large commercial banks with assets of more than $1 billion significantly dominate home mortgage loans. This difference deserves an examination. A look at the character and the changes in the behavior and the composition of institutional investors in real estate (commercial) financing is necessary. Such information is of great interest to academia, banks, and policy makers.

This paper is structured as: Section 1 provides literature surveys. Section 2 describes markets for commercial realestate lending and the major lending participants that provide the kinds of commercial real-estate loans. Section 3 describes the growth of market shares in commercial realestate mortgages by commercial banks of different asset categories. Section 4 reports statistical results of the comparative performance of national and state chartered banks as well as conclusions.

Literature Survey

There are many studies conducted on mortgage market. This paper focuses on those studies that are related to the theme of this paper.

Neveloff (1996) observed that banks and insurance companies became active in real estate lending in 1996. He suggested that institutional lenders must learn and act in a timely manner in order to compete with the "new breed of private lenders" (p. 26). He further suggested that "lending officer should bone up on specialized market niches so they can evaluate and react to loan proposals fast" (p. 26).

Smith (1990) provided an insight as to what to do when a property gets into trouble. According to Smith, troubled real estate properties can be salvaged in many ways. By giving an analogy of "Making Stone Soup," he suggested six ingredients. Similar to preparing stone soup, concerted efforts of various parties are needed to rescue troubled real estate properties. In "the mortgage and real estate executives report," Arnold (1990) provided information on total return by property types (for ten years since 1989) and discussed many issues on apartments and farm property outlook, world competition, environmental concerns, and compliance to flood insurance, etc. Cranmer (1990) believed that the real estate market was in trouble due to declining confidence in the banking industry. Bank stocks already had fallen 40 per cent in 1990. He thought that real estate loan problems were already severe and it would likely deteriorate further. According to Cranmer, one of the thorniest problems for bank analysts was to "determine the loss content of non-performing assets – that is, how much will ultimately be written off" (p. 27). He listed several factors for the real estate problems in the banking industry. Among those he said was "The most underrated factor is that banks (and real estate developers) were whipsawed by tax legislation related to real estate" (p. 28). The second was management behavior. "Management behavior is a second major cause of real estate problems among banks" (p. 28).

Corcoran (1987) presented a model of the commercial real estate market that explained the paradox of high and rising vacancy rates (combined with falling rents) and at the same time the increasing prices of existing commercial real estate. The model separates the temporary business cycle from structural factors influencing real estate. The key point in the first section of his paper is that real estate was both a factor of production and assets. So, the price for commercial real estate as a factor of production is the rental income on building space. The price of commercial real estate as an asset is the rate of return which must be consistent with other assets, such as stocks and bonds. McNulty (1995) evaluated the causes of overbuilding and determined whether the economic base multiplier effect was stronger in the long run. He found that the cause of overbuilding was embodied with two lags – "the lag in the transmission mechanism between basic and nonbasic economic activity and the lag between approval and completion of real estate projects" (p. 49). Samad (2005) examined the U. S. commercial banksrole in real estate financing from a historical perspective.

COMMERCIAL MORTGAGE MARKET AND ITS PARTICIPANTS

Commercial Mortgage Market

The U.S. realestate mortgage market is classified into four categories–residential, multi-family, commercial real estate, and farm.

Residential/home mortgages are loans secured by one-to-four family properties.

Multifamily real estate lending is a loan secured by multi-family units, including owner occupied condominium units.

The commercial real estate mortgages are income generating properties. They consist of the following four categories:

- Construction and land development
- Commercial or non-farm nonresidential
- Farmland
- Multifamily

However, in the truest sense, commercial real estate mortgages are loans secured by non-farm nonresidential properties, including properties owned by nonprofit organizations such as universities, hospitals, and churches. Commercial loans involve investments in office buildings, shopping centers, and warehouses.

Commercial realestate loans differ from a residential loan in many respects. Commercial loans are usually much larger in amount than a residential loan. Commercial mortgages are loans which are given on property that generates an income stream throughout the life of the property. The income generated from the property is used to make loan payments, pay expenses, and provides profits.

Among the categories of commercial real estate lending, non-farm nonresident is the largest component. Table 1 which shows the market share of mortgage debt secured by different categories of property. The total mortgage debt totaled $3762 billion ($3.7 trillion) in 1990. Out of $3762, one-four family mortgage lending was $2647 billion ($2.6 trillion). This was the largest component of mortgage debt. The rest of the mortgage debt was commercial lending.

Table 1
Mortgage Debt Outstanding by Type of Property in 1990

Secured by Property Type	*$Billion*	*Market Share %*
Nonfarm nonresident	758.3	20
Multifamily residences	309.3	8.2
Farmland	78.9	2

Table 1 shows that among the commercial lending, non-farm nonresidential lending is the largest one. The total mortgage debt for the non-farm nonresidential loans was $758.3 billion in 1990. They constituted 20% of the total mortgage markets.

Multi-family and farmland share a distant position – 8.2 and 2 per cent–in the total mortgage markets in the United States.

Mortgage Market Participants

In the primary mortgage[2] market of the real estate lending, there are six major lending providers. They are:

- Commercial banks
- Savings institutions
- Life insurance companies
- Federal and related agencies
- Mortgage pools and trusts
- Individuals and others

In the1960s, the principal lender in real estate mortgages was Savings and Loan Associations (S&Ls). They were the largest loan providers of one-to-four (1-4) family residential properties. Their market share in the mortgage lending/market drastically declined in the 1980s and 1990s. This was mainly due to a S&Ls crisis in the late 1970s and the early 1980s when the market interest rate increased dramatically. The increase in market interest increased S&Ls cost of payment to depositors and their borrowings, while their mortgage interest remained low.

Table 2 presents a snapshot of the market share of these major players in the total mortgage market during 1990.

Table 2
Mortgage Debt Outstanding by Type of Holder 1990

Holder	*$Billions*	*Market Share (%)*
Commercial banks	884	23
Savings institutions	801	21
Life insurances	267	7
Federal and related Agencies	239	6.8
Mortgage pool and Trusts	1,079	28.3
Individual and others	530	13.9
Total	3,800	100

Source: Federal Reserve Bulletin

Table 2 shows the total value of mortgage debt outstanding and the market share of various loan providers. The value of total mortgage debt outstanding at this time was approximately $3,800 billion.

It appears from Table 2 that S&Ls were no longer a primary lender in the mortgage market. Their market share was reduced to a third. Their share was only 21 per cent of the total mortgage market. Commercial banks became a dominant player, second to mortgage pools and trusts. Commercial banks real estate outstanding mortgage debt and their market shares were $884 billions and 23 per cent respectively. Mortgage pools and trusts occupied 28 per cent mortgage loans.

However, the allocation of mortgage funds among various commercial real estate categories shows that commercial banks became dominant players. This is substantiated from Table 3.

Table 3
Mortgage Holdings among Financial Institutions in 1990 (million $)

	Multifamily	*Nonfarm nonresident*	*Farmland*	*Total*
Commercial Banks	37,015	334,648	17,231	388,894
Savings Institutions	91,806	109,168	500	201,474
Life Insurance Cos	28,979	215,121	10,756	254,856

Source: Federal Reserve Bulletin

Table 3 shows commercial banks, savings institutions, and life insurance company loans outstanding in commercial properties. Commercial banks are the principal lenders in commercial, non-farm nonresidential properties. They supply the highest amount of commercial loans. Commercial banks supplied $334,648 million loans to nonfarm non-residential properties. S&Ls and life insurance companies supplied $109,168 million and $215,121 million respectively. In financing farmland, commercial banks were significantly ahead of S&Ls.

The total loans of commercial banks, and savings institutions were $388,894 million and $201,474 million respectively out of total commercial real estate mortgages $1,146,584 million in 1990.The total commc.cial real estate mortgages held by life insurance companies were $254,856 million.

The relative market shares of various mortgage lenders did not remain constant over the years. Table 4 shows the comparative percentage allocation/relative market shares of commercial banks, savings institutions, and life insurance companies in commercial mortgages consisting of non-farm nonresidential, farmland and multifamily properties between1990 and 2005.

Table 4
Relative Commercial Mortgages held by Financial Institutions, in 1990 and 2005 (Millions of $).

Category of Institutions	*Commercial Real Estate Mortgages1990*		*Commercial Real Estate Mortgages in 2005*	
Commercial banks	388,894	34%	$1,094,200	42.4%
Savings institutions	201,474	18%	$191,400	7.4%
Life insurance Cos	254,856	22%	258,700	10%

Source: Federal Reserve Bulletin

Table 4 shows the relative market share of financial institutions in commercial mortgage lending. Commercial banks were the most dominant participants in the commercial real estate market. The market share of commercial banks in commercial mortgages increased from 34 per cent in 1990 to 42.4 per cent in 2005. Their market shares were the highest in both 1990 and 2005. They held 34 per cent and 42.4 per cent of commercial mortgages in 1990 and 2005 respectively.

The market share of savings institutions declined from 18 per cent in 1990 to 7.4 per cent in 2005. Savings institutions no longer occupied the second position. Life insurance companies occupied the second place in commercial real estate lending.

It is clear from the examination of relative market shares of various financial institutions that commercial banks were the most important and number one player in commercial real estate mortgage markets.

GROWTH OF COMMERCIAL REAL ESTATE LENDING AND COMMERCIAL BANK

Within the banking industry, the development of commercial mortgage lending is not the same. In 1990, 1995, 2000, and 2004, commercial banks commercial real estate lending was a percent of the consolidated assets. The evidence is shown in Panel A through E in Table 5.

Table 5
Commercial Banks Real Estate Lending as a Percentage of Average Consolidated Assets, Selected Years by Bank Size

	Type of Loan (Domestic)			
Panel A. All Commercial Banks	1990(%)	1995(%)	2000(%)	2004(%)
Construction and land development	4.00	1.59	2.51	3.25
Farmland	0.51	0.56	0.56	.54
Multifamily Residential	0.62	0.81	0.99	1.06
Commercial (nonfarm nonresidential)	6.76	6.97	7.48	7.97
Total domestic	11.78	9.93	11.54	12.82
Memo: Domestic volume ($ billions)	393	412	681.5	1,012
Total assets ($ billions)	3,338	4,149	5,906	7,879
	Type of Loan (Domestic)			
Panel B. Ten Largest Banks	*1990(%)*	*1995(%)*	*2000(%)*	*2004(%)*
Construction and land development	3.79%	0.58	0.98	1.4
Farmland	0.08%	0.06	0.11	0.10
Multifamily Residential	0.68%	0.38	0.60	0.45
Commercial (nonfarm nonresidential)	3.51%	2.83	3.42	3.55
Total domestic	8.06%	3.85	5.11	5.5
Memo: Domestic volume ($ billions)	58	40	114	200
Total assets ($ billions)	725	1,051	2,234	3,654
	Type of Loan (Domestic)			
Panel C. Banks Ranked 11-100 by assets	*1990(%)*	*1995(%)*	*2000(%)*	*2004(%)*
Construction and land development	4.91%	1.50	3.00	3.51
Farmland	0.12%	0.13	0.22	0.19

Contd.

Multifamily Residential	0.46%	.077	1.11	1.34
Commercial (nonfarm nonresidential)	6.01%	6.54	7.28	7.41
Total domestic	11.50%	8.94	11.61	12.45
Memo: Domestic volume ($ billions)	114	120	235.7	295.8
Total assets ($ billions)	995	1,338	2,031	2,376

	Type of Loan (Domestic)			
Panel D. Banks Ranked 101-1,000 by assets	*1990(%)*	*1995(%)*	*2000(%)*	*2004(%)*
Type of loan (Domestic)	1990(%)	1995(%)	2000(%)	2004(%)
Construction and land development	4.37%	2.21	4.15	6.98
Farmland	0.28%	0.40	0.65	0.91
Multifamily Residential	0.74%	1.21	1.58	2.24
Commercial (nonfarm nonresidential)	9.12%	9.47	13.36	17.82
Total domestic	14.51%	13.29	19.74	27.95
Memo: Domestic volume ($ billions)	136	145	195	302
Total assets ($ billions)	937	1,094	986	1,080

	Type of Loan (Domestic)			
Panel E. Banks Not Ranked among the 1000 largest by assets	*1990(%)*	*1995(%)*	*2000(%)*	*2004(%)*
Construction and land development	2.37	2.38	3.70	6.00
Farmland	1.86	2.48	3.06	3.22
Multifamily Residential	0.66	0.95	1.04	1.41
Commercial (nonfarm nonresident)	8.09	10.37	13.06	16.93
Total domestic	12.28	16.08	20.86	27.56
Memo: Domestic volume ($ billions)	84	107	136.6	211.9
Total assets ($ billions)	681	666	655	769

It is clear from Panel A through E that among the commercial real estate loans, commercial loans (non-farm nonresidential) dominated the commercial mortgage market. In terms of percentage, commercial loans (nonfarm nonresident) are the most dominant item in the asset portfolio of commercial banks.

In terms of relative percentage, the rankings for 2004, from Panel A are presented in Table 6.

Table 6
Ranking of Commercial banks Real Estate Lending in 2004

Type of Loans	*Rank*	*Percent of Assets*
Commercial (nonfarm nonresidential	1	7.97
Construction and land development	2	3.25
Multifamily Residential	3	1.06
Farmland	4	0.54

As far as real estate lending is concerned, commercial real estate (non-farm nonresidential) loans were dominant and became number one in the assets of commercial banks. Construction and land development became the second distant source of assets. The third and fourth items in the assets of commercial bank mortgage lending were multifamily and farmland respectively.

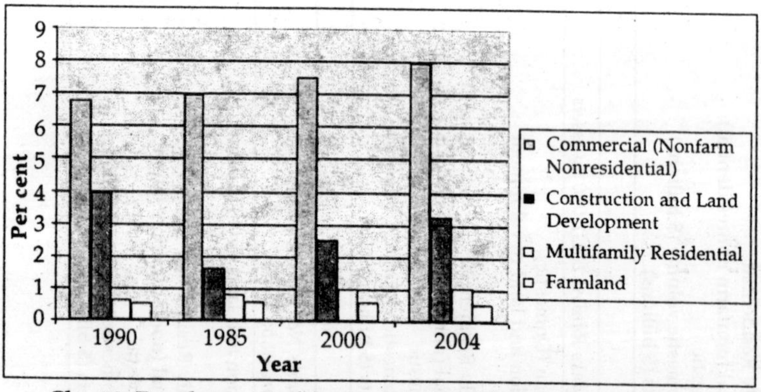

Chart 1: Development of Commercial Real Estate Loans Held by Commercial Banks as a Percentage of Assets
Source: Table 6, Panel A.

Chart 1 presents a snapshot of the development of market shares in the commercial mortgage lending during 1990-2004.

Table 5 and Chart 1 show that construction and land development loans of commercial banks were most cyclical in nature. It swings from 4 per cent of total assets in 1990 to 1.5 per cent in 1995 and back to 3.25 per cent. These swings of lending were caused by the cyclical fluctuation of total real estate lending from 12 per cent of the total assets in 1990 to10 per cent in 1995 and 13 per cent in 2004.

Commercial loans were dominant and becoming increasingly popular. The percentage of total assets allocated to non-farm non-residential real estate increased from 6 percent in 1995 to 8 per cent in 2004.

Farmland shows the most stable form of commercial lending for commercial banks. Refer to Table 5.

The data for the 10 largest banks presented in Panel B showed that commercial banks commercial real estate business differed from the rest of the banking industry. They provided relatively fewer loans secured by farmland. Only 0.07 per cent of the loans of the ten largest banks were secured by farmland in 1990 compared to 1.32 per cent for the banks not ranked among the 1,000 largest.

The data for the 90 banks ranked 11-100 by assets size presented in Panel C show lending behavior similar to the 10 largest banks. That is, these super-regional banks were less active in loans secured by farmland. They issued relatively fewer loans secured by farmland.

The data for the 900 banks ranked 101-1,000 by assets presented in Panel D showed that these banks are the largest lending providers of total real estate loans. This group provides the largest percentage of total real estate financing. They provided 32 per cent ($67 billion real estate loans out of $209 billion total domestic real estate loans) in 1990, 35 per cent ($136 billion out of $393 billion) in 1995, 29 per cent ($195 billion out of $681 billion) in 2000, and 30 percent ($302 billion out of $1,012 billion) in 2004.

The data for the banks not ranked among the 1,000 largest by assets is presented in Panel E and shows that these banks provided more commercial real estate loans than the 10 largest banks in the U.S. For example, in 1995, these banks proved $107 billion real estate loans compared to $40 billion provided by the 10 largest banks. However, the ten largest banks participation increased during the subsequent periods. In 2000 and 2004, banks commercial real estate lending was $114 billion and $200 billion respectively. In terms of percentage for total assets, banks commercial real estate loans were 5 per cent and 5.4 per cent in 2000 and 2004 compared to 4 per cent in 1995. This increased activity in commercial real estate loans was mainly due to the robust performance of the U.S. economy.

In addition to the above factors, Table 5 provides the following interest points:

- The smaller the bank size (by assets) the larger the percentage of banks commercial real estate loans. For example, the top 900 banks ranked 101 through 1,000 by assets had 18 per cent of their assets as commercial real estate loans in 2004 compared to 12 per cent and 6 per cent for the top 90 banks ranked 11 through 100 and the ten largest banks respectively. This is true for other years.

Non-farm Non-resident Mortgage (Commercial Mortgage) and Commercial Banks

Within the category of commercial real estate lending, commercial banks lending to non-farm nonresidential property was a phenomenon. It was the most dominant sector among the commercial real estate lending–construction and development, non-farm non-residential, multi-family, and farmland.

The growth of commercial real estate loans (commercial mortgages) held by commercial banks and savings institutions during 1992-2004 is presented in chart 2.

Chart 2 shows commercial banks as the principal lender in the commercial mortgage market. Savings institutions were least important players. Commercial banks average commercial mortgage loans (Table 4) was $492.1 billion dollars during 1990-2004. During the same period, savings institutions average loans in commercial mortgages were $70.2 billion.

Chart 2 also shows the rapid growth of commercial mortgages, except for the years 1991-1994. During these years the growth of commercial banks, total as well as commercial mortgages, declined significantly. During 1991-1994 the changes of commercial mortgages were –13.6 billion, –43.6 billion, 34.1 billion, and –12.5 billion (Federal Reserve Bulletin Z.1).

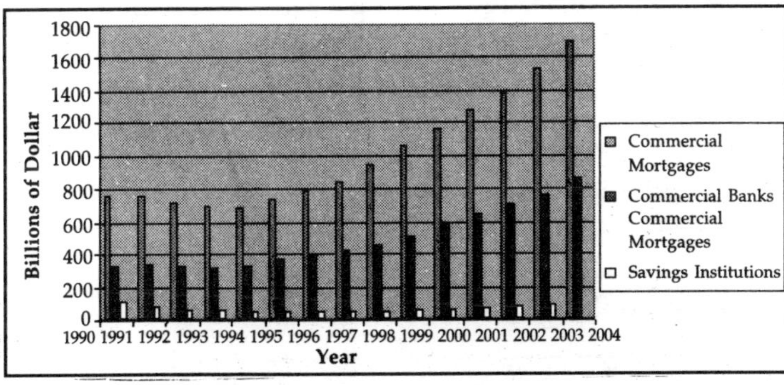

Chart 2 Development of Commercial Mortgages, Commercial Banks and Savings Institutions During 1992-2004
Source: Federal Reserve Bulletin

The negative growth of commercial mortgage lending was captured by the outflow of funds. In 1992, the total was almost $57 billion–more than one half of the 1986 inflow (Sinkey, 1998, pp. 513). Savings institutions accounted for the bulk of the outflow – about 61 per cent.

Since 1992 the commercial mortgage market began to recover slowly. Until 1995, most of the recovery was mainly a reduction of outflow of funds. The recovery became real during the first quarter of 1995 when $28.6 billion flowed into commercial mortgages.

Total mortgages as well as commercial mortgage markets witnessed rapid development during 1995-2004 with the exception of 2001. The decline in the mortgage market in 2001 was linked to the loss of confidence caused by the September 11 attack on the World Centers. The rapid growth of the mortgage market during the 1990s and 2000s was mainly due to a record low mortgage interest rate.

Commercial banks were major lending providers for commercial mortgages. The development of the commercial banks market share in commercial mortgages is provided in Chart 3.

Chart 3 shows commercial banks were the dominant market share in the commercial (non-farm nonresidential) mortgage market in the U.S. commercial banks market share of commercial mortgages during 1990-2004. A descriptive statistics of the commercial mortgage market shares for commercial banks and savings is provided in Table 8.

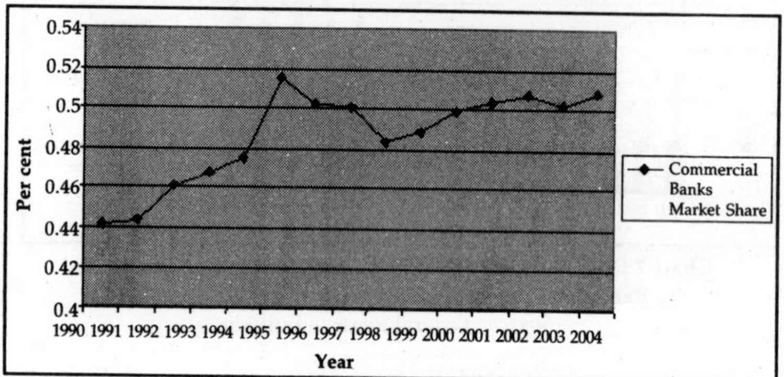

Char 3 Commercial Banks Market Share in Commercial Mortgages
Source: Federal Reserve Bulletin

Table 8
Descriptive Statistics of Commercial Mortgages and Market Shares for Commercial Banks and Savings Institutions During 1990-2004

Deviation	*Mean*	*Standard*
Commercial banks	$492.1 billion	$178.8 billion
	48.7 per cent	2 per cent
Savings institutions	$72.2	$17.9 billion
	7.2 per cent	2 per cent

In the U.S. the commercial real estate mortgage market, commercial banks were dominant lenders. Commercial banks averaged a market share in commercial mortgages of 48.7 per cent with standard deviations of 2 per cent. On the other hand, savings institutions market share was only 7.2 per cent.

The increased market share by commercial banks vis-à-vis the decrease market share of savings institutions in the commercial mortgage market can be explained by several factors.

The innovation of securitization of commercial loans has significantly improved the liquidity position of commercial real estate loans and thus reduced the liquidity risk of commercial banks. This has a tremendous impact on commercial banks increased market share in commercial mortgages.

The decline of the savings institutions market share in commercial as well as home mortgages was mainly due to the S&Ls crisis in the 1980s.

Commercial Mortgages by Bank Size

Within the banking industry, there are different sizes of commercial banks. Bank sizes–small, medium, and large–are measure by assets size. The mortgage lending of the U.S. commercial banks is not the same. The development of market shars of commercial mortgages held by commercial banks with assets less than $100 million, assets between $100 million and $1 billion, and assets more than $1 billion during 1990-2004 is different. Chart 4 substantiates this fact.

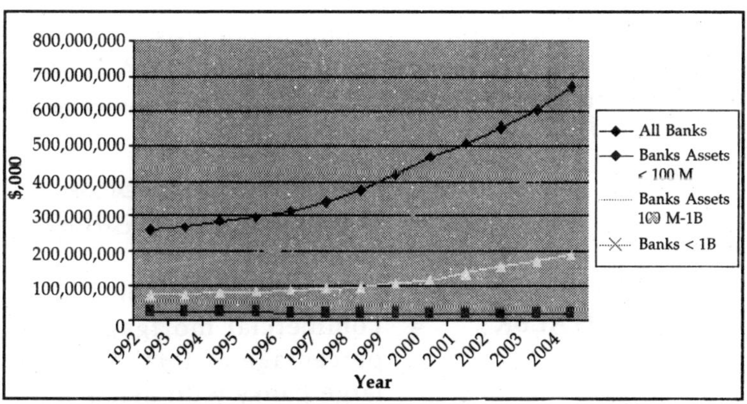

Chart 4: Development of Commercial Mortgages of Commercial Banks by Assets

Chart 4 shows that banks with large assets held large volumes of commercial mortgages more than banks with medium and small assets. The average commercial mortgages held by the commercial banks with assets less than $100 million, assets between $100 million and 1 billion, and assets more than $1 billion during 1992-2004 were $24 billion, $112 billion, and 274 billion respectively.

STATISTICAL METHODS AND RESULTS

In order to examine their comparative performance in commercial mortgages, it is appropriate to consider commercial mortgages as a percent of their total assets. Loan volume itself is not a good measure for comparative analysis. Ratio analysis has many benefits (Chen & Shimerda, 1998, O'Connor, 1973) and has been widely used for comparative analysis (samad 1999, 2004, Elyasiani and Mehdian, 1995, Sabi 1996). Mortgage loans as a percentage of total assets compensates the disparity of bank sizes.

The Following Variable is Used in This Study

CMTA ratio = Commercial mortgages to total assets. The CMTA ratio is estimated as total commercial mortgages of ith bank divided by total assets of ith bank.

ANOVA is applied to the mean ratio of commercial mortgages to total assets (CMTA) for the commercial banks of different assets categories.

The test procedure is: the null hypothesis (H_0) of the equality of mean commercial mortgage ratio, CMTA of banks with different assets category is tested against the alternative hypothesis (H_a).

Where H_0 : $\mu_{CMTALBK} = \mu_{CMTAMBK} = \mu_{CMTASBK}$

H_a : $\mu_{CMTALBK} \neq \mu_{CMTAMBK} \neq \mu_{CMTASBK}$

Where H_0 : Null hypothesis

H_a : Alternative hypothesis.

Where CMTALBK = commercial mortgages as a percentage of total assets of large banks with assets more than $1 billion.

CMTAMBK = commercial mortgages as a percentage of total assets of medium banks with assets between$100 million and $1 billion.

CMTASBK = commercial mortgages as a percentage of total assets of large banks with assets less than $100 million.

The result of comparative performance in commercial mortgages by asset size with a different asset category is presented in Table 5.

Variables	μ_{CMTA}	*SD*	*Hypothesis*	*ANOVA F-statistics*	*P-value*	*Decision Rule*
CMTALBK	0.06	0.002	$\mu_{CMTALBK} =$	58.66	0.0000	Reject H_0
CMTAMBK	0.14	0.030	$\mu_{CMTAMBK} =$			
CMTASBK	0.09	0.014	$\mu_{CMTASBK}$			

ANOVA result in Table 5 show that there was a significant difference among the commercial banks of different asset categories. The null hypothesis of the equality of performance among the commercial banks of different assets categories is rejected with a very low level of significance. This is substantiated by high *F*-statistics, 58 and very low *p*-value, 0.0000.

The pair-wise t-test results provided in Table 6 suggest that the performance of small and medium banks in issuing commercial mortgage loans as a percentage of their total assets was far better than large banks.

Variables	μ_{CMTA}	*Hypothesis*	*t-statistics*	*P-value*	*Decision Rule*
CMTASBK	0.09	$\mu_{CMTASBK} = \mu_{CMTALBK}$	8.8	0.0000	Reject H_0
CMTALBK	0.06				
CMTASBK	0.09	$\mu_{CMTASBK} = \mu_{CMTAMBK}$	5.2	0.0000	Reject H_0
CMTAMBK	0.14				
CMTAMBK	0.14	$\mu_{CMTAMBK} = \mu_{CMTALB}$	9.7	0.0000	Reject H_0
CMTALBK	0.06				

The pair-wise test results in Table 6 suggest that there was a significant differences among the commercial banks with different assets categories. Medium size banks with assets between $100 million and $1 billion issued more commercial mortgage loans than large banks with capital more than $ 1 billion. Banks with capital between $100 million and $1 billion held 14 per cent of their assets as commercial mortgages compared to only 6 per cent of the large banks with assets more than $1 billion. This difference in mortgage loans performance is statistically significant. The null hypothesis, $H_0 : \mu_{CMTAMBK} = \mu_{CMTALB}$, is rejected. The level of significance associated with the *t*-test is very low. This is substantiated by *t*-statistics = 9.7 and *p*-value = 0.0000.

The pair wise *t*-test between small banks with assets less than $100 million and large banks with assets more than $1 billion shows that small banks issued a significantly high percentage of commercial mortgage loans than large commercial banks. Small commercial banks held 9 per cent of their total assets in commercial mortgages compared to 6 per cent of the large banks. This difference in mortgage loans performance is statistically significant. The null hypothesis, $H_0 : \mu_{CMTASBK} = \mu_{CMTALBK}$, is rejected. The level of significance associated with the *t*-test is very low. This is substantiated by *t*-statistics = 8.8 and *p*-value = 0.0000.

Commercial banks regressive behavior in domestic commercial mortgage lending–the larger the bank size the smaller the commercial lending–can be attributed to several factors.

The examination of the balance sheet of commercial banks of different assets categories reveals that large commercial banks with assets more than $1 billion are more interested in foreign mortgage lending than domestic mortgage lending.

During 1992-2004, the average total foreign real estate lending of small banks with assets less than $100 million was $4.4 million, (1.48581E-05 per cent of total assets) compared to $31.6 billion (0.07 per cent of total assets) of large banks with assets more than $1 billion. The difference is statistically significant.

The average total foreign real estate lending of medium banks with assets between $100 million and $1 billion was 46.8 million, (6.52E-05 per cent of total assets) compared to $31.6 billion (0.07 per cent of total assets) of large banks with assets more than $1 billion during 1992-2004. This difference is statistically significant.

Similarly, there were significant difference in foreign real estate lending between banks with assets less than $100 million and assets between $100 million and $1 billion. The average lending of banks with assets between $100 million and $1 billion held significantly higher foreign mortgages than banks with assets less than $100 million. The average foreign mortgages held by commercial banks with assets between $100 and $1 billion was $4.4 million, (1.48581E-05 per cent of total assets) compared to 46.8 million, (6.52E-05 per cent of total assets) during 1992-2004.

The above discussions reveal that the larger the bank sizes the higher the amount and percentage of foreign real estate lending vis-à-vis regressive nature of domestic mortgage lending.

CONCLUSION

The major participants of the total real estate lending are commercial banks, savings institutions, and life insurance companies. Among them commercial banks are the most dominant players in total commercial real estate lending. Commercial banks held 42.4 per cent of the total commercial real state mortgages compared to savings institutions with 7.4 per cent in 2004.

Within the banking industry, the performance of commercial banks in total (domestic) commercial real estate lending varied widely. Banks behavior in total commercial real estate lending was found to be regressive. Large commercial banks held significantly less total commercial real estate mortgages than medium and small commercial banks. The ten largest banks held only 5.5 per cent of their assets in total commercial real estate mortgages compared to 12.45 per cent and 27.96 per cent for the banks ranked 11-100 by assets and banks ranked 101-1000 by assets respectively.

Within the category of total commercial real estate lending, commercial (non-farm non-residential) mortgage lending was the most important component of the total commercial real estate lending. It constituted for 9 per cent of the total commercial real estate lending compared to 1 per cent and 0.5 per cent for multifamily and farmland in 2004.

The growth of commercial (non-farm non-residential) mortgage lending was spectacular during 1992-2002. Commercial banks average commercial mortgage lending was $492.1 billion with a standard deviation of $178.8 billion. Commercial mortgage lending (non-farm non-residential) varied widely among the commercial banks by asset size. There was a significant difference in commercial mortgages among banks with assets less than $100 million, assets between $100 million and $1 billion, and assets more than $1 billion. The large commercial banks with assets more than $1 billion issued far less commercial real estate loans in both volume and percentage than banks with assets less than $100 million and assets between $100 million and $1 billion.

REFERENCES

Arnold Alvin A., (1990), "The Prime Real Estate Report," *The Mortgage and Real Estate Executives Report*, (May), Vol. 23, No. 5, pp. 1-8.

Chen K. H., & Thomas Shirmerda, (1981), "An Empirical Analysis of Useful Financial Ratios," *Financial Management*, Vol. 10, No. 1, pp. 51-60.

Corcoran Patrick J., (1987), "Explaining the Commercial Real Estate Market," *Journal of Portfolio Management*, (Spring), Vol. 13, pp. 15-21.

Cranmer Charles N., (1990), "Commercial Banks; Real Estate – Real Trouble," *Issues in Bank Regulation*, (Summer), pp. 26-32.

Elyasiani Elyas, & Seyed Mehdian, (1995), "The Comparative Efficiency Performance of Small and Large U.S. Commercial Banks in the Pre and Post Deregulation Era," *Journal of Applied Economics*, Vol. 27, pp. 1069-79.

McNulty James E., (1995), "Overbuilding, Real Estate Lending Decisions, and the Regional Economic Base," *Journal of Real Estate Finance and Economics*, Vol. 11, pp. 37-53.

Neveloff Jay A., (1996), "Institutional Lenders Must Speed Up To Profit on Return of Realty Market," American Bank, (January, 26), p. 26.

O'Conner Melvin C., (1973), "On the Usefulness of Financial Ratios to Investors in Common Stock", *Accounting Review*, (April), pp. 339-53.

Sabi Manijeh, (1996), "Comparative Analysis of Foreign and Domestic Bank Operation in Hungary," *Journal of Comparative Economics*, Vol. 22, No. 2, pp. 179-88.

Samad Abdus, (2005), "U.S. Commercial Banks' Real Estate Financing: An Examination of Antebellum Banking History," *Regional Business Review*, Vol. 24, (May), pp. 90-103.

—(1999), "Comparative Efficiency of Islamic Bank vis-à-vis Conventional Banks in Malaysia," *IIUM Journal of Economics and Management*, Vol. 7, No. 1, pp. 1-25.

—(2004), "Performance of Interest Free Banks vis-à-vis Interest Based Conventional Banks of Bahrain," *IIUM Journal of Economics and Management*, Vol. 12, No. 2, pp. 115-130.

Smith David A., (1990) "Working on Real Estate Properties," *Real Estate Review*, (Spring), pp. 20-25.

NOTES

1. The state of the Nation's Housing, 2002, Cambridge, MA (Joint Center for Housing Studies of the Harvard University).
2. The total flow of home mortgages is $917.2 billion in 2004 and constitutes 72.2 per cent of the total mortgages.
3. Primary mortgage market consists of lenders who originate and/or service mortgage loans.

CHAPTER 16

GLOBALISATION AND STATE LEVEL FISCAL REFORMS IN INDIA SINCE 1991

Ratna Vadra

INTRODUCTION

Globalization and Economic Reforms have enormous potential for economic growth and economic development .The term Globalization gained prominence among the economists since the early 1980s. Ever since the end of the Second World War, the need was felt to facilitate the movement of capital and other factors of production across geographical borders. It was to enable this, that the process of globalization was adopted. Globalization is one of those words that seem to be all things to all people. Some use it in the narrow sense to mean increased trade and capital flows between nations. Spectacular technical change, especially in information and communication, which has facilitated this integration, is also included by some others under the heading of globalization. To yet others, the perceived increase in economic and political power of mobile capital and skilled labor at the global level, vis a vis unskilled labor and sovereign governments. At the same time as discussion of globalization has come to dominate the international discourse many economies have adopted the Liberalization, Privatization and Globalization approach, commonly known as LPG approach. The national discourse is dominated by the issue of "Economic Reforms". Globalization and economic reforms are related because one of the key tenets of Economic Reforms in the last ten years has been the opening up the national economy to international competition through more openness in trade and in capital flows. The other, and related, key tenet has been the rolling back of the state in major areas of economic and social activity.

In the era of globalization, economic policy reforms have assumed paramount importance specially in developing economies. With the international economic situation changing rapidly, the need was felt by developing countries to introduce economic reforms to accommodate the process of globalization. While globalization is an international phenomenon, economic reforms at national levels was required to promote the growth of globalization and make it a truly global feature. This would also help to spread the benefits of globalization to the developing nations.

The year 1991-92 was one of the toughest years for the India economy. All the macro economic indicators become adverse. The overall growth slumped to mere 1.1 per cent. The gross fiscal deficit stood at 8 percent of the GDP and revenue deficit on the current account at 3.5 per cent in 1990-91.

The new government decided to adopt in June 1991 a programme of macro-economic stabilization to restore viability to fiscal balances and contain prices. At the same time it undertook a for reaching programme of structural reforms involving bold initiatives in external trade exchange rate, industrial policy, fiscal crisis, all aiming at moving the country to a higher growth. India also adopted the Liberalization, Privatization and Globalization approach, known as LPG approach under "New Economic Reforms" in 1991.

GLOBALISATION AND ROLE OF STATE

India's experience in its transition to globalisa-tion over the years was clearly very different from the pessimistic perceptions and projections of the anti-globalisers. The overall growth perfor-mance improved significantly and poverty as conventionally measured also declined. But it is also true that the achievements in these di-mensions were less than was expected and there were distributional problems. The bene-fits of growth were not seen to be evenly dis-tributed among different states and some of the poorer and most populous states actually expe-rienced a deceleration in growth. The main reason assigned to such performance can be that the reforms that were implemented were too slow and some of the reforms that were essential were not taken. One of them can be in the area of State Level Fiscal Reforms. States level fiscal policies play a vital role in Indian public finance. States maintain law and order provide economic and social infrastructure to its people. Most developmental and other normal administration functions are assigned to them so their expenditure obligations are relatively high. States too are major partners in the development process Agriculture, Irrigation, rural development and social services are crucial areas that happen to be the sole responsibility of the states. Further a large part of power development, transport and communication is also under purview, of the state governments. Thus a true reform is required in these areas.

It must be recognized that India has twenty-Nine Governments, 28 states level ones and one at the Centre. The States have a significant role to play in a globalizing economy. For citizens to take advantage of the opportunities of globalization, they need access to high quality education, health care, information and communication technologies (ICT), social safety nets, and infrastructure. The role of government is to secure for the citizens affordable access to these services. In countries characterized by weak State institutions and inadequate social policies, it may be difficult to minimize the costs of globalization.

That is why strengthening State institutions and social welfare is essential in a globalizing world. With the advance of globalization, the State has an important role to play in the establishment and preservation of an "even playing field" and an enabling environment for private enterprise, individual creativity and social action. It can also contribute to the establishment and maintenance of social safety nets; promote as well as facilitate social dialogue at the sub-national, national, and international levels; establish and maintain mechanisms for mediation of disputes, mitigation of conflicts and reconciliation of rival cultures or interests in the increasingly diversified contemporary societies. States also play important role in creating an enabling environment for the private sector. The State encourages, through appropriate rules and regulations, healthy competition among businesses. The State, in partnership with civil society and the private sector, has a major role to play in the quest for peace, greater freedom, social equity and sustainable development. Improving and reforming public administration and governance systems is critical in addressing a number of issues, including making globalization work for all.

Fiscal consolidation has been high among the reform priorities of the government. The government decided to adopt in June 1991 a programme of macro-economic stabilization to restore viability of fiscal balances and the balance of payments and to contain prices. At the same time it took a far-reaching programme of structural reforms involving bold initiatives in external trade, exchange rate and industrial policy etc. Out of them one of the important components of the reform was 'Fiscal Reforms'.

Over the years, the Centre has seen a burgeoning of non-plan expenditure in the face of inadequate buoyancy of revenues. They have responded by resorting to larger and larger volumes of borrowing to finance plan expenditure, which is shrinking as a percentage of GDP. This process has led to steady build up of debt, which in turn has generated a rising interest burden. One of the crises that India faced in 1990-91 was the unsustainable imbalance between government revenues and expenditure. Revenue deficit have been financed by running up surpluses on the capital account of the budget. Such surpluses on capital account of the budget will prove harmful for the long run growth prospects of the economy. The steady deterioration in the revenue account caused enlargement of gross fiscal deficit.

Unlike the Centre which had surpluses on revenue account in the budget till 1978-79, the states seemed to be managing their finances relative better but in the late eighties they also began to run revenue deficits which led to the steady deterioration in the revenue account which caused increase in states gross fiscal deficit. Revenue deficit have been financed by running surpluses on capital account of the budget. The rising fiscal deficit of the states became a matter of concern for Central government. To overcome the fiscal crisis of the states, Centre gave some bold and drastic measures or steps which will have to be taken on all fronts, if states want to come out of its fiscal crises. Such measures came to be known as "Fiscal Reforms Programme for states".

INDIA'S STATE LEVEL FISCAL CRISES-CAUSES

The fiscal deterioration in both the Central and states fiscal position in the second half of the 1990's and prevailing still now were due to the out come of many causes:

1. The first and the fore most culprit as stressed by Acharya (2001, 2002) is the Fifth Pay Commission Award, the decision of the Government of India in 1997 under the United Front (Gujaral) Government to implement large (40 to 60 per cent) pay increases for Central employees. Under employee pressure, most state governments followed suit in the next couple of years starting in 1998-99 resulting in a massive ballooning of the salary at the state level. The Fifth Pay Commission has been called the single largest adverse shock India's strained public finances in the last decade and an act of fiscal profligacy without parallel (Godbole, 1997, Acharya, 2001). There is a wide range of criticism against the pay commission. State governments are autonomous body and they have the right to decide salaries of their employees. State governments had their pay commission till 1972. But after 1972 they are following the same salary pattern of the Central government employees. So it a wrong policy of state governments which had given rise to such fiscal crises.

2. The second factor one can point to after public sector salary increase is a secular deterioration in the finances of the states over the last twenty years.
3. The third factor is that the states were hit over the nineties by high interest rates. Even at the start of the nineties, the states faced high interest rates than the Centre but the gap increased over the course of the nineties from 2.5 per cent in 1990-91 to as much as 5.1 per cent ten years later in 2001-01.
4. The fourth contributing factor to the state level fiscal crises was the inability or unwillingness of the Central government to limit the borrowing of state governments.
5. The fifth and the final factor behind the state level fiscal deterioration of the late nineties is the rise of off-budget liabilities particularly the acute financial weakening of the power sectors and the rise of off-budget borrowing.

TIME PROFILE OF FISCAL COMPONENTS OF STATES

Deeping Deficits

Deficits are a comprehensive indicator of fiscal health of the health of the states. Fiscal deficits (total receipts (except borrowings minus total expenditure expressed as proportion of GDP) for the state governments to indicate the stability in the finances of State GDP. It is the crucial factor computed which has been an increasing trend in the in the fiscal deficit. It is useful to begin recounting the crisis of state finances by examining the trends in deficits of state governments during the period 1990-91-2007-08, presented in Table 1 and Graph 1.

Regarding the position of fiscal deficit of states as percentage of GDP is concerned it was 3.3 per cent in 1990-91, which further went up to 4.6 of GDP in 1999-2000.After that due to certain fiscal measures taken by the government, it showed a declining trend and it declined to 3.4 per cent in 2004-05 and further to 2.3 per cent of GDP in 2007-08(B.E).

The revenue deficit was 0.9 per cent of GDP in 1990-91 which increased to 2.8 per cent in 2002-03 and then declined to -0.3 per cent of GDP in 2007-08 (B.E.) .Primary deficit was 1.8 per cent of GDP in 1990-91, decreased further to 0.9 per cent of GDP in 1997-98 but further increased to 1.5 per cent of GDP in 2003-04 and then declined to 0.1 per cent in 2007-08 (B.E). To sum up, it may be mentioned that the State Governments have witnessed visible reduction in the deficits indicators in recent years due to strict measures taken by state governments.

Table 1
Macro Indicators of States Fiscal Health

(as % of G.D.P)

Year	*Gross Fiscal Deficit*	*Revenue Deficit*	*Primary Deficit*
1990-91	3.3	0.9	1.8
1991-92	2.9	0.9	1.2
1992-93	2.8	0.7	1
1993-94	2.4	0.5	0.5
1994-95	2.7	0.7	0.8
1995-96	2.6	0.7	0.8
1996-97	2.7	1.2	0.8
1997-98	2.9	1.1	0.9
1998-99	4.2	2.6	2.2
1999-00	4.6	2.8	2.3
2000-01	4.2	2.6	1.8
2001-02	4.1	2.6	1.4
2002-03	4.1	2.3	1.2
2003-04	4.4	2.3	1.5
2004-05	3.4	1.3	0.7
2005-06	2.5	0.2	0.2
2006-07	2.6	0.2	0.2
2007-08(B.E.)	2.3	-0.3	0.1

Source: Reserve Bank of India Bulletin, Various Issues

From Table 1 we see that deficits are still there and improvement in fiscal balance in the recent years should be undertaken fastly. The trend in major deficit indicators as set out in Graph 1 reveals significant improvement witnessed in recent years after recording progressive deterioration from the second half of the 1990s.

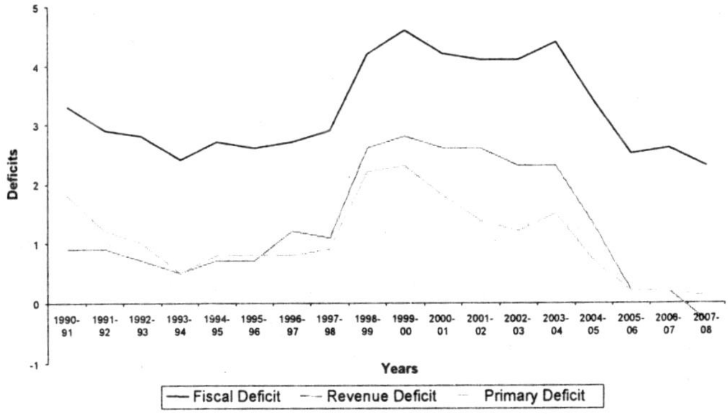

Graph 1: Macro Economic Indicators of States Fiscal Health

Receipts of States

Causes of imbalances of states are well known. The widening of deficit in recent years is due to both sharp rise in revenue receipts and rising expenditure, the latter factor being more significant. On the receipt side, there was some slow down in the ratio of states revenue receipt to GDP. Nearly half of the states revenue receipts come from own tax revenue, about 60 per cent of which is generated through the sales tax. Thus rather than tax revenues, slowdown in the revenue receipts during the second half of nineties, was on account of the states own non tax receipts and Grants from the Central government the non-tax revenue is decreasing due to no. of factors.

Table 2
Tax and Non –Tax Revenue of States

Years	*Tax Revenue*	*Non-Tax Revenue*
1990-91	44586.3	21880.5
1991-92	52603.9	27931.8
1992-93	60448.4	30642.7
1993-94	68818.9	36744.8
1994-95	80619.2	41664.5
1995-96	92912.8	43890.6
1996-97	106139.1	46697.3
1997-98	121640.6	48660.2
1998-99	128416.5	48031.3

Contd.

Years	*Tax Revenue*	*Non-Tax Revenue*
1999-00	146703	60498.1
2000-01	168714.7	69238.3
2001-02	180311.9	75363.2
2002-03	198798	81541.3
2003-04	229313.1	104976.9
2004-05	267683	104392
2005-06	306332	124690
2006-07	372817	158612
2007-08	430222	176511

Source: Reserve Bank of India Bulletin, Various Issues

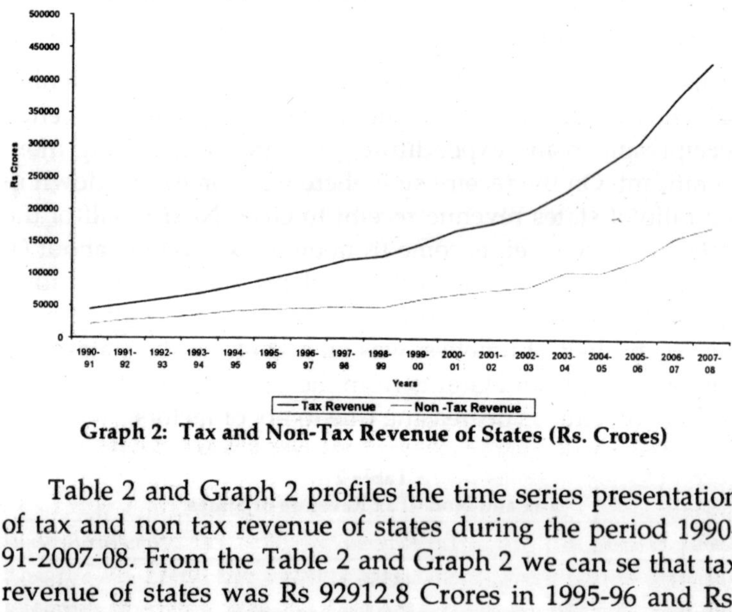

Graph 2: Tax and Non-Tax Revenue of States (Rs. Crores)

Table 2 and Graph 2 profiles the time series presentation of tax and non tax revenue of states during the period 1990-91-2007-08. From the Table 2 and Graph 2 we can se that tax revenue of states was Rs 92912.8 Crores in 1995-96 and Rs. 215048.5 Crores in 2002-03 and further to Rs. 430222 Crores in 2007-08(B.E).

As far as the condition of non tax revenue of states is concerned it was Rs. 21880.5 crores in 1990-91 which increased to Rs. 43890.6 crores in 1995-96 and further to Rs. 91894.3 crores in 2003-04 and then to Rs. 176511 crores in 2007-08 (B.E).

It is clear from the Table 2 and Graph 2 that growth in states revenues both tax and non tax revenue does not present a satisfactory picture. The tax revenue and non tax revenue both showed an increasing trend but the growth of non-tax revenue was less than that of tax revenue. It is thus obvious that states need to take steps to strengthen their fiscal situation by taking suitable measures to mobilize additional resources from their own tax and non-tax revenues.

Expenditure of States

On the expenditure side of states, there are two types of expenditure, development and non developmental which are causes of worry. The non developmental expenditure is growing at a faster pace than the growth in the development expenditure. There are two main areas where non developmental expenditure has increased quite sharply, interest payments and pensions. These two expenditures are eating about one-fifth of the states, revenue receipts. On both of these items the states have little control. The rising proportion had made the fiscal management of states difficult.

Table 3 and Graph 3 shows the time profile series of developmental and non developmental and non developmental expenditure of states during the period 1990-91 to 2007-08. The developmental expenditure of states was Rs. 63370 crores in 1990-91 and Rs. 114819 crores in 1995-96, increased further to Rs. 467696 crores in 2007-08 (B.E).

Table 3
Developmental and Non Developmental Expenditure

(Rs Crore)

Year	*Developmental*	*Non-Developmental*
1990-91	63370	22600
1991-92	74588	27143
1992-93	80567	32104
1993-94	88791	37859
1994-95	102629	48,964
1995-96	112888	54,544
1996-97	129363	61,353
1997-98	142266	70,652
1998-99	161200	85,174
1999-00	183540	108,451

Contd.

Year	*Developmental*	*Non-Developmental*
2000-01	205670	116,823
2001-02	211086	135,505
2002-03	221799	149,554
2003-04	272848	166,538
2004-05	286473	185,152
2005-06	330,044	190,021
2006-07	419050	224,475
2007-08	467696	246,130

Source: Reserve Bank of India Bulletin, Various Issues

As regard the percentage increase of development expenditure to total expenditure it was 69.5 per cent in 1990-91 declined to 64.7 per cent in 1995-96 and then to 57.1 per cent in 2002-03 and then increased to 61 per cent of GDP in 2007-08 (B.E).

The non developmental expenditure of states was Rs. 22600 crores in 1990-91, further went up to Rs. 160391 crores in 2002-03 and then to Rs. 246130 crores in 2007-08. (B.E). The percentage increase of non developmental expenditure in terms of total expenditure was 24.8% which ballooned up to to36.5 % in 2002-03 and then declined to 32.1% in 2007-08 (B.E).

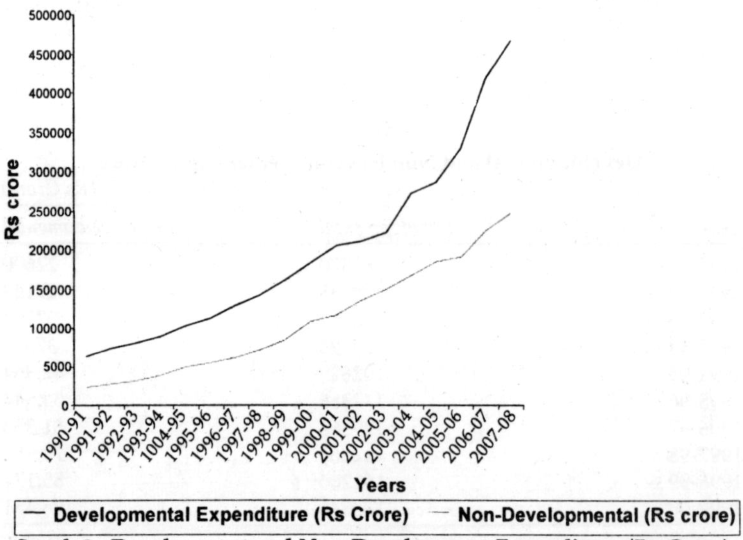

Graph 3: Development and Non-Development Expenditure (Rs Crore)

The key deficit indicators of the State Governments, viz., RD, GFD and PD recorded significant reduction. The correction in the revenue account in 2005-06 (Accounts) was largely due to a sharp reduction in the revenue expenditure, mainly non interest revenue expenditure which fell byRs. 22,928 crore (6.1 per cent). It is significant to mention that the State Governments have budgeted a consolidated surplus on the revenue account after two decades. In this context, it may also be mentioned that several State Governments have achieved the targets of reduction in RD and GFD ahead of the path of restructuring recommended by the TFC and their own FRL.

Discretionary Changes and Steps Taken by States

To improve the fiscal performance of states, the states have come up with reforms in the field of expenditure management, more resource mobilization, PSU reforms, disinvestments, sectoral reforms which increased its pace after 2001.

For expenditure management some states have undertaken steps like comprehensive rationalization of post, voluntary retirement scheme (VRS) and also introduced the concept of zero based budgeting. The state governments of Maharashtra and Madhya Pradesh are conscious of the impeding wage revisions on state finances. They have decided what in future all teachers Primary and Secondary schools will be recruited by panchayats and not by the state governments .The salary would also be paid by the panchayats.

For increasing the pace of fiscal reforms of states, various funds have been formulated with the recommendations of Eleventh Finance Commission. The Consolidated Sinking fund was set up in 1999-2000 to meet market redemption of loans of state governments. The Incentive Fund was also formulated which would provide incentive for states to implement fiscal reforms programmes in time bound manner. States Fiscal Reform Facility (2000-01 to 2004-05) was created to encourage states to undertake fiscal reforms. Under this facility, medium term fiscal reforms programmes (MTFRPs) are drawn up by the states. A significant development in respect of State finances in the recent period has been progressive enactment of Fiscal Responsibility Legislation (FRL) by the State Governments (twenty-six States so far). The Reserve Bank, on its part, has been advising the State Governments on several issues, besides providing support in the form of WMA/OD and raising of market borrowings.

States have continued to take steps to flow private investment in infrastructural sectors. Andhra-Pradesh has set up a fund to improve agricultural production and road Development Corporation. Many states like UP, Karnataka, A.P, Tamil Nadu and others have set up Electricity Regulatory Commissions. Many states have set up cyber parks and information technology parks to increase the pace of direct investment. For sectoral development Tamil Nadu has set up a wasteland development authority and also set up industrial garments, biotechnology and floricultural parks. Uttar Pradesh in recent policy initiatives decided to set up two power houses at Allahabad and Anpara with the cooperation of private investors, upgrade one engineering institute to develop it on the lines of Indian Institute of Science, Bangalore to promote technical education. Upgrade another engineering institute to IIT level and set up two new State Homeopathic Colleges and two new Allopathic Medical colleges.

Interest payment is a major item of revenue expenditure. To reduce the interest burden of states a Debt Swap Scheme has been formulated in 2004, so that states can swap up their high cost central government loans. The process of swapping high cost debt under the scheme is completed in respect of states. For proper resource mobilization, states have taken measures for the rationalistion of taxes, levy of proper user charges for all services like power, irrigation, transport, water etc. one of the important component of fiscal reforms in terms of resource moblisation is the introduction of state valve added tax (VAT) in place of sales tax. An empowered committee of states was not fully prepared. Thus after a great thrust from the government it was finally implemented on April 1, 2005 in the states of India. In initial stages are facing some problems in implementation. But in due course of time these problems will be sorted out. According to Asim Das Gupta there is an increase in revenue of receipts after the adoption of VAT in the states. The recommendations of Twelfth Finance Commission (2005-10) include a plan for restructuring of public finances of the Centre and the states through improvement in revenue mobilization and bringing down debt levels, and through enactment of fiscal responsibility legislation by states. The Commission recommended debt relief to states linked to fiscal reform, doing away with the present system of Central assistance to state plans in the form of grants and loans and transfer of external assistance to states on the same terms and conditions as attached to such assistance by external funding agencies. The TFC raised the share of states in shareable Central taxes from 29.5 per cent to 30.5 per cent. Total transfers to states recommended by the TFC amount to Rs. 755752 crore over the five years period, 2005-10. Of this, transfer by way of share in Central taxes and Grant-in-Aid amount to Rs. 613112 crore and Rs. 142640 crore, respectively. The total transfers recommended by the TFC be higher by 73.8 per cent over those recommended by the Eleventh Finance Commission (EFC). Within the total transfers, while the share in Central taxes is higher by 62.9 per cent Grants-in-Aid recommended by the TFC are higher by 143.5 per cent over those recommended by the EFC. .

International financial institutions like World Bank and Asian Development Bank have focused on state level reforms and extended loans to state undertaking economic restructuring programmes. The World Bank is assisting Andhra Pradesh, Uttar Pradesh and Karnataka. The Asian Development Bank has similar programmes with Gujarat and Madhya Pradesh.

CONCLUSION

The fiscal and institutional reforms aimed towards fiscal correction and consolidation coupled with the implementation of recommendations of TFC and improvement in tax buoyancy on the strength of macroeconomic fundamentals have contributed in bringing about substantial improvement in the consolidated fiscal position of the State Governments since 2005-06.

An overview of the finances of states governments helped us arriving at a much focused conclusion that states are still experiencing a high deficits and declining revenue effort and declining development expenditure. Unless the fiscal scenario of India is not improved, it cannot reap the benefits of globalization. Improvement in fiscal scenario will have more productive use of national resources, better infrastructure and rapid capital formation. The fiscal deficit (especially the revenue deficit) needs to be quickly reduced. India must sincerely implement the Fiscal Responsibility and Budget Management Act. Simultaneous action is required at both Central and state levels to raise the tax-to-GDP ratio by expanding the tax base (for example, by taxing services and rich agriculturists) and improving tax administration (for example, through computerization). The revenue deficit must be brought to zero within five years.

Thus now the moot question arises that whether States are doing enough and it there enough incentive to get them to do so? The reform process taken by states needed a deep -seated changes at the state level and the present reforms taken by states should be further intensified. We must recognize that the national government has sub national governments below it, and that all these layers of government simultaneously interact with foreign governments and corporations in a global economy. To some degree, these reforms in federal governance hold the key to opening the door to further reform elsewhere, by reducing the fiscal burden placed on the private sector by government deficits. States government should think and act accordingly so that they are not only committed to people of the state in a democratic set up but they are also the custodians of future generations.

India has clearly managed the transition from a relatively closed economy to a more open economy fairly well. The change has been slow, but the cumulative effect of the reforms that have already taken place is to put the economy in a much better position today than it was 10 years ago. The macroeconomic environment is broadly favourable for growth. India has been able to increase its savings and investment rates steadily. Investor interest in India is definitely increasing and many potentially big investors–Microsoft, In-tel, Dell, Toyota, POSCO, to name only a few–has announced their intention to in-crease investment in India. In order to ensure that society at large benefits from globalization, and to minimize its negative effects, Indian states need to reinforce an efficient public administration, an effective strategy of resource mobilization and improve tax administration systems and build capacity in for the private sector investment for development.

India's economy clearly is on the move and most certainly has the potential to cope up with globalization and challenges its throws up. Experience has shown that globalization requires strong, not weak States. However, this potential can be made a reality only if India mobilizes adequate political will and quickly commits itself to reduce its budgetary deficits in recent years by implementing reforms.

REFERENCES

A. Muhannad, and El-Mefleh, (2005), *"Economic Role of the State in the Era of Globalization" http://aabss.org/journal*

Ahluwalia S. Montek, (2002), *Economic Performance of States in Post-Reforms Period*, Economic and Political Weekly, May, Vo.; 6, pp. 1637.

Ahluwalia Montek, (2004), *"Understanding India's Reform Trajectory: Past Trends and Future Challenges"*, India Review, Vol. 3, No. 4.

Ahluwalia S. Montek, (2005), "India's *Experience with Globalisation"*, David Finch Memorial Lecture at Melbourne University, Australia on September 22.

Amin Samir, *Capitalism in the Age of Globalization*, London and New.

Anand Mukesh, Amaresh Bagchi, and Tapas K. Sen, (2002), *Fiscal Discipline at the State Level: Perverse Incentives and Paths to Reform*, National Institute of Public Finance and Policy, New Delhi.

Bertucci Guido, and Adriana Alberti, *"Globalization and the Role of the State: Challenges and Perspectives"*.

Bank World, (2005), *"State Fiscal Reforms in India, Progress and Prospects,* A World Bank Report.

Krueger O., and Sajjid Chinoy, (Ed.), (2002), "*Economic Policy Reforms and the Indian Economy*", Chicago: Chicago University Press.

Mukherji Rahul (2005), "*The Indian State and Globalization*", Background Paper for the Ford Foundation's Project Administered by the National Foundation of India.

Rao M. Govinda (1992), "Proposals for State-Level Budgetary Reforms", *Economic and Political Weekly*. Feb1.

Report on Currency and Finance, Various Issues. Mumbai. R.B.I.

Reserve Bank of India, A Study of Budgets, Bulletin, Various issues.

Sandy Gordon (1997), "Globalisation and Economic Reform in India", *Australian Journal of International Affairs*, Vol. 51, Issue 1, April, pp. 73-89.

Srinivasan T. N., (2002), "*Indian Federalism, Economic Reform and Globalization*".

United Nations (2000), "*Globalization and State: An Overview*", Report Prepared by the Secretariat Nations Programme in Public Administration and Finance, Fifteenth Session, 8-12 May.

INDEX